D0218612

Voyage to the Other World

Medieval Studies at Minnesota

Published in cooperation with the Center for Medieval Studies, University of Minnesota

Volume 5. Edited by Calvin B. Kendall and Peter S. Wells
Voyage to the Other World: The Legacy of Sutton Hoo

Volume 4. Edited by Barbara A. Hanawalt
Chaucer's England: Literature in Historical Context

Volume 3. Edited by Marilyn J. Chiat and Kathryn Reyerson
The Medieval Mediterranean: Cross-Cultural Contacts

Volume 2. Edited by Andrew MacLeish
The Medieval Monastery

Volume 1. Edited by Kathryn Reyerson and Faye Powe
The Medieval Castle

Voyage to the Other World

THE LEGACY OF SUTTON HOO

✣

Calvin B. Kendall and Peter S. Wells, editors

Medieval Studies at Minnesota, Volume 5

University of Minnesota Press
Minneapolis

Published with assistance from the Carl D. Sheppard Fund

Copyright 1992 by the Regents of the University of Minnesota

All rights reserved. No part of this publication may be
reproduced, stored in a retrieval system, or transmitted, in any
form or by any means, electronic, mechanical, photocopying,
recording, or otherwise, without the prior written permission
of the publisher.

Published by the University of Minnesota Press
2037 University Avenue Southeast, Minneapolis, MN 55414

Printed in the United States of America on acid-free paper.

Library of Congress Cataloging-in-Publication Data

Voyage to the other world : the legacy of Sutton Hoo / Calvin
  B. Kendall and Peter S. Wells, editors.
    p.   cm. — (Medieval studies at Minnesota ; v. 5)
  Includes bibliographical references and index.
  ISBN 0-8166-2023-7. — ISBN 0-8166-2024-5 (pbk.)
  1. Sutton Hoo Ship Burial (England)   2. Anglo-Saxons —
Kings and rulers — Death and burial.   3. Excavations
(Archaeology) — England — Suffolk.   4. Suffolk (England) —
Antiquities.   5. Anglo-Saxons — England — Suffolk.   6. Ship
burial — England — Suffolk.   7. Beowulf.
I. Kendall, Calvin B.   II. Wells, Peter S.   III. Series: Medieval
studies at Minnesota ; 5.
DA155.V69   1992
936.2'646 — dc20   91-42865
                                                              CIP

The University of Minnesota is an
equal-opportunity educator and employer.

Contents

❖

Acknowledgments

❖

The essays collected in this volume are the fruit of the conference on Sutton Hoo, jointly sponsored by the Center for Ancient Studies and the Center for Medieval Studies at the University of Minnesota, which was held in Minneapolis in May 1989. It is a pleasure to thank the organizers of that conference and especially the director of the Center for Medieval Studies, Professor Kathryn Reyerson, for their help in making this volume possible. We also wish to acknowledge the invaluable editorial assistance of John Bedell, Elizabeth Dachowski, Alice Klingener, Edward Schoenfeld, and Gregory Waltigney.

CBK/PSW

Introduction

⁂

Sutton Hoo and Early Medieval
Northern Europe

Calvin B. Kendall and Peter S. Wells

The essays in this volume were occasioned by the fiftieth anniversary of the discovery of the ship burial at Sutton Hoo. Scholars
from around the world gathered at special sessions on Sutton Hoo
at the Twenty-fourth International Congress on Medieval Studies at Western Michigan University in Kalamazoo and at a conference at the University of Minnesota in Minneapolis in May 1989 to share their findings and
to exchange ideas. In the essays collected here, participants from the Minnesota conference review the impact of Sutton Hoo over the past half-
century and reconsider aspects of the culture of Anglo-Saxon England in
the broad context of its connections with Scandinavian and Merovingian
Europe.[1]

The Sutton Hoo grave was richly outfitted, and study of the diverse
materials included in the burial brings to bear a wide range of disciplines,
including archaeology, art history, economic history, folklore, literary
studies, and numismatics, on attempts to understand the significance of
the find. From the perspective of European archaeology, Sutton Hoo
belongs to a large group of exceptionally rich burials, dating from the
Neolithic period until the practice of placing lavish objects in graves
ended with the adoption of Christianity, well into the medieval period in
northern Europe. The importance of Sutton Hoo for historians depends
upon its chronology in the early periods of historical record keeping in
Britain. For the great majority of rich graves of prehistoric and early medieval date, we have no chance of associating the burial with a specific
individual. The hypothesis that Rædwald of East Anglia was buried (or
memorialized) at Sutton Hoo has not been proved, and there are other
candidates. It is even possible that this was not a royal burial. But the
mere fact that we can speculate in an informed way about the identity of
the man buried at Sutton Hoo forms a bridge between archaeology and
history. Resemblances between the epic poem *Beowulf* and the Sutton
Hoo grave provide a link between archaeology and literary tradition, as
Rosemary Cramp and others demonstrated many years ago,[2] though the
significance of this link is far from undisputed. In her essay in this volume, Roberta Frank cautions that "the material culture of *Beowulf* is the
conventional apparatus of heroic poetry" (p. 53).

The grave at Sutton Hoo was discovered in 1939.[3] In 1938 Edith May Pretty had employed Basil Brown, a local archaeologist, to investigate several mounds on her property near Woodbridge in East Anglia. The excavations uncovered a number of graves containing objects that included items of distant origin. As a result of these early finds, Mrs. Pretty in the following year authorized Brown to explore the largest mound of the group (now known as Mound 1). Early in the investigation, Brown noted iron rivets and quickly concluded that the mound contained a ship of considerable size. In view of the special significance of the find, authorities at the British Museum and at the Inspectorate of Ancient Monuments were notified. In the course of careful excavations in the summer of 1939, the burial was fully excavated and the spectacular objects from it were recovered. The principal excavations of the burial were directed by C. W. Phillips. W. F. Grimes, Stuart Piggott, and Margaret Guido carried out much of the digging and drawing of the deposit. Special expertise was lent by Grahame Clark, J. B. Ward-Perkins, J. W. Brailsford, and O. G. S. Crawford. The excavation was thus carried out by leading professional archaeologists of the day, employing the most current techniques of excavation, mapping, and photography.

Shortly after the completion of the fieldwork, the Second World War began. The material objects that had been recovered were removed to a place of safety and the excavations filled in. C. W. Phillips published an early report on the excavations in *Antiquaries Journal* 20 (1940). A reexcavation of Mound 1 was carried out as part of the British Museum campaign of 1966-71 in order to study again the boat and the structure of the mound. The growing number of major analyses and synthetic works on the burial and its contents was now augmented by the three volumes edited by Rupert Bruce-Mitford — *The Sutton Hoo Ship Burial*, vols. 1-3 (London, 1975, 1978, 1983).[4]

Since Sutton Hoo is the richest early medieval burial found in Britain, and indeed in Europe, special treatment has been given to the study, analysis, and interpretation of the objects found in it. The presentation and handling of the objects from the grave, and the questions addressed to them, are in essence the same as those applied to any archaeological find, though the resources that were made available for analysis of the Sutton Hoo complex have been much greater than those available for most archaeological materials. Moreover, Sutton Hoo is unusual not only in its exceptional wealth, but also in its connection with the politics and personalities of seventh-century England. This link with the historical tradition makes Sutton Hoo of special interest to scholars who focus on the development of early medieval Europe.

From the perspective of European archaeology, Sutton Hoo is a typical example of a richly equipped grave. From as early as the Neolithic period, but especially during the Late Bronze Age (1200–800 B.C.), the Iron Age (800 B.C.–birth of Christ), the Roman Iron Age (birth of Christ–A.D. 400), and the early medieval period (A.D. 400–800), marked differences in wealth are apparent in burials. Many cultural contexts are characterized by the presence of especially richly outfitted graves, commonly called "chieftains' graves," "kings' graves," or *Fürstengräber*. From the Late Bronze Age through Merovingian times and as late as the Conversion period in Scandinavia, recurring categories of objects distinguish these exceptionally rich graves from the majority of burials. Both men's and women's graves occur among this richest category; since Sutton Hoo contains objects characteristic of a man's grave, we shall limit our discussion here to rich male burials, but the interested reader will find further information on women's graves in Else Roesdahl's essay in this volume.

The standard features of rich male graves in late prehistoric and early medieval Europe are (1) an exceptionally large covering mound of earth or a combination of stone and earth, (2) a wooden chamber in which the burial was placed, (3) a horse or a vehicle (wagon, cart, boat), (4) weapons (sword, spear, helmet, shield, arrows, dagger), (5) vessels, usually ornate and often of foreign manufacture, associated with the consumption of special beverages (jugs, cups, mixing vessels, bowls, drinking horns), and (6) other ornamental objects from distant places. The striking recurrence of most or all of these categories of objects in hundreds of richly equipped graves all over Europe during a period of more than two thousand years is testimony to the existence of a shared system of signification of status and power through the manipulation of a specific set of material symbols. Even in landscapes in which the local material cultures vary considerably, where, for example, each local area has its own distinctive types of pottery and bronze jewelry, the rich burials are often very similar in their character. This interregional similarity of the richly equipped burials indicates the existence of regular contact and exchange of information between elite groups in different parts of Europe from about 1200 b.c.[5] Sutton Hoo must be viewed in the context of this long tradition of burial ritual, in which a standard grammar of material culture is employed to convey particular meanings about the buried individual and his place in society. The task of deciphering this grammar is difficult, and the results are controversial. One of the reasons for the special significance of the Sutton Hoo burial is that interpretation is supported by data from other fields of inquiry that are not usually available to the archaeologist.

During the past decade, anthropologically oriented archaeologists have been particularly interested in questions regarding the significance of burial ritual. They have shown that many traditional assumptions about the meaning of particular practices or grave goods are unwarranted and that the practices evident in any given grave or cemetery need to be evaluated in relation to our understanding of the whole cultural context.[6] Useful comparisons could be made between the Sutton Hoo grave and the burial of Childeric, a Frankish king and father of Clovis, who died in 481 or 482 and whose grave was discovered at Tournai (in modern Belgium) in

1653. The Childeric grave is unusual in that it is one of the very few early medieval burials of a historically known individual. Like Sutton Hoo, the burial of Childeric contained ornate iron weapons, lavish gold ornaments, and coins. Also like Sutton Hoo, the objects in the Childeric grave reflect not only vast wealth and high status, but also long-distance connections with peoples across much of Europe.[7]

So too the traditions reflected in Anglo-Saxon poetry can contribute to our interpretation of the significance of the ritual reflected in the burial structure and goods of Sutton Hoo. A coroner's jury was summoned in the summer of 1939 to decide whether the rich objects found at Sutton Hoo were treasure trove — that is, objects that had been buried for safekeeping in order that they might be dug up later — and thus crown property, or whether they had been laid in the ship as part of a ritual ceremony, in which case they would belong to Mrs. Pretty. Legend has it that the jury listened to a recitation from the Anglo-Saxon poem *Beowulf* of the burials of Scyld Scefing and of Beowulf before giving its verdict in favor of Mrs. Pretty.[8] Although the parallels are far from exact, and the jury may never have heard of them, it is certainly true that there are striking similarities between the Sutton Hoo ship burial and the burial practices described in *Beowulf*.

The similarities cannot be used to prove a close proximity in space or time between the grave and the poem. The *Beowulf* poet may have been a monk; he was almost certainly a Christian.[9] The Christian elements in the poem, which nineteenth-century scholars liked to dismiss as monkish interpolations, form a seamless whole with the rest of the poem. There is no objective criterion by which they can be excised.[10] And if he was a Christian, a monastic community becomes a likely setting for his work. It was the place, above all, where words could be set to parchment, and we know that Anglo-Saxon monks enjoyed listening to the deeds of their pagan ancestors. Alcuin implicitly rebuked the monks of Lindisfarne on just this ground: "Let the Word of God be heard at the meals of the brethren. There it is proper to hear a reader, not a harper, the sermons of the Fathers, not the songs of the pagans. What has Ingeld [a Germanic hero who is mentioned in *Beowulf*] to do with Christ? The house is narrow; it cannot hold both of them."[11] There is no necessary reason to suppose that the *Beowulf* poet lived in East Anglia, and he might have composed the poem at any time from the later seventh to the tenth century.[12] His was a retrospective vision of the pagan past, seen through the filter of Christianity.

To what extent the *Beowulf* poet was personally familiar with the burial practices that he describes in the poem we cannot say. We do not know whether the ship funeral rites of Scyld Scefing at the beginning of the poem (which differ from Sutton Hoo in the important respect that the ship is set afloat in the sea instead of being buried under a mound) were a traditional variant of the rites implied by Sutton Hoo, a variant that by definition has left no trace in the archaeological record, or the confused

and distorted memory of a ritual that had long since ceased to be practiced. The same can be said of the cremation of Beowulf at the end of the
poem, which is followed by the building of a great funeral mound into
which his ashes are placed. Perhaps the poet had heard stories of a ceremony like the one that must have taken place at Sutton Hoo circa 625 and
from them imagined the several different burials that take place in the
poem; perhaps he was repeating narrative themes of burial that he had
learned from the traditional oral culture in which he had grown up.

What the evidence of *Beowulf* encourages us to do is to interpret the
ship burial at Sutton Hoo as implying that in this culture death was felt to
involve a voyage to the Other World. Death was not annihilation. In some
sense it extended the occupations and procedures of life. The dead person
had to accomplish the passage, and it required the accoutrements of the
living—armor and weapons, money, lamps, bowls, and cups, a drinking
horn, a lyre. Such conceptions may have become attenuated by the seventh century, the material objects no more than dispensable items from
the marginal surplus of a prosperous society in a ritual that had been emp-
tied of meaning. We cannot be sure. Nevertheless the implicit symbolism
is important. Some belief, strong or weak, in an existence in the Other
World apparently activated the burial. Else Roesdahl puts the same interpretation on the later ship burials in Scandinavia.

Aron Gurevich remarks that the boundary separating life from death
was "at least partially transparent" in the popular consciousness of the
Middle Ages.[13] Nothing in the Sutton Hoo burial requires us to suppose
that the people who buried Rædwald (if we can accept the identification)
looked upon the the voyage as in some sense reversible, as implying the
possibility of two-way communication. They may have. At the end of
Beowulf, the dead hero is carried to the funeral pyre *in a wagon* together
with quantities of gold (*Beowulf*, 3134-36). After the pyre is lit, the poet
remarks that it is fitting to praise one's lord, "when *he must be carried
forth* from his body."[14] The scene preserves at least a vague notion of a
physical journey to the Other World. The poet follows his account of the
launching of Scyld Scefing's burial ship into the sea with the ambiguous
comment, "men are not able to say for certain, hall-counselors, warriors
beneath the heavens, who received that freight."[15] Beowulf and the other
human inhabitants of the lands of the Danes and the Geats never encoun-
ter revenants from the Other World, however much Beowulf's dive into
the underwater hall of Grendel and his mother may remind us of epic de-
scents into hell. The dragon that terrorizes Beowulf's people in the second
part of the poem is a living embodiment of a curse laid on a treasure by
men long dead. It therefore represents a kind of continuity between the
dead and the living, but not direct contact. Yet it may be that the poet has
screened from our view the full extent of pagan beliefs in intercourse between the living and the dead, leaving us with an impression in *Beowulf*
of unidirectional movement toward, but not back from, the Other World.

The oral culture of early, pre-Christian Anglo-Saxon England is almost irretrievably lost. We can approach it only indirectly, through triangulation, as it were. Sutton Hoo is one partial, mute witness of the material culture of those pagan Anglo-Saxons at the moment of transition to Christianity. In the language of *Beowulf* we hear distant echoes of their voices. Robert Creed has uncovered in that language a stratum below the level of the traditional formulas—a stratum that he sees as formed of "Ideal Structures." He argues that in the "sound-linked syllables" of the poem we have a guide to the ideas and ideals of the ancient Germanic culture that the Anglo-Saxons brought with them to England and that underlay the distinctive Anglo-Saxon Christian culture, based on writing, that came into being in the seventh century. Sutton Hoo gives us material evidence of the wealth and power of an Anglo-Saxon king or chieftain. Creed's analysis of one of the Ideal Structures of *Beowulf* opens a window on the community's probable attitude toward that wealth and power: apparently, it expected its leader not only to provide it protection, but also to seek its advice. Since the collective wisdom of traditional oral societies was maintained and transmitted in the songs they listened to, the fragments of a lyre that were found in the Sutton Hoo burial might be interpreted in this sense—just as the weapons can symbolize the protection that the leader has to offer, the lyre is a reminder of the body of tradition and culture that will guide his actions.

Both Sutton Hoo and *Beowulf*, then, offer essential materials for the construction of a model of early Anglo-Saxon culture. The value of constructing a model, a necessarily simplified, paradigmatic schema of an early culture, is that it provides us with a means of integrating and testing our assumptions about the meaning of such data as can be recovered. No models are perfect; each must and will be challenged and modified over time, or even finally discarded. A case in point is the influential concept of the "Bretwalda," which has been used to interpret the great whetstone of Sutton Hoo. Since the man commemorated at Sutton Hoo may have been Rædwald the "Bretwalda," the whetstone begins to look like part of the regalia of the office of Bretwaldaship. It becomes in the eye of the modern beholder a ceremonial scepter. Yet Simon Keynes demonstrates in his essay that the idea of the "Bretwalda" was largely a construct of nineteenth-century historiography. And so we must take a fresh look at the whetstone and consider its meaning anew. In the words of James Campbell, "The study of the relationship of Sutton Hoo to social and political reality has to be in large measure not the establishment of new certainties, but the creation of new hypotheses, in a sense the creation of new uncertainties" (p. 96). Without these "new uncertainties," our efforts to glimpse the past in a truer or at least stronger light would be in vain.

One crucial element in the model is the story of Rædwald as narrated by Bede. This does *not* depend upon the identification of Rædwald as the man buried (or not buried, as the case may be) in Mound 1 at Sutton Hoo.

Rather it has to do with what Bede says about Rædwald's attitude to paganism (that is to say, the oral, pre-Christian, Germanic culture carried by the Anglo-Saxon invaders into England in the fifth and sixth centuries) and Christianity (the written, Latinate, Mediterranean culture spread by Christian missionaries sent over from the continent, in the first instance on the initiative of Pope Gregory the Great). According to Bede:

> Rædwald had long before been initiated into the mysteries of the Christian faith in Kent, but in vain; for on his return home [to East Anglia], he was seduced by his wife and by certain evil teachers and perverted from the sincerity of his faith, so that his last state was worse than his first. After the manner of the ancient Samaritans, he seemed to be serving both Christ and the gods whom he had previously served; in the same temple he had one altar for the Christian sacrifice and another small altar on which to offer victims to devils. . . . Rædwald . . . was noble by birth though ignoble in his deeds.[16]

What alarmed Bede about Rædwald's behavior is, of course, precisely what fascinates us. The line between paganism and Christianity, once crossed, could not be recrossed with impunity. Bede does not deny a kind of reality to the old gods; in truth they were demons. When Rædwald, having accepted Christianity, set up pagan and Christian altars side by side, he became in Bede's eyes an apostate, but he left us a precious trace of the grinding pressures at the point of intersection of cultures in conflict. Bede's response was to offer Rædwald as an exemplum of the antihero, the negative saint, the man whose end was worse than his beginning. The early Christian saint assimilated the characteristics of the Germanic hero. He came from noble parentage; his youth was distinguished in some way; his later deeds exceeded his early promise; his death was carefully noted; his glory increased after his death. The reverse trajectory of Rædwald's life is summed up in the inverted formula that describes him as "noble by birth though ignoble in his deeds" (*natu nobilis, quamlibet actu ignobilis*).[17]

From the triple conjunction of Sutton Hoo, Bede's story of Rædwald, and *Beowulf* we can construct an interpretative model for a culture on the boundary between competing ideologies and contrasting social systems. Common to them all is the mixture of Christian and pagan elements. The model will consist of certain common elements: nobility, aristocratic society, military equipment, riches, gold, splendid eating and drinking vessels, ships, trade, plunder, burial, memory, fame, concern with the Other World, visible monuments, abstract linear stylization, animal imagery; and of dichotomous elements held in simultaneous suspension: oral traditional, Iron Age culture ("archaic") versus writing-based culture ("modern"); northern European, Germanic versus Mediterranean, Latin influences; the power of the word versus the power of the book; raiding versus trading.

Although the model is derived from elements that belong to, or look back to, the seventh century and earlier, it maintains its explanatory power over a considerable period of time—perhaps the whole period of Anglo-Saxon England. All of Anglo-Saxon and Anglo-Viking England might be described as a richly fertile but unstable mix of competing cultures with a constantly shifting boundary between them. The stylized, patterned, zoomorphic art of some of the Sutton Hoo treasures derives from archaic traditions of Iron Age European culture, as Gloria Greis and Michael Geselowitz demonstrate in their essay. At the same time, the mixing of this art with designs from Christian Europe (the silver bowls with inscribed crosses, the baptismal spoons) and the possible Christian symbolism in some motifs (the man between monsters, the stag) seem to anticipate the interlace designs of the Anglo-Saxon manuscript illumination of the monasteries and the artful ambiguities of Christianized Anglo-Saxon poetry.[18] The older, traditional culture of the North tenaciously held its ground, although the dynamic missionary zeal of the early monastic movement, directed from Rome, and later the educational initiatives pushed forward by King Alfred insured the ultimate triumph of the literate culture of the Mediterranean.

Little is specifically known of the political and cultural organization of East Anglia in the first half of the seventh century.[19] But Wesley Stevens's investigation of the scientific achievement of Anglo-Saxon England reveals a pattern of unexpectedly rich and diverse traditions of learning being rapidly diffused throughout the island. Scarcely forty years from the time of the Sutton Hoo burial, there were scholars present at the Synod of Whitby (664) who came from Frankish, Irish, and English schools and who advocated competing mathematical systems for reconciling lunar and solar cycles of time. These systems were developed in order to calculate the date of Easter, and since their results differed, the need to decide among them was imperative. Stevens shows that interest in these systems went beyond the utilitarian purposes for which they were devised, and also that the systems themselves were too complicated to be transmitted and applied in a mechanical fashion. In order for monastic schools to train scholars in the *computus*, they had to maintain contact with centers of learning throughout western Europe, particularly in Merovingian, and later in Carolingian France.

Henrik Jansen provides a perspective on the broader context of northern Europe in the first millennium after Christ with his discussion of recent research on major archaeological sites in Denmark. He begins with a discussion of the important, recently discovered trade center at Lundeborg. This site is changing our understanding of the development of trade ports in northern Europe. The Scandinavian connections of the Sutton Hoo materials are clear, and Jansen shows how many of the issues raised by the grave are important in the archaeology of first-millennium Denmark, including the growth of long-distance trade, wide-ranging political and military changes, and a growing tension between indigenous systems of ritual and symbolism and those of the new Christianity.

The present implied by the ship burial at Sutton Hoo is less archaic than the past reconstructed by the *Beowulf* poet. No coins change hands in Heorot or anywhere else in the Scandinavian lands of the poem;[20] wealth is buried in a treasure hoard in the form of cups and bowls, the weapons and armament of war, and "heathen gold" (line 2276). This latter is a curious item. How does "heathen gold" differ from Christian gold? Is it possible that the *Beowulf* poet thought of coinage (whether gold or some less precious metal) as a material sign of a Christian culture, and therefore consciously excluded it from his reconstruction of the pagan past of his continental forebears? The thirty-seven Merovingian coins in the purse at Sutton Hoo do not make the man who was commemorated in the burial a Christian, but they do indicate at least a modest circulation of coins in seventh-century East Anglia and trade with Merovingian Gaul, because, as Alan Stahl's analysis clearly implies, these coins cannot be regarded as a princely sum (such as might be gathered as plunder) or even as a unique selection of coins from representative mints in Gaul. They look instead to be the sort of odd assortment that a merchant might carry in his purse — an assortment that could be conveniently gathered from coins in local circulation.

The meaning of the "wealth" of the Sutton Hoo ship burial may ultimately prove to be not that the man buried there must have been a great king to merit so rich a burial, but rather that the material resources and commerce of East Anglia must have been greater and more extensive than anything previously suspected if the chance survival of a single rich grave seems so impressive. In their assessment of the economic value of the Sutton Hoo burial, Edward Schoenfeld and Jana Schulman draw attention to the diverse skills and sheer number of man-hours of labor that went into the manufacture of the various items involved, from the ship to the weapons, household utensils, and jewelry. They suggest that this implies that the economic, manufacturing, and perhaps commercial infrastructure of society in East Anglia was well developed in the early seventh century.

In the final essay, Martin Carver looks ahead. The future of Sutton Hoo appears to be rich with promise. If in the past fifty years we have concentrated our attention on the magnificent ship burial, it is not only because of its intrinsic importance, which is undeniable, but also because Sutton Hoo has had as yet little else to teach. As a result of the current excavations directed by Carver, attention will certainly shift to the larger significance of the site. Mound 1 is only one of twenty tumuli. The site shows evidence of two principal uses — as a prehistoric settlement, dating to circa 2000 B.C., and as an early medieval burial ground from the seventh century A.D. From the latter period of use come the enigmatic "sand bodies," so called because the shapes of human bodies, which have completely decayed, are preserved in packed sand. These are from flat graves. Some of the sand bodies appear to have been persons who were executed. Since sand bodies are associated with at least one of the mounds (Mound 5), it seems likely that the executions were connected with the royal burials.

Was human sacrifice part of the ritual of elite burial in East Anglia? What does this burial ground tell us about the politics and ideology of the East Anglian kingdom? Does it represent an assertion of traditional pagan values in the face of the tide of Christianity flowing in from the south? If so, which values were particularly being asserted? These are some of the kinds of questions that we will have to take up in order to come to terms with the new information that is emerging about Sutton Hoo. Other questions still lie buried in the earth. Scholars at the centenary conference in 2039 will have much to talk about.

Notes

1. Overviews of Anglo-Saxon archaeology that provide essential information include David M. Wilson, ed., *The Archaeology of Anglo-Saxon England* (London, 1976); C. J. Arnold, *An Archaeology of the Early Anglo-Saxon Kingdoms* (London and New York, 1988); and Richard Hodges, *The Anglo-Saxon Achievement: Archaeology and the Beginnings of English Society* (Ithaca, N.Y., 1989).

2. See especially Rosemary Cramp, "*Beowulf* and Archaeology," *Medieval Archaeology* 1: 57-77.

3. The following information about the excavations has been drawn from R. Bruce-Mitford, *The Sutton Hoo Ship-Burial: A Handbook*, 3rd ed. (London, 1979), pp. 15-21. Martin Carver's chapter in this volume includes additional discussion of the history of the excavations and summarizes the status and objectives of the current campaign.

4. James Campbell and Roberta Frank survey in greater detail work on the Sutton Hoo burial and the use historians and literary scholars have made of it in their chapters in this volume.

5. For a survey of such burials from the Late Bronze Age, see P. F. Stary, "Das spätbronzezeitliche Häuptlingsgrab von Hagenau, Kr. Regensburg," in *Vorzeit zwischen Main und Donau*, ed. K. Spindler (Erlangen, 1980), pp. 46-97. A recent overview of Early Iron Age rich graves is C. F. E. Pare, "Der Zeremonialwagen der Hallstattzeit," in *Vierrädrige Wagen der Hallstattzeit* (Mainz, 1987), pp. 189-248. For the early medieval period, see O. Doppelfeld and R. Pirling, *Fränkische Fürsten im Rheinland: die Gräber aus dem Kölner Dom, von Krefeld-Gellep und Morken* (Bonn, 1966); and Y. Duval and J.-Ch. Picard, *L'inhumation privilégiée du IVe au VIIIe siècles en Occident* (Paris, 1986).

6. See, e.g., R. Chapman, I. Kinnes, and K. Randsborg, eds., *The Archaeology of Death* (Cambridge, 1981); and J. O'Shea, *Mortuary Variability: An Archaeological Investigation* (London, 1984).

7. For discussion of the Childeric grave, see P. Périn and L.-C. Feffer, *Les Francs*, 1: *A la conquête de la Gaule* (Paris, 1987), pp. 117-32.

8. Roberta Frank shows in chapter 4 how this story has hardened into "fact."

9. The possibility that the poet was a woman cannot be excluded, though at least in the present state of our knowledge of Anglo-Saxon culture it seems unlikely.

10. See Lawrence Moe, "The Christian Passages of *Beowulf*" (Ph.D. diss., University of Minnesota, 1990).

11. Letter to Higbald, Bishop of Lindisfarne, trans. D. W. Robertson, Jr., *The Literature of Medieval England* (New York, 1970), p. 98. The letter was written in A.D. 797.

12. For various views on the dating of the poem, see the essays gathered in Colin Chase, ed., *The Dating of Beowulf* (Toronto, 1981).

13. Aron Gurevich, *Medieval Popular Culture: Problems of Belief and Perception*, Cambridge Studies in Oral and Literate Culture 14 (Cambridge, 1988), p. 109.

14. *Ponne he forð scile / of lichaman (læded) weorðan (Beowulf, 3176b-77).*

15. *Men ne cunnon / secgan to soðe, selerædende, / hæleð under heofenum, hwa þæm* hlæste onfeng (*Beowulf*, 50b-52).

16. Bede, *Historia ecclesiastica gentis Anglorum* II.15; in *Bede's Ecclesiastical History of the English People*, ed. Bertram Colgrave and R. A. B. Mynors (Oxford, 1969), p. 191. For discussion of this passage, see chapter 7 by Simon Keynes in this volume.

17. The true saint would have been "noble by birth but *more noble* in his deeds."

18. See, for example, Roberta Frank, "Some Uses of Paronomasia in Old English Scriptural Verse," *Speculum* 47 (1972): 207-26; Stanley B. Greenfield, "Esthetics and Meaning and the Translation of Old English Poetry," in *Old English Poetry: Essays on Style*, ed. Daniel G. Calder (Berkeley and Los Angeles, 1979), pp. 91-110; and Fred C. Robinson, "Artful Ambiguities in the Old English 'Book-Moth' Riddle," in *Anglo-Saxon Poetry: Essays in Appreciation*, ed. Lewis E. Nicholson and Dolores Warwick Frese (Notre Dame, Ind., and London, 1975), pp. 355-62.

19. See the remarks of Simon Keynes in chapter 7 of this volume, esp. pp. 114-15.

20. *Feoh* and *sceatt* and their compounds are glossed "money," but they cannot be taken as evidence that coins, rather than valuable property in some form, were necessarily involved in any episode in *Beowulf*.

PART I

✙

The Sutton Hoo Objects

CHAPTER 1

✛

The Nature of the Sutton Hoo
Coin Parcel

Alan M. Stahl

The purse of the Sutton Hoo ship burial contained thirty-seven coins, three unstruck coin blanks, and two small ingots, all of gold. The coins whose origins can be determined were all struck in Merovingian Gaul in the late sixth and early seventh century.[1] The inclusion of these coins was a deliberate act by those who constructed the burial and must be seen as some sort of symbolic expression. This chapter examines whether the specific coins included also reflect a deliberate choice by these individuals or rather can be seen as a random sample of those coins that would have been readily available for inclusion. In other words, was the Sutton Hoo coin parcel a consciously selected collection or was it the contents of a purse that could have been assembled for commercial use?

There were few sources of coins in the period, and France appears to have supplied England with most of its currency until the beginning of the Anglo-Saxon issues. Besides Merovingian coins, the only issues available for use in sixth- and seventh-century England appear to have been Byzantine, Visigothic, and Anglo-Saxon. The only known coin hoard of the period found in England, that discovered at Crondall (Hampshire) in 1828, contains 1 Byzantine coin, 24 Merovingian (and imitative Frisian) coins, and 69 Anglo-Saxon gold coins.[2] Of 144 coins of the sixth and seventh century found before 1975 in England, either singly or in small groups, 26 are Byzantine issues, 8 are Visigothic, 85 are Merovingian and related (Frisian, "Alemannic") coinages, and 25 are Anglo-Saxon issues.[3] Most Byzantine coins found in England are of the sixth century,[4] and most Visigothic coins are imitations of these. The beginnings of Anglo-Saxon coinage are not well dated, but it appears unlikely that there was significant minting in England before the assemblage of the Sutton Hoo parcel.[5] The fact that all of the Sutton Hoo coins are from Merovingian mints cannot then be seen as resulting from a deliberate choice; it is what one would expect in an English hoard from the early seventh century.

All of the coins in the Sutton Hoo parcel are gold tremisses. As it appears that no silver and little bronze circulated north of the Mediterranean coast in the sixth and early seventh centuries,[6] the presence of coins of any metal other than gold in the parcel would have been remarkable.

Merovingian gold coins are of two denominations, the large solidus and its third, the tremissis. Though lacking from the Sutton Hoo parcel, Merovingian solidi were available; they comprise fifteen of the seventy-one stray finds of Merovingian coins in England.[7]

Only 5 of the coins in the Sutton Hoo parcel bear the name of a ruler. One has the name of the Frankish king Theodebert II (595-612) and no indication of the mint [SH.2]. Merovingian coins, especially of Neustrian and Austrasian mints, rarely bear the name of a Frankish monarch; of about 2,500 tremisses in the collection of the Bibliothèque Nationale, Paris, only one specimen bears the name of Theodebert II.[8] Another coin in the Sutton Hoo parcel bears the name of the Byzantine emperor Justin II (565-78) [SH.1], and 3 are in the name of Maurice Tiberius (582-602) [SH.11, 26, 27].[9] These coins have initials on their reverse that are interpreted as identifying mints in the Provence region of Merovingian Gaul: Uzès on the Justin coin [SH.1] and Venasque [SH.11], Valence [SH.26], and Arles [SH.27] on those in the name of Maurice.[10] This group is generally termed the quasi-imperial coinage of Provence, as distinct from pseudo-imperial coins, on which no mint is identified. The remaining 32 Sutton Hoo coins identify only their mint on one side and an individual sometimes specified as "monetarius" on the other; this type of coinage is conveniently referred to as the mint-and-minter type.

The Sutton Hoo parcel then contains only tremisses and has 5 "signed" coins, on which a governmental authority is identified, and 32 "anonymous" coins. The absence of solidi and this proportion of signed coinage might indicate a process of intentional selection or may simply be typical of current monetary circulation. For comparison, it is helpful to examine finds in which coins have been treated as nonmonetary objects and contrast them to hoards that appear to represent circulating money put in the earth with the intention of retrieval for future commercial use.

Two finds of the period comprise only coins that have been mounted as jewelry, an indication of conscious demonetization. The poorly documented Faversham (Kent) grave find contains 6 tremisses of the late sixth century with loops attached; 3 of these are of the quasi-imperial type.[11] The Wieuwerd (Netherlands) pot find of gold jewelry contains 29 coins in mounts of varying degrees of elaborateness; the latest coins are of the early seventh century.[12] Of these mounted pieces, there are 9 imperial Byzantine solidi and 3 imitations of these, 1 imperial tremissis, 1 quasi-imperial solidus and 1 quasi-imperial tremissis, 10 royal Merovingian solidi and 1 royal tremissis (all of the mint of Marseille), and 1 Visigothic royal tremissis. Only 2 of the coins in this assemblage are of the mint-and-minter type. In these two finds, which are almost contemporary with Sutton Hoo and which show clear evidence of selection, signed coins are represented equally with mint-and-minter coins in the Faversham burial and far more frequently in the Wieuwerd treasure. The large solidi are especially prominent among the Wieuwerd coins.

To these can be compared other finds from the same period that appear to be monetary hoards, circulating coinage buried with the intention of eventual recovery. The Escharen (Netherlands) hoard is the only sizable find containing mint-and-minter coins that appears to predate Sutton Hoo.[13] Its 65 known pieces include 5 Byzantine solidi, 1 pseudoimperial solidus, 2 quasi-imperial solidi, and 3 quasi-imperial tremisses; among its 54 mint-and-minter coins are 3 solidi and 51 tremisses. The Buis (Burgundy) hoard of 56 tremisses, apparently composed about a decade after the Sutton Hoo parcel, has 2 quasi-imperial coins and 1 Merovingian royal; the rest are mint-and-minter issues.[14] The Nietap (Netherlands) hoard of about the same period has 1 Byzantine solidus, 1 quasi-imperial tremissis, and 34 mint-and-minter tremisses.[15] The Crondall hoard contains a Byzantine tremissis from Ravenna among its 26 Continental coins; the remainder are mint-and-minter tremisses.[16] The Saint-Aubin (Lorraine) hoard is the latest about which we have reliable information as to numbers of coins; it comprises 3 Merovingian royal tremisses and 25 mint-and-minter tremisses.[17] In these hoards, whose assemblage and burial appear to have been commercial, signed coins comprise from 10 percent to 20 percent of the contents, with mint-and-minter coins comprising the balance. The proportion of signed coins appears to decrease with time as does the proportion of solidi. In both these respects, the Sutton Hoo parcel, all tremisses and with 5 signed coins to 32 mint-and-minter pieces, resembles the commercial hoards far more than it does the Faversham and Wieuwerd burials of selected coins.

The 37 coins in the Sutton Hoo parcel each bear a different mint name. This has led to the inference that "it is as though the coins had been hand-picked . . . to represent different types and mints."[18] In a typical national coinage the representation of so many mints by one specimen each would indeed be so extraordinary as to imply a conscious selection, but the Merovingian coinage is no typical series. In the 1890 catalog of about 2,500 Merovingian coins in the collection of the Bibliothèque Nationale, 420 mints are assigned to specific districts of Gaul; many other mint names cannot be located or are too garbled to be legible.[19] Among the Sutton Hoo coins, 2 lack any mint designation [SH. 2, 19] and 5 have mint names too fragmentary or garbled to be read with any confidence [SH. 9, 12, 14, 15, 34]. Five identify mints not previously known from other specimens, which have been identified with Merovingian settlements only speculatively, if at all [SH. 7, 10, 13, 16, 36]. An additional coin [SH. 8] identifies a mint classed among the "uncertain" mints and not assigned by Prou to any district.

There remain 24 coins from the Sutton Hoo parcel that name mints among those identified by Prou. If all of these 420 mints were active at the time of production of the Sutton Hoo coins and were producing at the same rate, the probability of getting no mint duplication in a random selection of 24 specimens would be about fifty-fifty.[20] However, the Sutton

Hoo parcel appears to be from the beginning of the mint-and-minter coin-age, and it is by no means certain that such a large number of mints were, in fact, in operation at that time.

Very little work has been done to determine the chronology of operation of various mints; only a few mints, most notably that of Paris and a handful in the south of France, produced a significant number of coin issues with royal or other datable names. There are certain groups of Merovingian coins defined by style and iconography that bear the names of a group of mints; in some cases these can be seen to have had a short duration and can be used to infer the simultaneous operation of a group of mints. The best studied of these groups, however, should offer a strong caution to such an inference. The anchored cross reverse with a highly stylized obverse style (*à l'appendice perlé*) was long considered a discrete series that must have been of limited chronological duration. It was this assumption that led to the original dating of the Sutton Hoo parcel to the second half of the seventh century.[21] In his reexamination of the Escharen hoard, Jean Lafaurie discovered that the anchored cross type can be found among the earliest of mint-and-minter coins.[22] It also appears in the Saint-Aubin hoard, the latest hoard of mint-and-minter coins for which accurate descriptions are available.[23]

There is, however, another group in the Sutton Hoo parcel that appears to have been produced over a short period; it is known as the Type 2 style of northeast Gaul.[24] Characterized by a distinct portrait style and reverse type closely modeled on the earliest quasi-imperial issues of Provence, this group of coins is represented by 7 specimens in the Escharen hoard [E.26-30, 38, 45] and one in Sutton Hoo [SH.4]. Of the dozen mints identified on this issue and apparently active in the early period of mint-and-minter coinage, four are represented in the Sutton Hoo parcel: SH.4 of Huy is of Type 2 and is die-linked to a coin in the Escharen hoard, while SH.23 (Laon), SH.29 (Metz), and SH.31 (Sens) are of different (probably later) types. Within this very limited early issue of mint-and-minter coins, the Sutton Hoo parcel then represents only about a third of the mints known to be active in the period.

A more widely produced early group that appears in the Sutton Hoo parcel has as its reverse type a cross with a globe beneath and no circle or wreath surrounding (the Type 2 issue is actually a subgroup of this type). Coins of this description are common in the early Escharen hoard (15 of the 31 distinct issues are of this type), as well as in that of Sutton Hoo (7 of 37 issues), but are entirely lacking from the later Crondall and Saint-Aubin hoards. A total of seventy-six mints are illustrated in the Belfort corpus as having produced this type.[25] Of these, twelve are represented by coins in the Sutton Hoo parcel. Again, the Sutton Hoo coins can be seen to represent only a small percentage of the mints active in this phase of the coinage. It appears then that a large number of mints were indeed active at the time of the assembly of the Sutton Hoo parcel and that the lack of duplication of coins in it can be attributed to random selection.

If the lack of duplication of mints does not need to be explained by conscious selection, what of the observation that "the hoard contains no geographical concentrations, however small"?[26] A glance at the map of mint locations published as Figure 413 of the Sutton Hoo report would tend to confirm this statement. However, we should not be too quick to accept the caption that notes that "the mints at which those [coin numbers] shown in circles were struck can be positively identified and located."[27] For eight of the twenty-seven locations marked with a circle on this map, the identification in the accompanying catalog is actually somewhat less than "positive." The coin of King Theodebert with no mint [SH.2] is assigned by Kent to Clermont-Ferrand (Arvernus in Aquitaine) because the only other known coin of this king was struck there;[28] his corollary argument based on the stylistic similarity of this piece to a coin of Arvernus is contradicted by his own observation that a coin of very similar style (and with the name of the minter of the Arvernus coin of Theodebert) in the Sutton Hoo parcel [SH.28] bears the mint name of Mouzon in Austrasia.[29] Kent gives no explanation for his attribution of SH.7, read with difficulty as ROSSONTE, to Ressons-sur-Matz (Oise), nor is any documentation provided for Merovingian settlement at this site: the mint name is known from no other coin.[30] For SH.8, Kent rejects Lafaurie's new attribution,[31] as well as Prou's old one,[32] for "an uncertain mint in the Rhine-Moselle region."[33] In the catalog entry for SH.13, Kent notes that Lafaurie's attribution for the "very common" name of Montiniaco "must be considered provisional."[34] A coin with a mint name conceded by the catalog to have been "widely distributed in Gaul" [SH. 32] is assigned by Kent to Provence on the basis of a stylistic resemblance to quasi-imperial coins of that region; these were, however, imitated in mints throughout the Merovingian realm.[35] Kent has moved three coins with the anchored cross reverse [SH. 20, 21, 24] from the mint locations ascribed by Prou to the region near Paris on the basis of stylistic arguments; for all three pieces, the catalog entry admits doubts about these new attributions.[36] In view of the fact that pieces in the Sutton Hoo parcel attributed to Bordeaux [SH. 22], Laon [SH. 23], and Quentovic [SH.25] have anchored cross reverses, it is doubtful that this reverse type was limited to the region around Paris at this period, and the use of the "appendice perlé" style for geographical attributions is no better supported than its discredited use for chronology.

There remain 19 coins whose mint identifications have been established with some degree of certainty. Of these, 13 bear the names of *civitates*, the urban centers of Roman administration, which were, for the most part, also the Merovingian episcopal sees. It appears that the coinage of the *civitates* was relatively more important in the early period of Merovingian mint-and-minter coinage than in the later. *Civitates* strongly outnumber the coinage of other mints in the early Escharen (9 *civitates* of a total of 15 mints) and Buis hoards (18 *civitates* out of 26 mints) and represent about half the mints in the Crondall hoard (6 *civitates* out of 10 Merovingian mints); they are only a small minority of mints in the late Saint-Aubin hoards (2 *civitates* out of 10 mints). In a region whose Merovingian coinage has been studied in detail, a progression has been discerned from coinage concentrated in *civitas* mints in the earlier period of the mint-and-minter coinage to a coinage dominated by mints of other settlement types in the later period.[37] In its predominance of coins of *civitas* mints, the Sutton Hoo hoard appears to reflect the general coinage of its time at the beginning of the mint-and-minter coinage and is consistent with the early commercial hoards.

While the *civitas* mints in the Sutton Hoo hoard are not concentrated in a specific region of the Merovingian kingdom, their identities do not suggest a conscious selection. While many of the main *civitates* of Merovingian Gaul are represented (e.g., Paris [SH.17], Metz [SH.29], Angers [SH.3]), others that were important as mints as well as political and ecclesiastical centers, such as Reims, Tours, and Marseille, are absent. To the extent that some geographical concentration of the *civitas* mints is evident, this can be seen as reflecting patterns of settlement and commercial activity. Five mints are in Mediterranean Gaul: Valence [SH.26], Venasque [SH.11], Arles [SH.27], Uzès [SH.1], and Javols [SH.35]. Most of the remainder were centers on or near major rivers: the Seine (Paris [SH.17], Sens [SH.31], Troyes [SH.6]); the Loire (Angers [SH.3]); the Moselle (Metz [SH.29]); and the Garonne (Bordeaux [SH.22]). Laon [SH.23] and Sion [SH.19] do not fall into these classes, but their appearance among commercially active *civitates* of Merovingian France is not surprising.

The remaining 6 identified mints in the Sutton Hoo parcel are of smaller settlements, typically *vici*, stopping places on roads and regional centers of production and marketing. Such smaller settlements were an important source of Merovingian coinage; in Prou's catalog, 340 non-*civitas* mints are identified and assigned to specific districts. In the former province of Belgica I, the number of issues known from the 11 identified small mints is about equal to that known from the 4 *civitates*.[38] One of the small mints represented in the Sutton Hoo parcel [SH.33], read on the coin as ICCIOMO, is attributed by Kent to Usson in the district of Poitiers,[39] following the attribution by Prou of a die-linked specimen [BN.2314]. Prou's attribution was apparently based on style; he cited without comment a tentative attribution to the Touraine and gave no documentation for his choice.[40] Other than this problematic mint, the small settlements represented in the Sutton Hoo parcel are all in the extreme northeast of Gaul and on waterways tied in to the communication between France and the North Sea region: Mouzon [SH.28], Dinant [SH.5], and Huy [SH.4] on the Meuse; Andernach [SH.30] on the Rhine; and Quentovic [SH.25] on the North Sea coast itself.

The mints identified with a reasonable degree of certainty within the Sutton Hoo hoard then can be seen to fall into two groups: issues of *civitates* throughout Gaul and issues of small settlements in the Northeast. This same pattern is true in the distribution of mints in the Crondall hoard. Coins of 6 widely scattered *civitates* are present in the Crondall hoard: Rodez, Chalon-sur-Saône, Paris, Amiens, Cologne,[41] and Metz. Two of these *civitas* mints are from the northeast of Merovingian Gaul: Cologne and Metz. Metz, the main mint in the northeast of Merovingian Gaul, is represented by three specimens in the hoard. The 4 small mints represented in Crondall are possibly all from the northern region as well: Marsal and Meuvy are on the Meuse, Quentovic is on the North Sea coast, and "Palaciolo" is usually placed in the Rhineland.[42] The representation of mints in the Sutton Hoo parcel is basically similar to that of the Crondall hoard, the only other hoard of Merovingian coins found in England and one whose monetary nature is generally accepted.[43]

There then appears to be nothing in the origin of the coins in the Sutton Hoo parcel that leads to an inference of conscious selection. Is there anything about the number of coins or the presence of unstruck blanks and ingots that sets this parcel apart from monetary hoards? In 1970 Philip Grierson proposed that the parcel was too small to have been commercially important, so the size must have had some symbolic significance. The presence of three unstruck blanks suggested that a certain number of coins was sought; the total number of small pieces (forty) coincided with the number of oarsmen, so each one could be seen as a payment for passage to the Other World for these oarsmen. The heavier ingots would have been for the steersman.[44] This explanation was taken up in the 1975 excavation report, where it was noted that the number of forty oarsmen, which had been only hypothetical before, had since been demonstrated.[45] Grierson's explanation is intriguing and, if true, implies only a conscious selection of the number of pieces, not any attention to the mints or types of the coins. However, the equivalence of the number of coins to the number of oarsmen raises a number of unanswered questions. Why were there two ingots for a single steersman? If more valuable pieces were sought for him, why not solidi, which figure in other English and North Sea finds of the period? If a "Charon's obol" in the form of a coin was needed as fare to the Other World for each of the crewmen, who were not included in the burial, why was there none for the individual who was buried? As there are no parallel cases in analogous burials, the whole concept of the coins as payment to or for the boatmen must remain speculative.

Grierson contended that the three blanks and two ingots could not have been included in order to make up a certain weight, as there would have been no reason to hammer out individual blanks for such a purpose. This argument assumes that the blanks were made specifically for inclusion in the burial. An alternative possibility is that unstruck blanks and ingots were in circulation alongside struck coins and that the parcel is representative of this. Unstamped coin blanks are present in the Nietap, Crondall, and Dronrijp hoards, and ingots are also present in the Dronrijp hoard.[46] These three monetary hoards are from outside the Merovingian kingdom; for commerce beyond the Frankish realm it appears that unstruck pieces of gold could be used alongside Merovingian coins. The flans and ingots in these hoards are different in appearance from those in Sutton Hoo, but as their deposition is later, this may reflect a development in the nature of unstruck blanks in circulation.

If ingots of various sizes were included in the monetary circulation outside of the Merovingian realm, it would appear that the basis of payments was weight rather than count. The thirty-seven coins in the Sutton Hoo parcel have a combined weight of 47.00 grams; the three blanks together weigh 3.93 grams, and the two ingots together weigh 10.18 grams, yielding a total weight of 61.11 grams for the parcel. Grierson has argued that even before striking their own coins, the Anglo-Saxons had a monetary weight unit of gold, the shilling, equivalent to twenty sceattas, or barley grains.[47] These grains were equal in weight to later ones, so the troy grain of 0.0648 grams can be taken as the theoretical basis for the Anglo-Saxon monetary unit.[48] A shilling would then be a unit of 1.296 grams of gold. The 61.11 grams of gold in the Sutton Hoo parcel can then be seen as a monetary unit worth 47.15 shillings.

The idea that an indigenous English weight unit was applied to imported coins is, however, hypothetical. There is no way to know whether the Sutton Hoo coins were brought together within the Merovingian kingdom, in northern continental Europe, or in England. The Sutton Hoo parcel, made up entirely of Merovingian coins, might have been evaluated in terms of the Merovingian weight system, either by those including it in the burial or by someone assembling a parcel of coins on the Continent. The weight standard of Merovingian gold coinage was derived from the late Roman system, based on the classical Roman pound. The solidus from the fourth century on had been $1/72$ pound and was in turn the weight of 24 carats. This solidus had a theoretical weight of 4.54 grams; its third, the tremissis, would weigh 1.51 grams.[49] Around the year 538 special solidi of reduced weight were issued by the Byzantine government apparently for specific trade purposes, one series of 22 carats and one of 20 carats.[50] Around 585 a solidus of 23 carats was added.[51] The quasi-imperial solidi of Gaul usually bear the Roman numerals XXI on the reverse; the corresponding tremisses usually have VII. This has been taken as an indication that they were to weigh respectively 21 and 7 carats and represent another reduced-weight issue, though probably not an officially sanctioned one.[52] A solidus of 21 Roman carats would weigh about 3.97 grams; a tremissis about 1.32. The total weight of the Sutton Hoo coin parcel (61.11 grams) would then represent a value of 15.39 of these solidi, or 46.30 tremisses.

In practice, Byzantine solidi of the late sixth century appear to have been struck somewhat below their theoretical standard.[53] Merovingian coins following the quasi-imperial model also seem somewhat below the theoretical 21-carat weight of 3.97 grams for a solidus and the 7-carat weight of 1.32 grams for a tremissis. The quasi-imperial solidi published by Rigold have a modal peak in the 3.85-3.89 gram range, and the tremisses have a mode in the 1.25–1.29 gram range. This same weight distribution can be seen in the Merovingian mint-and-minter coinage; the modal weight for the mint-and-minter coins in the Escharen, Sutton Hoo, Nietap, and Crondall hoards also falls into the 1.25–1.29 gram range, and the mean weight of these coins is 1.32 grams for Escharen, 1.27 grams for Sutton Hoo and Nietap, and 1.28 grams for Crondall.

The best weight to use for the effective standard at the time of the assembly of the Sutton Hoo parcel derives from the Sutton Hoo coins themselves. While the 37 Sutton Hoo coins have a total range from 1.057 to 1.388 grams, all but 4 fall between 1.21 and 1.34 grams. They have a mean weight of 1.270 grams and a standard deviation of 0.053 grams. The modal weight (the class with the most coins) is from 1.270 to 1.279 grams. The weight standard for the 37 struck Sutton Hoo coins then appears to have been 1.27 grams. The 61.11 grams for the 37 coins, 3 blanks, and 2 ingots would then have a value of 48.12 tremisses or 16.04 solidi. This is as close as could practically have been achieved for a monetary sum of 16 solidi. Sixteen solidi or 48 tremisses or shillings may have been a sum of some symbolic significance, or this may just be the quantity of money that was in a coin purse intended for commercial use. It may also represent the total amount of coins and other monetary media that could be assembled in early seventh-century East Anglia for inclusion in a burial.

There is then nothing extraordinary about the types of coins included in the Sutton Hoo purse, their origins, or their number or weight. Had they been found in a regular purse in a nonburial context, it is unlikely they would have been considered a remarkable assemblage. There was certainly a conscious decision to include coins in the ornate purse of the Sutton Hoo burial, but the actual coins included may well have been the contents of a purse that was assembled for less specific purposes or a sample of coins circulating in the region.

Notes

1. The Sutton Hoo coins are published and discussed in J. P. C. Kent, "The Coins and the Date of the Burial," in *The Sutton Hoo Ship-Burial*, Rupert Bruce-Mitford, with contributions by Paul Ashbee et al., 3 vols. in 4 (London, 1975-83), 1:578-647; these coins are cited hereafter as SH. 1, etc., following the numbers in that catalog. The best introduction to Merovingian and contemporary coinages is Philip Grierson and Mark Blackburn, *Medieval European Coinage*, 1: *The Early Middle Ages* (Cambridge, 1986) (hereafter cited as MEC). In Alan M. Stahl and W. A. Oddy, "The Date of the Sutton Hoo Coins," in *Sutton Hoo: Past, Present, and Future*, ed. Robert Farrell and Carol de Vegvar (Kalamazoo, Mich., forthcom-

ing), an argument is set forward for a possible date of the Sutton Hoo parcel at the beginning of the seventh century rather than the 620-25 proposed by Kent, but the standard relative chronology of Merovingian coinage and coin hoards as summarized in Grierson and Blackburn is accepted. I would like to thank Lauris Olson for his helpful criticism of this chapter.

2. C. H. V. Sutherland, *Anglo-Saxon Gold Coinage in the Light of the Crondall Hoard* (Oxford, 1948); and Philip Grierson, "The Purpose of the Sutton Hoo Coins," *Antiquity* 44 (1970): 14-18.

3. S. E. Rigold, "The Sutton Hoo Coins in the Light of the Contemporary Background of Coinage in England," in Bruce-Mitford, *Sutton Hoo* 1: 653-77.

4. Jean Lafaurie and Cécile Morrisson, "La pénétration des monnaies byzantines en Gaule mérovingienne et visigotique du VIe au VIIIe siècle," *Revue numismatique*, 6th ser., 29 (1987): 93-94.

5. Grierson and Blackburn, *MEC* 1:161.

6. Lafaurie and Morrisson, "La pénétration," pp. 64-94.

7. Rigold, "Sutton Hoo."

8. Maurice Prou, *Catalogue des monnaies françaises de la Bibliothèque Nationale; Les monnaies mérovingiennes* (Paris, 1892), p. 354, no. 1713; these coins are cited hereafter as BN. 1713, etc.

9. The legend of the Justin coin is garbled and may in fact be derived from the name Justinian (527-65).

10. S. E. Rigold, "An Imperial Coinage in Southern Gaul in the Sixth and Seventh Centuries?" *Numismatic Chronicle*, 6th ser., 14 (1954): 93-133.

11. Rigold, "Sutton Hoo," pp. 668-71, nos. 48, 49, 51, 66, 69, and 78.

12. Jean Lafaurie, B. Jansen, and A. N. Zadoks-Josephus Jitta, "Le trésor de Wieuwerd," *Oudheidkundige mededelingen uit het Rijksmuseum van Oudheden te Leiden* 42 (1961): 78-107.

13. Jean Lafaurie, "Le trésor d'Escharen," *Revue numismatique*, 6th ser., 2 (1959-60): 153-210.

14. Pierre Le Gentilhomme, "Les monnaies mérovingiennes de la trouvaille de Buis," *Revue numismatique*, 5th ser., 2 (1938): 133-68; reprinted in his *Mélanges de numismatique mérovingienne* (Paris, 1940), pp. 95-130.

15. Arent Pol, "De 7e-eeuwse muntvondst Nietap," *Jaarboek voor Munt-en Penningkunde* 62-64 (1975-77): 23-62.

16. Sutherland, *Anglo-Saxon Gold Coinage*, pp. 9-12; Philip Grierson provided the correct attribution of the Byzantine coin to Phocas in "The Purpose of the Sutton Hoo Coins," p. 15.

17. L. Maxe-Werly, "Trouvaille de Saint-Aubin (Meuse)," *Revue numismatique*, 3rd ser., 8 (1890): 12-53.

18. Rupert Bruce-Mitford, "Introduction and Observations on the Dating of the Hoard and the Burial," in *Sutton Hoo* 1:585.

19. Prou, *Monnaies mérovingiennes*.

20. The "Classical Birthday Problem" of basic probability presents an analogous situation: in a population of 23 students, chances are about fifty-fifty that no two will have the same birthday. With our universe of 420 possible mints and 24 coins selected, the probability is .51 of having distinct mints in a random selection, about one chance in two. Even if all 37 Sutton Hoo coins are included and the total number of mints is held to the 420 located by Prou, the probability of having distinct mints in a random draw is still .20, that is one in five. The formula for calculating the probability (p) of getting no duplication of mints in n draws from a population of S mints is:

$$p = \frac{S(S-1)(S-2) \ldots (S-n+1)}{S^n}$$

21. Pierre Le Gentilhomme, "Aperçu sur quelques aspects du monnayage des peuples

barbares," *Revue numismatique,* 5th ser., 4 (1940): 33-35; and R. L. S. Bruce-Mitford, "Sutton Hoo—A Rejoinder," *Antiquity* 26 (1952): 76-82.

22. Lafaurie, "Le trésor d'Escharen," p. 165.

23. Maxe-Werly, "La trouvaille de Saint-Aubin," nos. 19, 20, 21, and 22.

24. Jacques Yvon, "Note sur deux groupes de monnaies mérovingiennes du Nord-Est de la Gaule," *Revue numismatique,* 5th ser., 15 (1953): 67-77; and Lafaurie, "Le trésor d'Escharen," pp. 158-59.

25. A. de Belfort, *Description générale des monnaies mérovingiennes,* 5 vols. (Paris, 1892-95). I have used this corpus rather than the more reliable Prou catalogue because it illustrates all coins, albeit with engravings.

26. Bruce-Mitford, "Introduction and Observations," p. 585.

27. Ibid., p. 581.

28. Kent, "The Coins," p. 609.

29. Ibid., p. 635.

30. Ibid., p. 614.

31. Jean Lafaurie, "Numismatique romaine et médievale," *Annuaire de l'Ecole Pratique des Hautes Etudes, IVe Section,* 1967-68, p. 260.

32. Prou, "Monnaies mérovingiennes," no. 2544.

33. Kent, "The Coins," p. 615.

34. Ibid., p. 620.

35. Ibid., p. 639.

36. Ibid., pp. 627, 628, and 631.

37. Alan M. Stahl, *The Merovingian Coinage of the Region of Metz,* Publications d'histoire de l'art de d'archéologie de l'Université Catholique de Louvain 30 (Louvain-la-Neuve, 1982), pp. 134-36.

38. Stahl, *Merovingian Coinage,* pp. 143-57.

39. Kent, "The Coins," p. 640.

40. Prou, *Monnaies mérovingiennes,* pp. 475-76; and G. de Ponton d'Amécourt, "Recherches sur les monnaies mérovingiennes de Touraine," *Annuaire de la Société Française de Numismatique* 3 (1868-70): 125-26. Belfort, *Description générale,* identifies this mint as "Hiesmes," without giving a location for this settlement (2:105 and 5:232).

41. See Grierson and Blackburn, *MEC* 1:127, for this attribution.

42. However, I have assigned this coin to Paliseau in Neustria (Stahl, *Merovingian Coinage,* p. 36).

43. Grierson, "Purpose," p. 15.

44. Ibid., pp. 16-17.

45. Bruce-Mitford, "Introduction and Observations," pp. 586-87.

46. Pol, "Nietap," pp. 57-58, nos. 35 and 36; Sutherland, "Crondall," p. 99, nos. 91a and b; and J. Dirks, "La trouvaille de Dronryp en Frise," *Revue Belge de Numismatique* 43 (1887): 92 and 103, nos. 29-30.

47. Philip Grierson, "La fonction sociale de la monnaie en Angleterre aux VIIe-VIIIe siècles," *Settimane di studio del Centro italiano di studi sull'alto medioevo* 8: *Moneta e scambi nell'alto medioevo* (Spoleto, 1961): 341-62.

48. Grierson, "La fonction sociale," discussion on pp. 367-68.

49. Wolfgang Hahn, *Moneta Imperii Byzantini,* 1: *Von Anastasius I. bis Justinianus I. (491-565),* Österreichische Akademie der Wissenschaften, Philosophisch-Historische Klasse, Denkschriften 109 (Vienna, 1973), p. 21 (hereafter cited as *MIB*).

50. Hahn, *MIB* 1: 25-26.

51. Hahn, *MIB* 2: *Von Justinus II. bis Phocas,* Denkschriften 119 (Vienna, 1975), p. 16.

52. Rigold, "An Imperial Coinage." Grierson has argued that the choice of 21 carats was to create a coin weight on the Germanic standard; the new Merovingian tremissis would then be the equivalent of the shilling: Grierson, "Fonction sociale," p. 352.

53. Arnold Luschin von Ebengreuth, *Der Denar der Lex Salica*, Österreichische Akademie der Wissenschaften, Philosophisch-Historische Klasse, Band 163, Abhandlung 4 (Vienna, 1910), pp. 70-73; and Howard L. Adelson, *Light Weight Solidi and Byzantine Trade during the Sixth and Seventh Centuries*, Numismatic Notes and Monographs 138 (New York, 1957), pp. 44-49. The weights of the coins used in these studies may be lighter than a random sample: weights of 98 solidi of Tiberius II, Maurice, Phocas, and Heraclius in the collection of the American Numismatic Society show a modal weight in the 4.45–4.49 gram class rather than the 4.40–4.44 gram class evident in the studies of Luschin and Adelson. The heavier modal weight is evident in the coins of these reigns published in Cécile Morrisson et al., *L'or monnayé, 1: Purification et altérations de Rome à Byzance*, Cahiers Ernest-Babelon 2 (Paris, 1985), pp. 205-6.

CHAPTER 2

✛

Sutton Hoo
An Economic Assessment
Edward Schoenfeld and Jana Schulman

In 1939, when archaeologists began to uncover Mound 1 at Sutton
Hoo, few dreamed of the wealth that was buried in it. The gold coins
and jewelry, the silver utensils, the weapons and armor of iron and gilt
bronze, and the imprint, preserved in the sand, of an exceptionally large
ship, as well as other valuable items, were intended to accompany a powerful individual on his final journey.[1] While no one would argue that the
burial was intended to send the person off in great style, scholars traditionally have tended to focus on the symbolic and the aesthetic approaches to understanding and appreciating the pieces found. Historians
of art have pointed to the gold jewelry as the epitome of Germanic Style II
animal work and as fine examples of the polychrome technique.[2] Political
and economic historians have used the 37 gold coins, each from a different mint, and the silver bowls and spoons, with their probable origin in
Byzantium, as evidence of wide-ranging contacts and possible trade.[3] Military and art historians have used the weapons and armor to reconstruct
the military equipment of the Dark Ages.[4] Finally, historians of technology have used the ship to show that the Anglo-Saxons possessed advanced
shipbuilding techniques.[5]

While earlier approaches have established that the items are indeed
valuable in artistic and symbolic ways, they have not considered what
makes them valuable in an economic sense, in the sense that they mate-
rially reflect the power and wealth of the ruler who is buried at Sutton
Hoo and the society that buried him there. In this chapter we assess several of these artifacts to see why and how we may call them economically
valuable and to speculate, at least, on their economic value to the society
that buried them. In essence, we are seeking to establish an economic
context for the items.

To establish such a context, we have employed various methodological
approaches. The first method we used to determine how the Anglo-Saxons might have valued particular pieces was to search documentary and
literary sources to find references to monetary values. Unfortunately, the
evidence of a few wills and of the wergelds set down in contemporary law
codes is all that supplements the remains of a poetic tradition not characterized by its precision in recording economic matters. As a result, we

were often forced to use later evidence to make our estimates; yet, by doing so, we succeeded in calculating the money equivalent in contemporary coinage of the weapons and the trees used to build the ship .

Our next method was theoretically to melt down each individual piece into its weight in either gold or silver and to use this weight to assess its equivalent value in currency. The studies done by Rupert Bruce-Mitford and Angela Care Evans, which gave the weights for the coins, the gold jewelry, and the silver bowls and spoons, facilitated this approach.[6] Once we had the weights, we assumed that gold was ten to fourteen times more valuable than silver and that each Germanic solidus weighed approximately 3.9 grams of gold.[7] Thus, for example, the Anastasius Dish, which is 5.64 kilograms (12.4 pounds) of silver,[8] is equivalent to between 424 and 583 grams of gold, for a monetary value of approximately 109 to 149 Germanic solidi. Since the price, in solidi, of everyday items like a cow are recorded, the monetary value assigned to an artifact like the Anastasius Dish can be understood as its cost, in terms of material resources, to the society that consigned it to burial. Since the seventh-century Ripuarian Laws set the value of a cow at one solidus, the value of the Anastasius Dish equals that of a herd of at least 109 cows.[9]

Our third approach for assessing the value of the artifacts was to consider the work process, that is the time and labor, required to make them. The work of Bernard Bachrach on castle building and of Carroll Gillmor on William of Normandy's naval operation in 1066 provided valuable guidance in this effort.[10] By evaluating work process in terms of an Average Working Day (AWD) of 7.5 hours,[11] we were able to draw some conclusions about the technology and general wealth of the society. If local artisans were commissioned to make these pieces, the society (the king) was wealthy enough to support those men and possessed a technical capacity sufficient to support their work. If the pieces were commissioned or obtained abroad, their origin has important implications for political contact and perhaps trade. Our work process calculations allowed us to begin quantifying a number of these factors.

Using these methods, we have arrived at an assessment of the value of several of the Sutton Hoo pieces: namely the gold coins, the gold jewelry, the silver, the weapons, and the ship. While we have been able to draw some conclusions, we must emphasize that the present study does not evaluate all of the artifacts found in the ship burial, since items such as the iron lampstand or the bronze hanging bowls lay outside the scope of our original research. Nor have we used each of the methods described to evaluate every item that is examined, as not all of the methods were equally applicable to all of the items. Still, within these limitations, we hope to show that the economic analysis of objects in the Sutton Hoo find can help us better understand their economic significance, their value, to the society that produced them.

The portion of the treasure easiest to evaluate is the hoard of 37 gold coins, 3 blanks, and 2 four-solidi ingots, with a total monetary value of 48 shillings or 16 Germanic solidi.[12] To put this number of coins into perspective, the wergeld of a freeman as defined in the Kentish Laws of King Æthelberht (d. 616) was 100 shillings, and 50 shillings was the fine for breaking the king's *mundbyrd* (protection).[13] While the Sutton Hoo coins make up less than a third of the latter sum, they do represent an amount of wealth sufficient to buy a herd of sixteen cows.[14] While this is a relatively modest amount of raw wealth, it is in line with the monetary value of several other Dark Age coin hoards, notably Escharen and Nietap.[15] Alan Stahl discusses the provenance of the coins in chapter 1. For our purposes it will be sufficient to note that the coins, which may have been selected from a larger hoard for die-relatedness (an argument that Stahl rejects), strongly imply at least political contact, if not trade, between East Anglia and the Merovingian realms.[16]

The gold jewelry found in the Sutton Hoo ship burial consists of some fifty pieces with a total weight of 1,661.5 grams, the equivalent of 426 Germanic solidi.[17] Most of the pieces are molded gold with cloisonné work, and many have filigree work, all of uniformly excellent workmanship and design. The Sutton Hoo jewelry, in fact, is so well executed that no paste or adhesives that might have secured the inlay work in place have been discovered, and the inlay pieces apparently are held in their compartments solely by pressure from the compartment walls and "trays" made of pointillé gold leaf set underneath the stones or glass. Since an experienced artisan using modern tools would need the better part of a day to cut and polish one inlay piece, all four thousand pieces of stone inlay would have required one person over eleven years to complete.[18] The jewelry also implies trade or political contact, as diffraction studies show that the garnets used at Sutton Hoo came from Bohemia.[19]

The major pieces of silver found at Sutton Hoo include a large footed dish, called the Anastasius Dish because of the four imperial control stamps bearing the monogram of Anastasius I (491-518) on its underside; a fluted bowl with the design of a female head; ten additional bowls, which were apparently intended to be a set; a smaller footed dish; two inscribed spoons; and a ladle. The purity of the silver reaches 97.3 percent, and these pieces yield a total metal weight of 10.993 kilograms of silver, equivalent to 827 to 1,137 grams of gold,[20] or approximately 212 to 292 Germanic solidi. Both the quantity of silver and its artistic quality place the Sutton Hoo silver in the first rank of late antique/early medieval silver hoards in Europe, including those found in the territory of Byzantium.[21] The workmanship of all of the pieces shows that the craftsmen were familiar with various types of punches and engraving techniques; the Anastasius Dish, at the very least, was polished on a lathe,[22] and all of the silver was probably embellished with niello to bring out the engraving lines.[23]

The evaluation of the silver presented several difficulties. Because of the deteriorated condition of two of the smaller silver bowls, it was hard to calculate the metal weight; however, since the small bowls are matched pairs and the fragmentary bowls match other, better-preserved bowls for which it is possible to determine weights, we were able to use the weight of the intact bowls to approximate that of their deteriorated partners. Anomalies in artistry also complicate the evaluation of the silver. While some of the bowls, for example, display extremely precise engraving, others seem almost sloppily executed.[24] Since the Anastasius Dish reveals similar imprecisions, some archaeologists (notably Ernst Kitzinger) have suggested that only the silver was produced in Constantinople and the decorative work added later, possibly in western Europe.[25] In fact, while an Eastern origin for at least the best-executed specimens of the silver is supported by their stylistic similarity to bowls found at Lampsacus in Turkey and Malaia Pereschepira in Armenia, the style and execution of the remainder, as well as the characteristically Merovingian engraving on the "Saulos" spoon, indicate Merovingian final manufacture.[26]

The weapons and armor found in the Sutton Hoo ship burial consist of the fragments of one helmet, an entirely oxidized mail coat, the fittings of a shield with some of the wood still intact, six spearheads and three angons, and a sword in its scabbard.[27] These items make Sutton Hoo one of the richest single finds of northern Dark Age military equipment in all of Europe and a very significant contribution to our knowledge of Dark Age warfare.

Of these, the easiest to assess using the methods we have chosen are the six spearheads and three angons, which are of conventional material (iron) and design for the period.[28] The precise method of construction shows some regional variation, which has been identified as Swedish and may be the result of trade or migration.[29] The shield was made of linden wood covered by hardened leather that was fastened down by metallic fittings and a gilt bronze rim, again a standard method of construction for the period.[30] The gilded fittings, however, take the item out of the realm of the ordinary and into that of treasure, and details of its construction confirm that it indeed was used only for ceremony or display.[31]

While the shield formed his basic defensive equipment, the spear was the primary weapon of the Anglo-Saxon warrior.[32] The seventh-century Ripuarian Laws set the value of a spear and shield at two solidi, the same as an ox or two cows.[33] Later Anglo-Saxon wills show that bequests of weaponry were common among the military class, usually given as a set: a spear and a shield together, often accompanied by a horse, sometimes by a sword.[34] In the eleventh-century Laws of Canute, two spears and a shield were the equipment required of a ceorl when he reported for war; a nobleman was required to send four warriors equipped in the same way.[35] The weapons found at Sutton Hoo were sufficient to outfit three or four warriors with spears, and although there is only a single shield, its richness and likely use for display indicate conspicuous consumption by a powerful lord.

The mail coat, or byrnie, was made of iron links that probably were cut out of sheet metal with a die, or from flat hammered wire cut into short lengths. A number of the links were then cut open, passed through solid links to "weave" the coat, and closed again with copper rivets.[36] This method of construction required a great deal of time, as well as a high level of skill. It took Jack Skogen, a Minneapolis blacksmith, 1.5 AWDs to construct a three-by-three-inch fragment of mail, beginning with wire and placing a rivet in each link.[37] By extension, a full-sized byrnie patterned after the Sutton Hoo coat would require about 135 AWDs to finish, not counting the time spent stamping out and cutting the links.

The gold-hilted sword, with its decorated scabbard, completes the offensive armament found at Sutton Hoo. The weapon falls well within the general description of Migration-and Viking-era swords,[38] and the construction of its blade with pattern-welded iron with a steel cutting edge[39] once again represents the best quality that an expert workman could reasonably be expected to achieve. A replica pattern-welded sword constructed by an acquaintance of H. R. Ellis Davidson for research purposes required 10 AWDs to complete and was a little smaller than the Sutton Hoo sword.[40] Not only the time, but also the skill needed to forge and decorate the sword, is remarkable.

In literary sources, the construction of this kind of weapon and armor seems to have been the exclusive province of master craftsmen such as the legendary Weland Smith, their possession a mark of great wealth and distinction, and their presentation an act worthy of the greatest kings.[41] In the Laws of Canute, only noblemen and warriors supported by the king were expected to equip themselves with byrnies; the "average" Anglo-Saxon soldier had to be content with his shield alone.[42] The Ripuarian Laws place the value of a mail coat at 12 solidi, the highest of any single piece of military equipment, and mail leggings at an additional 6 solidi, while an ordinary sword (with a sheath) is valued at 7 solidi.[43] Legal evidence shows that gold-hilted swords were expected to be the property of great lords, and it was a matter of note if a man of lesser rank obtained one. In the tenth-century wills of Beohtric and Duke Ælfeah, gold-hilted swords valued at 80 mancuses (or about 200 tenth-century shillings, the equivalent of about 75 to 95 seventh-century Germanic solidi) were given as bequests.[44] The Sutton Hoo sword, with its superior craftsmanship and extensive decoration, is definitely in this class of weapon, and the mail coat represents at least the state of the art in Dark Age defensive armament.

The final piece of military equipment found in the Sutton Hoo ship burial was the helmet. Its skull cap, cheek pieces, and neck guard were decorated in gilt bronze that was die-stamped with a series of designs showing combats or scenes of intertwined animals typical of the era's art. The crest, like the nasal and its moustache and eyebrow attachments, is entirely of gilt bronze and gives the helmet a very striking appearance. Overall, the piece demonstrates a high level of artistic ability and technical skill. The skull cap is unusual in that it is a single piece, rather than two or four held together by a crest, as was usual for helmets of Late Roman and Dark Age manufacture.[45] Furthermore, while the Ripuarian Laws do mention the value of a helmet as 6 solidi,[46] the helmet found at Sutton Hoo displays features that set its value as far above that of an ordinary helmet as that of the Sutton Hoo sword is above ordinary swords.

The last artifact that we have analyzed is the ship. Fortunately, even though no wood survived, the quite complete imprint left in the sand allowed archaeologists to ascertain the ship's length, the number of strakes, and the sizes and types of rivets. The ship was some 89 feet long with nine strakes on each side. She was clinker-built, with overlapping strakes fastened to each other with iron rivets; the gunwale strakes (those uppermost from the keel) were fastened with long spikes, also made of iron. The hull was strengthened by 26 ribs placed roughly 3 feet apart and attached by iron rib bolts (one per rib side) and trenails (wooden pegs).[47]

The ship's wood has not survived, but its grain pattern, preserved in iron oxides from the rivets, has a density similar to oak.[48] Assuming, along with Gillmor, that a large oak could provide two planks, each 12 inches wide and 18 feet long, the Sutton Hoo ship required 45 oaks for the hull, and approximately 2.5 to complete the keel, for a total of 47.5 trees. While Gillmor allows 10 trees for a mast and the rest of the ship, we need only add enough trees for the ribs—as there is no evidence of a mast—giving us a total of some 55 trees.[49]

Using modern comparative data, it is possible to assess the work time needed to cut and then transport the trees. A modern woodchopper, using steel axes and bucksaws, can cut down 3 oak trees in 1 AWD, sharpening his blade only once a day. The relative quality of tool metal suggests that seventh-century workmen would have had to sharpen their tools three times as often, thus requiring 55 AWD to cut down 55 oaks.[50] Estimates for the later Middle Ages hold "that the transport of heavy loads, such as logs, cost approximately one-third of an AWD per 1000 kilograms per 1.6 kilometers."[51] As overland transport was less than half as efficient before the eleventh century, it would have taken at least 20 AWDs to transport 55 oaks one mile in Anglo-Saxon times.[52] Thus, the total time spent in preparing and transporting the logs would be 75 AWDs.

The ship also required approximately 941 pounds of iron to build.[53] This is a significant amount, as the production of just 150 pounds of iron at the early medieval works in West Runyon, Norfolk, required workers to dig some 270 cubic feet of sand to find 600 pounds of iron-bearing pebbles.[54] To produce the 941 pounds of iron for the ship, workers would have had to dig away some 1,694 cubic feet of sand to find around 3,764 pounds of iron-bearing pebbles, requiring that they spend 27.7 AWDs just digging the sand for the iron ore.[55] Once the ore was dug and smelted, the iron had to be transported, and a worker could transport 941 pounds one mile in 2 AWDs.[56] At the shipbuilding site, the rivets would have to be installed, and we estimate that one worker could install all the rivets in 625 AWDs.[57]

These calculations show that to cut the wood, mine the iron ore, transport both to the shipbuilding site, and install the rivets would have cost a total of 739 AWDs. In other words, one man would have taken two years to do this work, while a crew of twelve could have finished in two months. Gillmor estimates that twelve men working together could finish a war ship in three months if all the building materials had been gathered in advance.[58] The only work to be done after the materials are gathered for which we have been able to calculate AWDs is installing the rivets, which would have taken a twelve-man crew 52 AWD. We have not, however, been able to calculate hard figures for such tasks as designing the ship, planing and fitting the wood, and installing the ribs, all of which would have had to be completed after the wood and iron had arrived at the shipbuilding site. Combining these tasks with the finding and transporting of raw materials, a time of five months for a crew of twelve (or five man-years) is not too long to build a large seagoing vessel, but is excessive if the ship were just to serve as a means of burial.[59]

We can appreciate the actual value of the ship even more if we look at the Laws of Ine of Wessex (688-725), which set the fine for cutting down a large oak tree at 60 shillings.[60] That many eighth-century shillings is equivalent to the value of a slave in Wessex and is sixty times more than the value of a sheep.[61] The value of a tree is also twenty times less than the 1,200-shilling wergeld for a member of the king's household.[62] Obviously, large trees were valued. The financial value of the trees used to build the Sutton Hoo ship would have been 3,300 shillings or almost three times the wergeld for a king's thegn. In comparison, a mail coat and sword together would probably be worth 40 eighth-century shillings (15 to 19 solidi in the seventh-century Ripuarian Laws).[63] Thus, the 3,300 eighth-century shilling value of the ship would approximate 1,238 to 1,568 seventh-century Germanic solidi.

Having assessed several of the Sutton Hoo artifacts, we would like to draw a few conclusions. First, trade and contact between Anglo-Saxon England and regions like the Baltic and Merovingian France seem likely to have existed earlier than historians have usually agreed. The existence of the ship confirms sea travel; her size and steering innovations indicate an ability for longer voyages. Among the weapons, the angons, at least, reveal Swedish stylistic influences and may even have been imported or brought by migration. Since iron mines in the Weald show little exploitation from the early medieval period, even the raw iron may have been brought from Sweden.[64] At least some of the silver came from Byzantium, and the rest of the finished silver pieces had to be brought from western Europe. The gold jewelry suggests trade as well, especially if Birgit Arrhenius is correct and a central goldsmith workshop existed at Trier with a satellite on the North Sea coast serving the British Isles, Merovingian Gaul, and Scandinavia.[65] The gold coins are from Merovingian mints; even if they were not a merchant's hoard, they do suggest political contacts of an extensive sort.

Taking advantage of trade—and thus confirming its existence—the Merovingian King Dagobert I granted permission to the town of Saint-Denis to establish an annual fair in 634.[66] If there were enough trade to justify the establishment of a fair just ten years or so after the burial of the Sutton Hoo ship, some trade must have been active when the ship was buried. In addition, the charters of Saint-Denis specifically mention the presence of Saxon traders at the fairs during the seventh century.[67] These fairs, then, may have served as the focal point for the acquisition of the gold coins, the silver, and perhaps even some of the weapons.

Trade, at fairs or by individual merchants; central workshops; and mints all bespeak a concentration of resources, basic industrial capacity, and the presence of skilled workers, all of which had to be supported by a social infrastructure. Some idea of the extent and complexity of this infrastructure can be gained from some of the items at Sutton Hoo. The ship, in particular, required the exploitation and concentration of a huge amount of raw material in the form of wood and iron and took two man-years of work to complete. In this sense, she is probably the most valuable single item in the burial.

The Sutton Hoo ship further displays both master craftsmanship and major technical innovations such as a fixed steering position and shorter and narrower planks for more flexibility. In fact, she is more sophisticated than any other before her and longer even than others that postdate her.[68] The weapons also display the hand of a master craftsman; the single skull piece of the helmet, in particular, represents a technical skill far above the norm for the early seventh century. As to the gold jewelry, the swivel-mount design of the shoulder clasps displays a technical innovation unique in Germanic archaeology;[69] Bruce-Mitford has called their creator (or creators) the most brilliant jeweler of the age.[70] Moreover, all these master craftsmen together devoted more than sixteen working years of labor to the man buried in the ship at Sutton Hoo.

In sheer metal weight alone, the Sutton Hoo treasure surpasses all but a few others in each category: almost 11 kilograms of silver (equivalent to 827 to 1,137 grams of gold or 212 to 292 Germanic solidi); over 1.5 kilograms of gold (equal to 426 Germanic solidi) and 40 coins with 2 ingots that equal 16 Germanic solidi in value. Taken together, these items form an almost incredible treasure; taken alone, each part of the Sutton Hoo treasure rivals the best that has been found in its category. Only the coins fall into the average category of treasure, but even they hint at more wealth than the solidi that they are worth.

Legal evidence has allowed us to put a monetary value on at least some of the raw materials. The trees used in constructing the ship had a monetary value of between 413 and 525 Germanic solidi, if one assumes that the fine in the Laws of Ine was a punitive one assessing the offender triple the value of the damaged or stolen goods. The spears and angons had a value of about 1 solidus apiece; the mail coat 12 solidi; and, if they are costly in proportion to the swords mentioned in later wills, the shield perhaps 11 to 14, the sword and scabbard 75 to 95, and the helmet perhaps 65 to 85 solidi or more.

If we were to take the monetary values that we have been calculating throughout this chapter as a guide, we could put the economic value of the Sutton Hoo ship burial at a minimum of 1,239 seventh-century Germanic solidi, over 15 pounds troy of gold. This is a minimum because it measures only some, not all, of the raw materials that were used to make the items we examined. It is a minimum because we have deliberately reduced or taken the lower extremes of some of the values suggested by the evidence, and it is a minimum because we have not been able to assess every piece of the Sutton Hoo treasure. Additional iron and wood from tools and utensils, an ivory rod and a stone scepter, three gilt bronze hanging bowls (more than have been found in any other burial in Britain), and a lyre would have to be considered not only for the value of the raw materials that went into making them, but also for the infrastructure of manufacturing ability, economic organization, and possible commercial activity that their presence implies.[71]

Further, even for the artifacts we have examined, a quantitative investigation of this sort is only the beginning of appreciating their economic value, of what they meant in economic terms to the society that produced them. Each artisan involved in the production of these items had to be provided with food and living quarters, at least during the period in which the work was being done, if not on a permanent basis. To provide such support, the society also had to support the individuals who produced the food and raw materials, collected and transported these supplies, took care of the living quarters, and administered the entire operation. Even in the case of items not actually made in East Anglia, their cost still reflected the overhead entailed in obtaining them by trade. Nor is the use of "monetary" values a simple and sufficient indicator of the cost of such items to the society as a whole; the "109-cow" cost of the Anastasius Dish represented not the loss of a single herd but the expenditure of a surplus, painstakingly gathered over time, from herds that not only had to be maintained, but also had to provide sustenance for the lord and the lowly people who spent their effort to honor him. An idea of the relative size of this effort can be gained by comparing the Sutton Hoo burial not only to other wealthy graves, but also to the graveyards of a simple village like the Frankish settlement at Krefeld-Gellep, where the efforts of a half dozen generations produced a number of so-called rich graves, the contents of any one of which do not have one one-hundredth the value of the treasure at Sutton Hoo.[72]

Yet in another sense, as useful as the investigation of the material value of objects can be, we have only served to confirm the general impression of wealth received by our predecessors in studying the Sutton Hoo ship burial, for value can mean many things, from many different points of view. The artifacts have an aesthetic value. They are well crafted and beautiful, able to evoke complex emotions even in a modern viewer. Along with aesthetic value, there is the personal value of such objects. The age of the Anastasius Dish, produced over a century before the time of the burial, suggests value as an heirloom. In addition to sentimental value, an aesthetically pleasing object has a great deal of "snob" value. Owning many things that are considered valuable by others is a great show of wealth and power. Previous scholars have also examined the value of the treasure in a symbolic sense: the fact of a ship burial indicates Germanic religious practices; the symbolism of the "Saulos" and "Paulos" spoons is a contribution from Christianity; and Grierson's idea that the coins were to pay the fee for 40 oarsmen and two ship's officers[73] recalls the influence of pagan antiquity, where the custom of burying the dead with a coin for the boatman originated. Finally, the Sutton Hoo treasure also has a historical value. To historians, archaeologists, and other scholars of the Middle Ages, such artifacts are priceless because they are often our only records of the past.

Notes

1. Rupert Bruce-Mitford, *The Sutton Hoo Ship-Burial*, with contributions by Paul Ashbee et al., 3 vols. in 4 (London, 1975-83), 1:685-98, argues that the individual buried at Sutton Hoo was Rædwald, King of East Anglia from 599-624.

2. George Speake, *Anglo-Saxon Animal Art and Its Germanic Background* (Oxford, 1980), p. 25 (on Style II art); and Jean Hubert, *Europe in the Dark Ages*, trans. Stuart Gilbert and James Emmons (London, 1969), p. 215 (on polychrome technique).

3. Bruce-Mitford, *Sutton Hoo* 1:585-87 (the coins), and 3:162-63 (the silver).

4. Bruce-Mitford discussess the armor and weapons, and their relations to other contemporary examples, in vol. 2. For the treatment of weapon finds in general, see R. Ewart Oakeshott, *The Archaeology of Weapons* (New York, 1960).

5. Bruce-Mitford, *Sutton Hoo* 1:352; Angela Care Evans, in Bruce-Mitford, *Sutton Hoo* 1:433.

6. Bruce-Mitford, *Sutton Hoo* 1:608-47 (coins); 2:615-16 (gold); 3:8, 48, 76-104, 147, and 152 (silver).

7. In Merovingian coinage of the "national" period (ca. 580-670), 40 silver denarii of 1.3 grams each were equal in value to a solidus of 3.9 grams fine gold, yielding a value ratio of gold to silver of approximately 13.3:1. Some of the denarii were, however, lighter, at 1.1 grams, and a comparison of these with the old Roman Imperial solidus of 4.55 grams fine gold yields a ratio of approximately 9.67:1 as the highest possible value of gold in relation to silver. See further Philip Grierson and Mark Blackburn, *Medieval European Coinage* (New York, 1986), pp. 102-7. Georges Duby, *The Early Growth of the European Economy: Warriors and Peasants from the Seventh to the Twelfth Century*, trans. Howard B. Clarke (Ithaca, N.Y., 1974), p. 99, remarks that the Carolingian currency reform set the value of gold to sil-

ver at 12:1, in accord with market prices. It is, however, possible that silver may have been less valuable in early seventh-century Britain, where the Laws of King Æthelberht of Kent suggest a ratio of 21:1. See *The Laws of the Earliest English Kings*, ed. F. L. Attenborough (Cambridge, Eng., 1922), p. 176 n. 16.1.

8. Bruce-Mitford, *Sutton Hoo* 3:8.

9. *Laws of the Salian and Ripuarian Franks*, trans. Theodore John Rivers (New York, 1986), pp. 185-86 (*Lex Ribuaria*, ch. 40.11).

10. Bernard Bachrach, "The Cost of Castle Building: The Case of the Tower at Langeais, 992-994," in *The Medieval Castle*, ed. Kathryn Reyerson, Medieval Studies at Minnesota, vol. 1 (Dubuque, Iowa, 1984), pp. 46-62; and C. M. Gillmor, "Naval Logistics of the Cross-Channel Operation, 1066," in *Anglo-Norman Studies VII: Proceedings of the Battle Conference, 1984*, ed. R. Allen Brown (Dover, N.H., 1985), pp. 105-31.

11. Many calculations of work process for the medieval period use an AWD of 10 hours, but one of 7.5 is more readily compared with modern data.

12. Bruce-Mitford, *Sutton Hoo* 1:578.

13. Attenborough, *Laws of the Earliest English Kings*, pp. 5 and 7; and Felix Liebermann, *Die Gesetze der Angelsachsen*, 3 vols. (Halle, 1898-1916), 1:3 (Æthelberht 8 and 21).

14. *Laws of the Salian and Ripuarian Franks*, pp. 185-86 (*Lex Ribuaria*, ch. 40.11).

15. W. A. Oddy, "Analysis of Four Hoards of Merovingian Gold Coins," *Methods of Chemical and Metallurgical Investigation of Ancient Coinage*, ed. E. T. Hall and D. M. Metcalf, The Royal Numismatic Society, Special Publication 8 (London, 1972), pp. 121-24; Grierson and Blackburn, *Medieval European Coinage*, pp. 107 and 124 (Escharen: 66 coins = 30 Germanic solidi); P. C. J. A. Boeles, "Merovingische munten van het type Dronrijp en de vondst van Nietap," in *Gedenkboek A. E. van Giffen* (Meppel, 1947); Grierson and Blackburn, *Medieval European Coinage*, p. 125; A. Pol, "De 7e-eeuwse muntvondst Nietap," *Jaarboek voor Munt-en Penningkunde* 62-64 (1975-77): 23-62; and Oddy, "Analysis of Four Hoards," pp. 124-25 (Nietap: 34 coins + 2 blanks = 13 Germanic solidi).

16. Bruce-Mitford, *Sutton Hoo* 1:585-87 and 605 (die-relatedness); Philip Grierson, "Commerce in the Dark Ages: A Critique of the Evidence," *Transactions of the Royal Historical Society*, 5th ser., 9 (London, 1958): 123-40, at 123-24 (political contact); J. Lafaurie, "Les routes commerciales indiquées par les trésors et trouvailles monétaires mérovingiens," *Settimane di studio del Centro italiano di studi sull'alto medioevo 8: Moneta e scambi nell'alto medioevo* (Spoleto, 1961): 231-78, and discussion on 313-37, and 246-48 (trade).

17. Bruce-Mitford, *Sutton Hoo* 2:615-16.

18. Ibid., 2:599-602.

19. Birgit Arrhenius, *Merovingian Garnet Jewellery* (Stockholm, 1985), p. 35.

20. Bruce-Mitford, *Sutton Hoo*, 3:41, 45, 69, 111, and 158.

21. Ibid., 3:1.

22. Ibid., 3:26.

23. Ibid., 3:7, 156, and 161-62.

24. Ibid., 3:116.

25. Ernst Kitzinger, "The Sutton-Hoo Ship Burial: The Silver," *Antiquity* 14 (1940): 48.

26. Bruce-Mitford, *Sutton Hoo*, 3:120 (the bowls) and 154-56 (the spoons).

27. Ibid., 2:xxv.

28. Ibid., 2:245-46, 248, 249-52, and 254; and Richard Wegner, "Die Angriffswaffen der Angelsachsen" (Ph.D. diss., Albertus-Universität at Königsberg, Prussia [now Kaliningrad, Russia], 1899), pp. 43-45. On the availability of iron in the Middle Ages, see Otto Johannsen, *Geschichte des Eisens* (Düsseldorf, 1953), pp. 98-109. Johannsen indicates that the earliest medieval iron-bearing sites to be exploited extensively were in Noricum (modern Austria) and date to the eighth century.

29. Bruce-Mitford, *Sutton Hoo* 2:264-65.

30. Ibid., 2:21-36; John Hewitt, *Ancient Armor and Weapons in Europe* (1860; repr. Graz, 1967), p. 31; Karl Pfannkuche, "Der Schild bei den Angelsachsen" (Ph.D. diss., Vereinigte Friedrichs-Universität in Halle-Wittenberg, 1908), pp. 53-55, 61, and 64-65; *An Anglo-Saxon Dictionary: Based on the Manuscript Collection of the Late Joseph Bosworth*, ed. T. Northcote Toller (1898; repr. London, 1972), s.v. *lind* (shield); and *Concordance to the Anglo-Saxon Poetic Records*, ed. Jess B. Bessinger (New York, 1978), s.v. *lind* for references to the poetry.

31. Bruce-Mitford, *Sutton Hoo* 2:97.

32. Wegner, "Angriffswaffen," p. 67; and Pfannkuche, "Der Schild," p. 72.

33. *Laws of the Salian and Ripuarian Franks*, p. 186 (*Lex Ribuaria*, ch. 40.11).

34. Pfannkuche, "Der Schild," p. 47.

35. Liebermann, *Gesetze* 1:357-59 (Canute 2, chap. 71), and 2.2:640 (concordance for "shield") and 657 ("spear").

36. Bruce-Mitford, *Sutton Hoo* 2:232-40.

37. Conversation with Jack Skogen, 3 May 1989.

38. Heribert Seitz, *Blankwaffen: Geschichte und Typenentwicklung im europäischen Kulturbereich von der prähistorischen Zeit bis zum Ende des 16. Jahrhunderts*, 2 vols., in Bibliothek für Kunst-und Antiquitätenfreunde 4 and 4a (Brunswick, Germany, 1965), 1:88-90.

39. Bruce-Mitford, *Sutton Hoo* 2:282; and Angela Care Evans, in Bruce-Mitford, *Sutton Hoo* 2:307.

40. H. R. Ellis Davidson, *The Sword in Anglo-Saxon England* (Oxford, 1962), p. 28.

41. Hewitt, *Ancient Armor*, pp. 38-42; and Toller, *Anglo-Saxon Dictionary*, pp. 949-50, s.v. *sweord*. For references to the poetry, see the *Concordance to the Anglo-Saxon Poetic Records*, s.v. *byrne* and *sweord*.

42. Liebermann, *Gesetze* 1:357-59 (Canute 2, chap. 71) and 2.2:606 (concordance for *panzer* = armor).

43. *Laws of the Salian and Ripuarian Franks*, p. 186 (*Lex Ribuaria*, ch. 40.11).

44. Hewitt, *Ancient Armor*, pp. 38-42; Liebermann, *Gesetze* 2.2:645-46 (*schwert*).

45. Bruce-Mitford, *Sutton Hoo* 2:138-52.

46. *Laws of the Salian and Ripuarian Franks*, p. 186 (*Lex Ribuaria*, ch. 40.11).

47. Bruce-Mitford, *Sutton Hoo* 1:352.

48. Care Evans, in Bruce-Mitford, *Sutton Hoo* 1:354.

49. Gillmor, "Naval Logistics," p. 114.

50. Gillmor, "Naval Logistics," p. 117. On early medieval iron tools in general, see Renée Doehard, *The Early Middle Ages in the West: Economy and Society*, trans. W. G. Deakin (Amsterdam, 1978), p. 14; and Duby, *Early Growth of the European Economy*, pp. 15, 75, and 194-96. Note that the durability of the metal's edge affects all phases of the work proportionately.

51. Gillmor, "Naval Logistics," pp. 117-18.

52. We are assuming that the logs were transported only a mile over land and floated the rest of the way to the building site. See Gillmor, "Naval Logistics," p. 118, for the weight of the logs, which she puts at 1,200 pounds (approximately 545 kilograms) each.

53. The 2,749 rivets (Bruce-Mitford, *Sutton Hoo* 1: fig. 325), each 2.25 inches long and averaging .75 inches in diameter (Bruce-Mitford, *Sutton Hoo* 1: fig. 227) yield 776 lbs.; 80 gunwale spikes (Bruce-Mitford, *Sutton Hoo* 1:425), each 6.5 inches long and averaging 1 inch in diameter (Bruce-Mitford, *Sutton Hoo* 1:363 and 398) yield 136 pounds; and 52 rib bolts (Bruce-Mitford, *Sutton Hoo* 1:425), each 2.25 inches long and averaging 3.32 inches in diameter (Bruce-Mitford, *Sutton Hoo* 1:400 and 402) yield approximately 29 pounds, for a total of 941 pounds. See *ASM Metals Reference Book*, 2nd ed. (Metals Park, Ohio, 1983), for the density of iron (0.284 pounds/cubic inch).

54. R. I. Page, *Life in Anglo-Saxon England* (New York, 1970), pp. 83-84.

55. A worker using modern hand tools can excavate 12 cubic yards, or 324 cubic feet, of loose sand in 1 AWD (*Cost Data for Landscape Construction, 1984*, ed. Kathleen Kerr [Min-

neapolis, 1984], p. 18). Since modern shovels, at 8.5 by 11 inches, are larger than their medieval counterparts, which were likely only 6 by 5 inches, volume comparison suggests that the digging would have taken over five times as long in the seventh century. See Page, *Life in Anglo-Saxon England*, p. 83. This estimate does not take into account the need to replace deteriorating equipment, which may have been especially important if most Dark Age hand tools were made of wood. See Duby, *Early Growth of the European Economy*, p. 15.

56. See Gillmor, "Naval Logistics," p. 118, and note 52 above. While Gillmor's calculations are applied to wood, the basic formula depends only on the weight of material to be transported.

57. *Means Mechanical Cost Data*, 11th ed. (Kingston, Mass., 1987), p. 29, shows that a skilled carpenter working with modern hand tools is able to install one 7/8-inch diameter bolt in approximately 34 minutes, or 13 such bolts in an AWD of 7.5 hours. Given that the efficiency of tools and techniques in the early Middle Ages was about one-third that of their modern counterparts, a workman would have been able to install 4.4 rivets in an AWD.

58. Gillmor, "Naval Logistics," p. 118.

59. Areas of the hull, however, had been overriveted and patched, and the ship may have been buried only because she had become unseaworthy. See Angela Care Evans, *The Sutton Hoo Ship Burial* (London, 1986), p. 29.

60. Attenborough, *Laws of the Earliest English Kings*, p. 51; and Liebermann, *Gesetze* 1:109 (Ine 44). The tree is defined as one able to shelter thirty swine; conversations with Richard Isaacson, librarian, Anderson Horticultural Library, Minnesota Arboretum, University of Minnesota, and B. G. Crabo, Department of Animal Science, University of Minnesota, on 7 August 1989 indicated that a tree with a 12-inch diameter trunk could do so.

61. Attenborough, *Laws of the Earliest English Kings*, p. 55; and Liebermann, *Gesetze* 1:101 (Ine 23.3), for a slave, and 115 (Ine 55), for sheep.

62. Attenborough, *Laws of the Earliest English Kings*, p. 43; and Liebermann, *Gesetze* 1:97 (Ine 19).

63. Attenborough, *Laws of the Earliest English Kings*, p. 55; and Liebermann, *Gesetze* 1:115 (Ine 54.1).

64. Helgö, in Lake Mälaren, near Stockholm, was a major center of international trade, producing iron and other goods for export. See Else Roesdahl, "The Scandinavians at Home," in *The Northern World: The History and Heritage of Northern Europe—AD 400–1100*, ed. David M. Wilson (New York, 1980), pp. 129-58, especially p. 148. Peter Hunter Blair, *An Introduction to Anglo-Saxon England*, 2nd ed. (Cambridge, Eng., 1977), pp. 283-84, suggests that the sword blade may have been forged in the Rhineland. For the Frisian trade route that connected these regions, see Robert LaTouche, *The Birth of the Western Economy: Economic Aspects of the Dark Ages* (New York, 1961), pp. 134-35.

65. Arrhenius, *Merovingian Garnet Jewellery*, pp. 158-59 (North Sea) and p. 195 (Trier).

66. Wilhelm Levison, *England and the Continent in the Eighth Century* (Oxford, 1946), p. 7.

67. Ibid., p. 24.

68. Bruce-Mitford, *Sutton Hoo* 1:352 (steering, length); Care Evans, in Bruce-Mitford, *Sutton Hoo* 1:433 (planks); and Gillmor, "Naval Logistics," p. 114 (length).

69. Bruce-Mitford, *Sutton Hoo* 2:473-76.

70. Ibid., 2:597.

71. Artifacts described in Bruce-Mitford, *Sutton Hoo* 3:2.

72. The statistical judgment is our own. For a catalog of the graveyard, see Renate Pirling, *Das Römisch-Fränkische Gräberfeld von Krefeld-Gellep* (Berlin, 1966).

73. Philip Grierson, "Purpose of the Sutton Hoo Coins," *Antiquity* 44 (Cambridge, Eng., 1970): 14-18, at 16.

CHAPTER 3

✣

Sutton Hoo Art
Two Millennia of History

Gloria Polizzotti Greis and Michael N. Geselowitz

It is well known among the recent generation of historians that the Dark Ages were not so dark as once supposed. Far from being the descent into barbarism envisioned by Henry Hallam, the centuries after the decline of the Roman Empire were a time of important political, spiritual, and artistic endeavor. The market structure of the Roman Empire was replaced by the Scandinavian emporia, which obtained through their Syrian partners goods from as far away as India and China.[1] The new Frankish kingdoms helped fill the political vacuum left by the dissolution of Roman rule, and the spread of Christianity forged economic and ideological links between the rising Byzantine Empire and even westernmost Europe. The burial at Sutton Hoo is a mirror of the European material culture of this period. Many of the artifacts included in the grave originated at distant locations, illustrating the far-reaching network of which the Sutton Hoo prince was a part.

The impact of this extensive network on the development of Anglo-Saxon artistic style has been widely debated, but remains problematic. In 1915, G. Baldwin-Brown wrote that "the Germanic art of the Migration Period . . . may have been affected by classical, by oriental and by Celtic traditions before it took a form and substance of its own."[2] This tentative conclusion is echoed by recent scholars.[3]

Perhaps the most intriguing aspect of the development of Anglo-Saxon art is the question of oriental influence. "Oriental," in this context, describes the parts of southern Europe and western Asia that are contiguous with temperate Europe, but culturally distinct: Asia Minor, the northern Near East, the steppes, and the northeastern rim of the Mediterranean. A common opinion among art historians holds that oriental styles were incorporated quite late into Germanic Europe, through the agencies of the Late Roman market system, the Scandinavian trade, the expansion of Christianity from Byzantium, and the nomadic incursions from the steppes that began in the fifth century A.D.[4] Nevertheless, a close look at the motifs of prehistoric European art demonstrates that orientalism was an important feature at least as early as the beginning of the Iron Age, in the eighth century B.C.[5] In other words, we are suggesting that certain motifs in Anglo-Saxon art do not represent new additions, but were already an integral part of both the European and Asian symbolic idioms. This is hardly surprising, because Europe is a geographical appendage of western Asia, and many aspects of European prehistory and early history can only be understood if the interaction between Europeans and Asians is explored.

Asia and the European Iron Age

The relationship between western Asia and temperate Europe is as old as European culture itself. The so-called Neolithic Revolution—the domestication of plants and animals and the establishment of settled village life—diffused into Europe from Mesopotamia and Anatolia; the earliest Neolithic villages in Europe are based on Anatolian prototypes.[6] As with agriculture, both bronze and iron metallurgy also reached Europe through contacts with western Asia,[7] as did the Indo-European family of languages.[8]

This long-standing relationship between Asia and Europe was most intensive during the first millennium B.C., which was a time of cultural resurgence in the Mediterranean region.[9] One of the effects of this resurgence was the well-recognized orientalizing of European artistic style that occurred as far north and west as Etruria and that spilled over into central Europe, as well.[10] The first contacts between Europe and the Near East were probably made by seafaring traders,[11] but also around this time the Scythians had developed true horse-nomadism and were in close contact with the peoples of Anatolia and northern Mesopotamia. By the beginning of the Early Iron Age (c. 800 B.C.), central and eastern Europe was marked by an influx of items of Scythian manufacture. The influence of these Asian cultures is most strongly seen in the flowering of the so-called Situla Style, which appeared on both sides of the Alps at the head of the Adriatic starting in the sixth century B.C.[12] This form of figural representation, done in repoussé on sheet bronze vessels, bears its closest resemblance to the bronzework of the Urartians in northeast Anatolia.[13]

Around the same time, there was direct Greek contact with the peoples of the upper Danube basin through the entrepôt at Massilia (modern Marseilles). This trade between the Greeks and the Central Europeans involved a large volume of Greek-made luxury goods and was an important factor in the translation of Mediterranean motifs and styles into central Europe.[14]

By the fifth century B.C., true Celtic art was born—called by archaeologists the Early La Tène style after its type-site in Switzerland. The inspiration for this art again seems to have come through northern Italy and the Adriatic. This process is probably due to a shifting of trade routes between temperate Europe and the Mediterranean as trade from Massalia began to decline and the focus of Greek trade shifted to the Po Valley.[15] By the third century B.C., the expansion of the Celts brought them into direct contact with the peoples of Greece, central Italy, and Anatolia, and the eastern influences on later La Tène art are even more pronounced.[16]

The imperial expansion of Rome, which was itself tied strongly into eastern trade, did not, therefore, begin a new chapter in European-Asian interaction; rather, it continued a trend that had already existed for at least a thousand years.

Vinica

The role of this trade in the development of European art is well attested in the archaeological record, and artifacts from two archaeologically re-covered burial assemblages can serve to illustrate this claim. The first is the well-known material from Sutton Hoo, the theme of this volume. The second is a collection from the Iron Age cemetery of Vinica, an important assemblage of Celto-Illyrian art from the crossroads of Europe and Asia, which predates Sutton Hoo by over five hundred years.

Vinica lies in the general region of the Head of the Adriatic, on the Kupa River at the border of the modern Yugoslav republics of Slovenia and Croatia, about twenty-five kilometers west of the city of Karlovac. While the hill-fort settlement has never been systematically explored, the asso-ciated cemetery was excavated by the Duchess Paul Friedrich of Mecklen-burg in 1906 and 1907. The Duchess was a self-taught but accomplished archaeologist who excavated extensively on her ancestral estates in Slovenia (at that time in the Austro-Hungarian province of Carniola). The Duchess and her field assistant Gustav Goldberg were well acquainted with the lead-ing European prehistorians of the day, especially Oscar Montelius and Joseph Déchelette; correspondence preserved with the collection attest to their high opinion of her work.[17] At Vinica the Duchess excavated some 330 graves, dating from the end of the Early Iron Age through the beginning of the Roman Period (350 B.C. to A.D. 50). The great majority of these graves date to the Late Iron Age (c. 200 B.C.), making Vinica the largest Late Iron Age cem-etery known from temperate Europe.[18]

Vinica apparently began in the Early Iron Age as a modest hamlet. At this time, the northern Adriatic region was part of the proto-Celtic cul-ture sphere, but was strongly influenced from Italy, from the southern Balkans, and from points east. Scythian imports, especially, are notable in finds from this period.[19] Other foreign materials present at Vinica include amber from the Baltic, ceramics from Italy, and bronze, whose constituent tin must have come ultimately from Austria.

At the beginning of the Late Iron Age, when the historic Celts invaded from the North,[20] Vinica became a large village of the Japodians, a tribe with both Celtic and Balkan affinities.[21] Vinica was the northernmost outpost of this group, and may have served as a fort. The finds from Vinica show influence of Early Celtic and southern Balkan styles, as well as cer-tain presumably indigenous elements unique to the site.[22] The finds from

Late Iron Age Vinica continued to include great amounts of imported material, especially amber, bronze, ceramics from east and west, and Mediterranean shell. The fact that this region should have such far-flung trade contacts is not surprising. Most contacts between Asian and temperate European societies at this time must have involved the area around Vinica, because the region lies on the crossroads of the major natural north-south and east-west routes that link the various parts of Europe. One route ran between Italy and the Hungarian Plain — what in Roman times became the Aquileia-Emona Road — and the other ran between the Balkans and transalpine Gaul — along the "Amber Route" in use since at least the Late Bronze Age.[23] The interactions along these routes intensified at the end of the first millennium B.C., and their record is preserved in the finds from Vinica.

Continuity of Early Motifs in Anglo-Saxon Art

In view of this extended Asian and European interaction, it should be expected that Asian styles and motifs would have been incorporated into European art at a very early date. The evidence of prehistoric European art clearly demonstrates that certain Asian-derived motifs, generally attributed by art historians to Roman and post-Roman cultural influences, were already present in the European artistic vocabulary many centuries *prior* to Roman imperial expansion. Using the Sutton Hoo assemblage as an example, we wish to illustrate certain elements of decoration and iconography, common in Anglo-Saxon art, that have their roots in the earlier art styles of prehistoric Europe and the Near East. The occurrence of some of these elements of design at Vinica and other Iron Age sites shows that their origins must have predated the Germanic context of Sutton Hoo. Among such designs are the dot-and-circle ("eye") motif, the guilloche (an interwoven design forming a series of circular spaces), running spirals, true spirals, fan-shaped peltas (shieldlike designs), and triskeles (designs with three bent arms radiating from a center). A similar but more complex example is the use of animal symbolism. Certain creatures, such as waterfowl, were important images in Near Eastern and European art from Neolithic times.[24] Others, such as the stag, the boar, the bird of prey, and a variety of fierce mythical beasts such as dragons and griffins, were more common during the first millennium B.C., especially in ritual contexts and as totems associated with warriors.[25] The meanings of these decorative motifs — if indeed they have specific meanings — are uncertain. In the case of the guilloche, for example, Allen Seaby has argued that the ubiquity of this motif in art, from the predynastic Near East through Late Prehistoric and even Early Christian Europe, represents continuity of meaning.[26] Such an assertion, however, is very difficult to prove, especially in the case of relatively simple geometric designs; the cultural and historical link must be traced, as well as a demonstrable similarity in the usage and symbolic context of the motif.[27] Nevertheless, whether such designs do constitute symbols or purely geometric decoration, they form a recurrent part of the design repertoire of West Asian and European art.

Apart from the more general similarities, certain objects from Sutton Hoo do bear complex motifs that can be specifically identified and that are pre-Roman in origin. In these cases, the consistent use of complex symbols cannot be explained away as coincidence or reinvention, especially since the temporal and spatial considerations allow the possibility of direct diffusion. Three major Sutton Hoo artifacts—Hanging Bowl 2, the whetstone, and the purse lid—can serve to illustrate this point.[28]

The Hanging Bowls

Piled among the many silver vessels in the Sutton Hoo burial were a trio of bronze hanging bowls. They are of a type well known in Britain and Ireland, both from domestic and ecclesiastical contexts. Bowls of this type are believed to be Roman or Romano-British in origin, with derivative forms persisting until the eighth century. The Sutton Hoo bowls were probably made in Ireland; they were repaired with silver plates bearing Germanic designs, suggesting that they were treasured possessions and probably quite old when buried. The most interesting feature of the Sutton Hoo hanging bowls is the escutcheons, the medallions that decorate the bases and hanging hooks. In all three examples, the escutcheons are characteristic of Insular Celtic rather than Anglo-Saxon work, in both motif design and material.

Bowl 1 is the largest of the three and has eight escutcheons, including the small sculpture of a fish. The designs—running spirals and peltas, with zoomorphic terminals—are at home in both the Celtic and Anglo-Saxon traditions, but the coloring materials are red enamel and millefiori inlay, rather than the Germanic cloisonné. Bowl 3 is similar to Bowl 1, though smaller and simpler. Bowl 2, however, is quite unusual. It bears three hook escutcheons and two basal escutcheons, one inside and one outside. One of its three hooks is plain, but the other two are covered with die-stamped foil reliefs depicting an anthropomorphic figure flanked by two zoomorphic figures (Figure 3.1); this is a variant of the Near Eastern Master of the Beasts motif. The significance of this design is discussed later, in the description of the purse lid. The basal escutcheons both bear a swastika arrangement of four animal heads, possibly horses (Figure 3.2, *a*). The parallels for this design, which Bruce-Mitford could not find in early Anglo-Saxon or Roman art,[29] are in fact Scythian. The escutcheons bear a striking resemblance to silver Scythian harness mounts that were found in Rumania (Figure 3.2, *b*), as well as pewter mounts, also Scythian in origin, from Slovenia (Figiure 3.2, *c*).

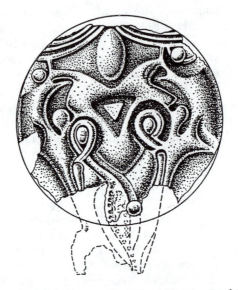

Figure 3.1. Die-stamped relief hook escutcheon from Hanging Bowl 2, showing a man between two open-mouthed beasts. Diameter, 2.25 cm. (From R.L.S.Bruce-Mitford, *The Sutton Hoo Ship-Burial 3*: fig. 189. Copyright 1983 by the Trustees of the British Museum; used by permission.)

The Whetstone

The Sutton Hoo whetstone, believed to be a kind of scepter, is unique in Anglo-Saxon art. Although scepters were known in Europe since Roman times, they tended to be relatively lightweight batons that could be easily carried. The Sutton Hoo stone is both long and heavy, and would either have to be rested on the knee while the holder sat or placed in a bracket. The scepter is made from a fine-grained sandstone, probably from a source near the borders of Scotland, or from central Germany. It is decorated at each end with a red-painted knob and four masklike faces. Like the designs on the hanging bowls, the faces are common to both Celtic and Germanic art. There are several examples of whetstones with faces carved at the top, such as the Iron Age stone from Hough-on-the-Hill[30] and the Saxon-period stones from Llandudno and Loch Carrane,[31] but only the Sutton Hoo whetstone is so large and so elaborately decorated.

The stag figurine attached to the top of the whetstone is cast of bronze and stands on a ring of iron wire. The stag is not Anglo-Saxon in style; Carola Hicks has identified Scythian and Romano-Celtic parallels for this figure, especially in the placement of the feet and the exaggerated realistic antlers.[32] Also, the bronze that makes up the figure is different in composition from that of the bands that hold it onto the scepter; this suggests

(a)

(b)

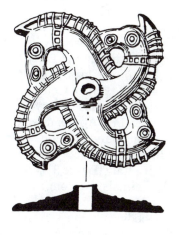

(c)

Figure 3.2. (*a*) Design from outer basal escutcheon of Sutton Hoo Hanging Bowl 2.
Diameter, 3.7 cm. (From Bruce-Mitford, *The Sutton Hoo Ship Burial* [London, 1975-83],
3: fig. 193. Copyright 1983 by the Trustees of the British Museum; used by permission.)
(*b*) Scythian silver bridle ornament from Rumania. Diameter, 7 cm. (After Emma Bunker
et al., *"Animal Style" Art from East to West* [New York, 1970], fig. 141.) (*c*) Scythian
pewter bridle ornament from Tumulus 5, Grave 31, Magdalenska gora, Slovenia.
Diameter, 4.25 cm. (From Hugh Hencken, *The Iron Age Cemetery of Magdalenska gora
in Slovenia*, fig. 151d. Copyright 1978 by the President and Fellows of Harvard College.)

that the stag was not originally made as the terminal for the scepter, but may instead have been a valued heirloom reused for this purpose.[33] Similar stag figures, standards set on pole tops, were excavated at Pazyryk in the Altai.[34] These are related to the zoomorphic bronze bells frequently used as pole tops by the Scythians and Eastern Europeans.[35] A similar bird-cage bell and several zoomorphic figures, in this case rams, were found by the Duchess of Mecklenburg in Slovenia.

The Purse Lid

The third artifact is the purse lid, decorated with several figural plaques. Of these, the most famous and interesting are the two that depict a man between open-mouthed beasts. Executed in cloisonné in Germanic style, this figure is familiar in La Tène and Asian as well as Anglo-Saxon art, and probably represents a motif of great antiquity known as the Master of the Beasts. W. Flinders-Petrie traced the Master of the Beasts motif back to ancient Mesopotamia;[36] it was a common design on Near Eastern cylinder seals, public art, and personal adornment during the last two millennia B.C. The Master of the Beasts is also ubiquitous in the art of the Lurs, steppe nomads and ancestors of the Scythians. Examples from the famous Luristan bronze hoard depict this character flanked by fierce beasts or by bird-headed serpents.[37] The motif must have entered Europe by contact with the Mediterranean world during the Early Iron Age and by contacts in eastern Europe with the nomads of the steppes, because by the later Iron Age the motif appears in all parts of Celtic Europe, from Iberia (Figure 3.3) to Fellbach-Schmiden in southern Germany (Figure 3.4)[38] to Gundestrup in Denmark. The most famous Iron Age representations are panels B and D from the Gundestrup Cauldron, found in Denmark but probably produced in the Carpathian region.[39] In more abstract representations, such as Late Iron Age belt hooks from northern Italy (Figure 3.5, *a*), the central figure is often reduced to an X, while the animals are elongated to become the decorative field;[40] in an openwork pendant from Vinica, clearly related to these Italian belt hooks, the X-shaped body and the serpentine beasts have actually merged (Figure 3.5, *b*). The increased degree of abstraction suggests that the motif and its usage had become sufficiently familiar that a simplified representation was nevertheless recognizable.[41]

The motif appears with regular frequency in both pagan and Early Christian contexts. As mentioned above, the hook escutcheon from Hanging Bowl 2 (Figure 3.1) falls into this category; in fact, the form of the man between two bird-headed beasts, his triangular "pectoral," and the intertwined legs are an abstract version of the gold purse plaque. Another example is the Riseley pendant (Figure 3.6, *a*),[42] which combines the arms-around posture of the Fellbach-Schmiden carving with the bird-headed beasts of the Sutton Hoo purse lid. The Torslunda die may be another example, although in this scene the man is killing the animals.[43]

Figure 3.3. Carved stone relief from Villaricos, Almeria, Spain, showing a Janus figure seated between two horses. (After Ministerio de Cultura, *Los Iberos* [Madrid, 1983], fig. 55.)

The Faversham hook escutcheon (Figure 3.6, *b*) is an important example of the Christian appropriation of this motif, in which the serpents have been transformed into open-mouthed fish, and the X-shaped man has become a Latin Cross.[44]

The Kells Market Cross has two panels that depict this figure: one is a man who apparently has horns and a tail, standing between two wolflike animals; the other is a clear representation of the biblical story of Daniel.[45] In fact, this motif of a man between two beasts is generally interpreted as Daniel in the lions' den.[46] However, as Helen Roe has pointed out in her study of this figure,[47] the so-called Daniels actually comprise several different motifs. True depictions of Daniel are quite common in Early Christian contexts, but must share certain invariable characteristics: Daniel is depicted with palms upraised in the conventional "orant" position, and the lions (usually two or seven in number)[48] are depicted in an attitude of submission. The belt clasp from Lavigny[49] is a classic example of this figure, as are the belt buckle from Bifrons[50] and the second Kells Market Cross panel. The Sutton Hoo purse and escutcheon figures show neither of these characteristics, nor do the Riseley pendant or the

37

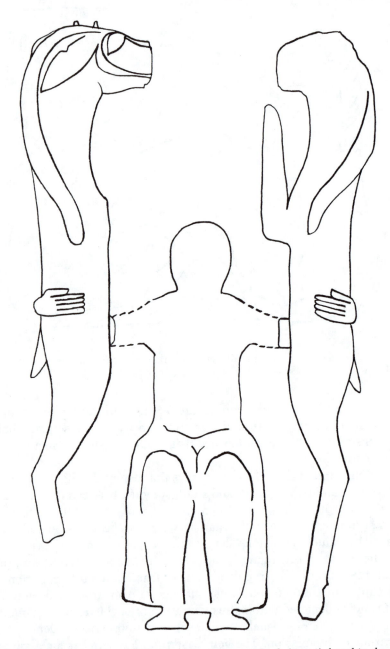

Figure 3.4. Carved wood statue of a man between two animals (rams?), found in the votive shafts at Fellbach-Schmiden (Rems-Murr-Kreis), Germany. Reconstruction of the central figure is conjectural. Height, 77 cm. (After Dieter Planck, "Eine neuentdeckte keltische Viereckschanze," [1982], fig. 24.)

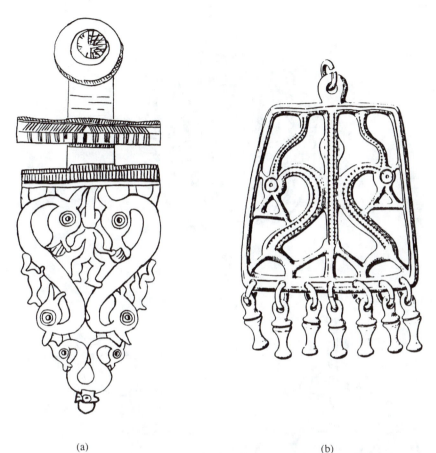

(a)   (b)

Figure 3.5. (*a*) Este-style belt hook from Holzelsau, Kufstein, Austria. Length, 16.2 cm. (After Paul Jacobsthal, *Early Celtic Art* [Oxford, 1944], fig. 360.) (*b*) Cast bronze pendant from Grave 268, Vinica, Slovenia. Length, 10.75 cm. (Courtesy of the Peabody Museum of Archaeology and Ethnology, Harvard University.)

first Kells Market Cross panel; these examples are closer in style to the pre-Christian depictions, such as the Luristan bronzes, the Este belt hooks, the Vinica pendant, the Gundestrup Cauldron, and the Fellbach-Schmiden carving.

Conclusion

The precise meanings of such pre-Christian symbols as the horsehead swastika or the Master of the Beasts are unknown to us, but the fact of their survival as meaningful symbols is illustrated by their recurrence in Anglo-Saxon Christian contexts. This syncretism, what Erwin Goodenough

(a)

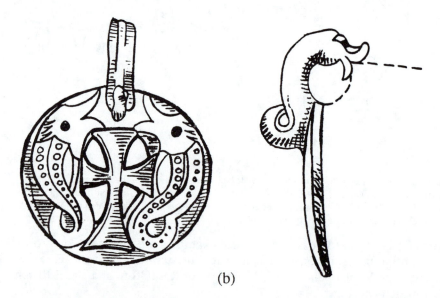

(b)

Figure 3.6. (*a*) Gold pendant from Grave 56, Risely, Kent. Diameter, 2 cm. (From Sonia Chadwick Hawkes et. al., "The Finglesham Man," *Antiquity* 39 [1965], fig. 3. Reprinted by permission of Sonia Chadwick Hawkes and Antiquity Publications Ltd.) (*b*) Bronze hook escutcheon from the Favesham (Kent) hanging bowl (5th c. A.D.). Diameter 2.5 cm. (After E. T. Leeds, *Early Anglo-Saxon Art and Archaeology* [Oxford, 1936], fig. 3.)

called the "migration" of symbols into new contexts,[51] attests to their continuing importance as both pagan and Christian religious symbols in early

Europe. The adoption of Christianity in Europe did not eradicate entirely the traces of past beliefs. In the case of an ambivalent convert such as Rædwald, the tokens of his two religions are to be expected, but the figure of the Master of the Beasts on the Kells Market Cross is more of a surprise. The Kells wolf/man, the pagan twin of Daniel on the other side of the shaft, represents the migration of the Master of the Beasts motif into an explicitly Christian context.[52] In this light, the Daniels and the Faversham escutcheon are best seen as syncretic representations of the much older Master of the Beasts motif, in which the role of "tamer" passes to Daniel and ultimately to Christ.

The examples presented in this paper have shown that Germanic art did not arise, as was once believed, out of the cultural ashes of post-Classical Europe. Because of the intensity of Asian and European contact throughout time, it is fruitless to discuss the origins of Anglo-Saxon or any European culture without consideration of the time depth of the cultures in both areas. To say that Sutton Hoo art represents two thousand years of history is not to deny Anglo-Saxon creativity, but rather to acknowledge that the complex of style and motif that we recognize as Anglo-Saxon is the inheritor of a long and active cultural legacy.

As Mildred Budny has pointed out, "In the rich Sutton Hoo ship burial, magnificent Anglo-Saxon jewelry and weapons were juxtaposed with Celtic or British objects such as hanging bowls, Scandinavian heirlooms, Byzantine silver and Merovingian coins, making the deposit emblematic of the complex interconnections between seventh-century pagan Anglo-Saxon art and its heritage and contacts."[53] In other words, it is the intertwining of culture and history, of ancient and new — the joining of the many individual threads — that weaves the fabric of art.

Notes

1. Richard Hodges, *Dark Age Economics* (New York, 1982); and George Duby, *Early Growth of the European Economy* (Ithaca, N.Y., 1974).

2. G. Baldwin-Brown, *The Arts in England*, 3 vols. (London, 1915), 3: 7.

3. George Speak, *Anglo-Saxon Animal Art and Its Germanic Background* (Oxford, 1980); David Wilson, *Anglo-Saxon Art* (London, 1984); and Mildred Budny, "Early Medieval Britain: The Visual Arts and Crafts," in *Cambridge Guide to the Arts in Britain*, ed. Boris Ford (Cambridge, Eng., 1988), 1:122-77.

4. Hodges, *Dark Age Economics*; Erwin Panofsky, "The Classical Tradition in the Middle Ages," in *Readings in Art History*, ed. Harold Spencer, 2 vols., 3rd ed. (New York, 1982), 1:415-42; Wilson, *Anglo-Saxon Art*; Nancy K. Sandars, *Prehistoric Art in Europe*, 2nd ed. (New York, 1985); and Lloyd Laing, *Later Celtic Art in Britain and Ireland* (Aylesbury, 1987).

5. Paul Jacobsthal, *Early Celtic Art* (Oxford, 1944), pp. 157-63; Vincent Megaw, *The Art of the European Iron Age* (New York, 1970), pp. 9-40 and 52ff; and Ruth and Vincent Megaw, *Celtic Art, from Its Beginnings to the Book of Kells* (New York, 1988), pp. 34-49.

6. Ruth Tringham, *Hunters, Fishers, and Farmers of Eastern Europe, 6000–3000 BC* (London, 1971).

7. Radomir Pleiner, "Early Iron Metallurgy in Europe," in *The Coming of the Age of*

Iron, ed. James D. Muhly and Theodore A. Wertime (New Haven, Conn., 1980), pp. 375-415; and R. Tylecote, *History of Metallurgy in Europe* (London, 1987).

8. The chronology and mechanism of this diffusion are debated; for two sides of the issue, see Colin Renfrew, *Archaeology and Language: The Puzzle of Indo-European Origins* (Cambridge, Eng., 1988); and J. P. Mallory, *In Search of the Indo-Europeans: Language, Archaeology and Myth* (London, 1989).

9. John Collis, *The European Iron Age* (London, 1984), chap. 2.

10. Jacobsthal, *Early Celtic Art;* David and Francesca R. Ridgeway, *Italy before the Romans* (London, 1979); and N. K. Sandars, "Orient and Orientalizing: Recent Thoughts Reviewed," in *Celtic Art in Ancient Europe,* ed. P. Duval and C. Hawkes (London, 1976), pp. 41-60. The exchange flowed in both directions, including ideas, technology, and materials, as well as art styles; see Collis, *European Iron Age;* and John Alexander and Sheila Hopkin, "The Origins and Early Development of European Fibulae," *Proceedings of the Prehistoric Society* 48 (1982): 401-16.

11. Collis, *European Iron Age.*

12. Ridgeway and Ridgeway, *Italy Before the Romans,* esp. chaps. 5, 6, 15, and 16; Larissa Bonfante, *Out of Etruria: Influence North and South,* British Archaeological Reports, International Series 103 (Oxford, 1981); and Zbigniew Bukowski, *The Scythian Influence in the Area of Lusatian Culture* (Warsaw, 1977).

13. T. G. E. Powell, "From Urartu to Gundestrup," in *The European Community in Later Prehistory,* ed. John Boardman, M. A. Brown, and T. G. E. Brown (London, 1971), pp. 181-210.

14. Peter S. Wells, *Culture Contact and Culture Change* (Cambridge, Eng., 1980).

15. Wells, *Culture Contact,* chap. 5.

16. Jacobsthal, *Early Celtic Art,* esp. pp. 141-63; Megaw, *Art of the European Iron Age,* pp. 9-40 and 52ff.; and Megaw and Megaw, *Celtic Art,* chaps. 3 and 4.

17. Peter S. Wells, "The Excavation at Stična in Slovenia by the Duchess of Mecklenburg, 1905-1914," *Journal of Field Archaeology* 5 (1978): 215-26.

18. The Duchess of Mecklenburg excavated principally at the sites of Hallstatt in Austria and Stična, Magdalenska gora, and Vinica in Carniola (modern Slovenia), with other excavations at smaller sites in the region. The Duchess's collections are now owned by the Peabody Museum of Archaeology and Ethnology, Harvard University. The Mecklenburg Collection has been partially published, and the material from Vinica has not yet been made available to scholars. However, the collection inventory has just been completed, and preparations are underway to publish the remaining material; see Hugh Hencken, *Mecklenburg Collection, Part 2: The Iron Age Cemetery of Magdalenska gora in Slovenia,* Peabody Museum, Harvard University, American School of Prehistoric Research Bulletin 32 (Cambridge, Mass., 1978); and Peter S. Wells, *Mecklenburg Collection, Part 3: The Emergence of an Iron Age Economy: The Mecklenburg Grave Groups from Hallstatt and Stična,* Peabody Museum, Harvard University, American School of Prehistoric Research Bulletin 33 (Cambridge, Mass., 1981).

19. For examples, see Hencken, *Magdalenska gora,* figs. 29, 52b, 151d, 364m; and Wells, *Emergence of an Iron Age Economy,* fig. 95e.

20. Collis, *European Iron Age;* and T. G. E. Powell, *The Celts* (New York, 1980).

21. Strabo, *Geography* 4.6.10.

22. For illustrations, see Peter S. Wells, "Prehistoric Charms and Superstitions," *Archaeology* 37:3 (1984): 38-43.

23. Collis, *European Iron Age;* and Peter S. Wells, "Socioeconomic Aspects of the Amber Trade in Early Iron Age Slovenia," *Journal of Baltic Studies* 16 (1985): 268-75.

24. André Parrot, *The Arts of Assyria* (New York, 1961); W. Flinders-Petrie, *Decorative Patterns of the Ancient World* (London, 1930); Emma C. Bunker, C. Bruce Chatwin, and Ann R. Farkas, *"Animal Style" Art from East to West* (New York, 1970), chaps. 2, 3, and 8; Sandars, *Prehistoric Art;* and T. G. E. Powell, *Prehistoric Art* (London, 1966).

25. Megaw and Megaw, *Celtic Art*, pp. 160-77.

26. Allen Seaby, "The Guilloche," *Antiquity* 7 (1933): 184-92.

27. Erwin Goodenough, "The Evaluation of Symbols Recurrent in Time, as Illustrated in Judaism," *Eranos-Jahrbuch* 20 (1951): 285-319; and Panofsky, "Classical Tradition."

28. For detailed descriptions of these, and the other Sutton Hoo artifacts, see Rupert Bruce-Mitford, *The Sutton Hoo Ship-Burial*, with contributions by Paul Ashbee et al., 3 vols. in 4 (London, 1975-83).

29. Bruce-Mitford, *Sutton Hoo* 3:282-86.

30. D. F. Petch, "Archaeological Notes for 1956, (25) Hough-on-the-Hill," *Architectural and Archaeological Society of the County of Lincoln, Reports and Papers* 7 (1956): 17-18.

31. C. A. Thomas, "The Animal Art of the Scottish Iron Age and Its Origins," *Archaeological Journal* 118 (1963): 14-64; and R. A. Smith, *British Museum Guide to the Anglo-Saxon and Foreign Teutonic Antiquities* (London, 1923). For other examples and citations, see Bruce-Mitford, *Sutton Hoo* 2:368-69.

32. Carola Hicks, "A Note on the Provenience of the Sutton Hoo Stag," in Bruce-Mitford, *Sutton Hoo* 2:378-82.

33. A. E. A. Werner, W. A. Oddy, and M. J. Hughes, "Scientific Examination of the Stag Assembly and the Bronze Fitments of the Stone Bar," in Bruce-Mitford, *Sutton Hoo* 2:385-93; and Hicks, "Provenience of the Sutton Hoo Stag," in Bruce-Mitford, *Sutton Hoo* 2:382.

34. Sergei Rudenko, *Frozen Tombs of Siberia* (Berkeley, 1970), pl. 137g, h.

35. Jan Bouzek, "Openwork 'Bird-Cage' Bronzes," in *The European Community*, ed. John Boardman et al., pp. 77-104.

36. Flinders-Petrie, *Decorative Patterns*.

37. Parrot, *Arts of Assyria*, figs. 148 and 151-54; and P. R. S. Moorey, *Ancient Bronzes from Luristan* (London, 1974), pp. 25-35, pls. 7b, 10a, 10b, 13a, and 13b.

38. Dieter Planck, "Eine neuentdeckte keltische Viereckschanze in Fellbach-Schmiden, Rems-Murr-Kreis," *Germania* 60 (1982): 105-72.

39. Powell, "From Urartu to Gundestrup"; Megaw and Megaw, *Celtic Art*, pp. 174-76, figs. 282-89.

40. For other examples, see Megaw, *Art of the European Iron Age*, figs. 95-99; and Jacobsthal, *Early Celtic Art*, pls. 169-71.

41. J. Clegg, "The Meaning of Schematization," in *Form in Indigenous Art*, ed. Peter J. Ucko (Canberra, 1977); and E. H. Gombrich, *Art and Illusion* (New York, 1960).

42. Sonia Chadwick Hawkes, H. R. Ellis Davidson, and Christopher Hawkes, "The Finglesham Man," *Antiquity* 39 (1965): 17-32, fig. 3.

43. Rupert Bruce-Mitford, *Aspects of Anglo-Saxon Archaeology* (London, 1974), chap. 1, pl. 15a.

44. E. T. Leeds, *Early Anglo-Saxon Art and Archaeology* (Oxford, 1936), fig. 1.

45. Helen Roe, "An Interpretation of Certain Symbolic Sculptures of Early Christian Ireland," *Journal of the Royal Society of Antiquaries of Ireland* 75 (1945): 1-23.

46. Bruce-Mitford, *Aspects*, chap. 1; and Leeds, *Early Anglo-Saxon Art*, pp. 18-19, pl. 16b.

47. Roe, "An Interpretation."

48. The number specified for this figure in the *Mount Athos Guide for Painters*; see Bruce-Mitford, *Aspects*, p. 43.

49. Bruce-Mitford, *Aspects*, pl. 15e.

50. Leeds, *Early Anglo-Saxon Art*, pp. 18-19, pl. 16b.

51. Goodenough, "The Evaluation of Symbols." See also Panofsky, "The Classical Tradition"; and Andre Grabar, "Origins of Christian Iconography," in *Readings in Art History*, ed. Harold Spencer, vol. 1, 3rd ed. (New York, 1982), pp. 213-34.

52. Pagan symbols are not uncommon even in churches of the early medieval period; examples include the head-niches in the doorways of the churches at Clonfert and Dysert

O'Dea, Ireland (twelfth century) and the fertility deity in the medieval church at Kilpeck, Hertfordshire. See Barry Cunliffe, *The Celtic World* (New York, 1986), pp. 72 and 84-86.

53. Budny, "Early Medieval Britain," p. 133.

PART II

✣

Sutton Hoo and *Beowulf*

CHAPTER 4

✛

Beowulf and Sutton Hoo
The Odd Couple
Roberta Frank

Nineteen thirty-nine was special. It saw the end of the Spanish
Civil War and the beginning of World War II. Hollywood's creative energy peaked and in a few miraculous months produced
*Ninotchka, The Wizard of Oz, Mr. Smith Goes to Washington, Stage-
coach, Goodbye, Mr. Chips, Dark Victory, Wuthering Heights, Gone with
the Wind*, and Bugs Bunny. The uranium atom was split, the New York
World's Fair opened, John Steinbeck published *The Grapes of Wrath*, and
Joe DiMaggio was named most valuable player in the American League. It
was also fifty years ago that the first ship rivet in Mound 1 at Sutton Hoo
was uncovered, on 11 May 1939.

One of my colleagues used to tell his *Beowulf* students the story of the
well-intentioned stranger who, late one night, seeing a man on hands and
knees beneath a streetlight searching for something, offered assistance.
"Are you sure this is the spot?" he asked. "No," came the answer, "but
this is where the light is." Sutton Hoo in 1939 lit up a bit of Dark Age
Britain; *Beowulf* responded, like a moth to a flame; and nothing has been
the same since. The glorious evidence dug up from Mound 1 was at once
asked to illuminate our unique poem, and *Beowulf*, to articulate the
burial deposit. The mutual affinity of *Beowulf* and Sutton Hoo was, in the
first flush of discovery, inevitably exaggerated. Scholars today who caution that "*Beowulf* has no necessary direct connection with Sutton Hoo"[1]
or that the link between the two "has almost certainly been made too
specific"[2] are in no danger of being hounded out of the profession. But
their carefully phrased warnings come too late: it is not nice to tell a couple on the eve of their golden anniversary that they have little in common, and besides, it is no longer true. Even if our rumbling poem and
silent mound did not have much to say to each other fifty years ago, they
do now. A lot of hard work, energy, and stubbornness went into making
this marriage stick. And in Auden's words: "Like everything which is not
the involuntary result of fleeting emotion but the creation of time and
will, any marriage, happy or unhappy, is infinitely more interesting and
significant than any romance, however passionate."[3]

The story of how *Beowulf* and Sutton Hoo got together, what they
came finally to mean to each other, and what the long-term effects of

their union were bears an uncanny resemblance to the plot of Greek New Comedy and, indeed, of most comedy down to our own day. The young couple had much to overcome: a certain difference in age (three and a half centuries, if you believe some people); the usual in-law problems (Vendel, Valsgärde, Suffolk and Uppland, Wuffings and Wylfings became inextricably, even incestuously, involved with each other). These and other obstacles to the marriage had to be removed by supporting players, stock characters of stage and scholarship like the miles gloriosus, the parasite, the lovable curmudgeon, and the bemused tyrant. The more complicated their maneuvers, the more absurd the gimmick that ensured a happy ending, the better the comedy.

The story of how *Beowulf* and Sutton Hoo met is well known. According to the received version, they first came face to face in a court of law. It was on a Monday, 14 August 1939. In the village hall of Sutton, some two miles away from the discovery, an inquest was being held to find out whether or not the grave goods were treasure trove.[4] What happened next was described in 1948 by Sune Lindqvist, a professor at Uppsala: "Much surprise was occasioned by the news of the Coroner's Inquest — something unfamiliar to Swedes — at which the legal title to the find was decided with the help of the passages in *Beowulf* describing the passing of Scyld and the lavish furnishing of Beowulf's memorial mound."[5] Lindqvist then quoted the relevant lines, concluding, "At all events it is obvious that the *rapprochement* that was at once made between the Sutton Hoo burial and the substance of *Beowulf* was fully warranted, and rich with possibilities. Everything seems to show that these two documents complement one another admirably. Both become the clearer by the comparison."[6] In other words, it was love at first sight. Charles Wrenn, who like Lindqvist had not been present at the inquest, spelled out in 1959 what Lindqvist had only hinted at, that *Beowulf* had been read aloud to an appreciative jury. The court decision, he reported, "was reached after the jurymen had listened to an exposition of the account of the ship-passing of Scyld Scefing in *Beowulf* with its astonishing parallels to the Sutton Hoo ship-cenotaph: and the matter was clinched by the reading of the story of the final disposal of the Dragon's hoard in ll. 3156-68."[7] Wrenn repeated his story in another 1959 essay, concluding with a complaint that "though this public citation of *Beowulf* and its parallels with Sutton Hoo in a court of law might be thought to have drawn the first attention to the light which the one might throw upon the other, it was not till 1948 that an outstanding scholar [Lindqvist] took especial pains to emphasize the fundamental importance of the new finds for the study of the poem."[8]

If in 1939 the recitation of *Beowulf* in the village hall of Sutton did not make as big a splash as Wrenn would have wished, it may be because it never happened. For it was not until 1948, when Lindqvist penned his piece, that anyone imagined that the words of the poem had been declaimed to the Sutton jury. The court deposition of Charles Phillips, the site archaeologist, simply stated, "There is contemporary literary evidence that the burial of chieftains among the northern nations in the Dark Ages was the occasion of celebrations and feasting, which lasted for several days, and nothing can be more certain than the public character of the Sutton Hoo burial."[9] Quotations from *Beowulf* did, however, form part of an editorial in the *East Anglian Daily Times* on 17 August 1939. And two days earlier, 15 August, the London *Times*, having reported the inquest decision along with Phillips's statement about "contemporary literary evidence," concluded that "the nature of the objects found reminds one . . . very strongly of the passage in 'Beowulf' in which jewels and treasures from different lands are piled round the dead king's body in the centre of a ship" (p. 9, col. 2). Reports of the excavation in *The Antiquaries Journal* and in *Antiquity* for 1940 include citations from *Beowulf*, with both Phillips and Hector Munro Chadwick quoting the poet's account of Scyld Scefing's funeral as "an interesting parallel."[10] In January 1947, in the first of many issues of *The Sutton Hoo Ship-Burial: A Provisional Guide*, put out by the British Museum, Rupert Bruce-Mitford, then Assistant Keeper in the Department of British Antiquities, quoted the usual passages from *Beowulf* and noted that "these literary accounts make it plain that the Sutton Hoo treasures were not buried in secret. They also make it plain that those who buried the treasure had no intention of recovering them later. It was these considerations which led the Suffolk jurors, in accordance with English law, to find that the gold and silver in the ship were not Treasure Trove."[11] Lindqvist's imaginative reconstruction the very next year of a courthouse drama, in which portions of *Beowulf* were read aloud to the jury, and Wrenn's repeated statements in the decade following that *Beowulf* "clinched" the Sutton Hoo case, go beyond the evidence of any of the published accounts available to them. Like so much in this torrid love story, the oft-recited tale of how the young couple first met rests on nothing more solid than "a conspiracy of romantic hopes";[12] the yearned-for hard facts melt, like popsicles, at our touch.

It is important to recall that *Beowulf*, though relatively young and clean-cut when hitched to Sutton Hoo, had a past. What the poem faced after 1939 was not unlike the gropings and assignations it knew in the second half of the nineteenth century. The first scholarly edition of the poem, by John Mitchell Kemble (a great Anglo-Saxonist and Fanny's brother), published in two volumes between 1835 and 1837, was accompanied by an English translation that made the poem accessible to a wider public.[13] Among the first antiquaries to cite from Kemble's edition was William J. Thoms, the English translator and annotator of Jens Worsaae's *The Primeval Antiquities of Denmark*. He noted in 1849 that the figure most often found perched on Germanic helmets was the boar, "and it is to this custom that reference is made in *Beowulf* where the poet speaks of the boar of gold, the boar hard as iron."[14] In 1852, Charles Roach Smith, in the second volume of his *Collectanea antiqua, etchings and notices of ancient remains, illustrative of the habits, customs, and history of past ages*, cited various passages from Kemble's *Beowulf* relevant to the ornamented swords, runic hilts, decorated ale cups, mail shirts, shields, and other objects that had been excavated from Saxon cemeteries. He, like Thoms, was particularly struck by the parallel between Beowulf's boar-crested helmet and the one found at Benty Grange; after quoting the relevant Old English lines, he concluded, "Nothing can be more satisfactory than the explanation of the hog upon the Saxon helmet found in Derbyshire presented by these citations from . . . *Beowulf.*"[15] *Beowulf* is similarly exploited in John Yonge Akerman's *Remains of Pagan Saxondom* (1855)[16] and in Roach Smith's 1856 introduction to *Inventorium sepulchrale: An account of some antiquities dug up at Gilton, Kingston, Sibertswold, Barfriston, Beakesbourne, Chartham, and Crundale in the County of Kent from A.D. 1757 to A.D. 1773 by the Rev. Bryan Faussett of Heppington.*[17] (This was the Faussett who boasted of digging up twenty-eight graves in one day, and nine barrows before breakfast.)[18] The excerpts from *Beowulf* in *Ten Years' Diggings in Celtic and Saxon Grave Hills in the Counties of Derby, Stafford, and York from 1848 to 1858, with Notices of Some Former Discoveries, Hitherto Unpublished, and Remarks on the Crania and Pottery from the Mounds*, published in 1861 by Thomas Bateman, come secondhand from Smith's *Collectanea*, but Bateman also describes one Dano-Norwegian burial custom not yet encountered in England: "Sometimes the bodies were placed in the small ships or boats of the period, which were dragged on shore and then buried under a barrow within view of the ocean. It is with interments of this late and peculiar description that the greatest variety of curious and rare objects is found."[19] The very next year, 1862, the first ship burial on English soil was dug up at Snape in Suffolk, only a few miles from Sutton Hoo. The coupling of objects mentioned in *Beowulf* with those excavated from Anglo-Saxon cemeteries continued unabated into the twentieth century: in 1923 the official British Museum *Guide* directed visitors curious about the ring-sword supposedly mentioned in *Beowulf* to the "top of Case 49 for specimens from Faversham and Gilton, Kent."[20] Sutton Hoo was not *Beowulf*'s first suitor, just the richest.

In the 1930s, *Beowulf* was sought after by social historians as well as by archaeologists. H. M. Chadwick, in 1940 one of the first to suggest that *Beowulf* and Sutton Hoo could do a lot for each other, had long criticized his colleagues for their reluctance to make use of archaeological and legendary material.[21] In 1935, Ritchie Girvan took up the challenge; his *Beowulf and the Seventh Century* attempted to show how closely the poem reflected the social and political realities of its time.[22] Even J. R. R. Tolkien, that most literary of Anglo-Saxonists, admonished readers of his 1936 essay, "*Beowulf*: The Monsters and the Critics," that "*Beowulf* is a historical document of the first order for the study of the mood and thought of the period, and one perhaps too little used by historians."[23]

Major studies between 1936 and 1939 by Swedish and Norwegian archaeologists express a similar optimism, praising *Beowulf* for its accurate por-
trayal of the material life of the age: "It can be shown from archaeological
evidence," note the authors of one book, "that the poem has preserved
accurately many details of the Scandinavian society to which the tradition originally belonged; as has been mentioned several times in this survey, the descriptions in *Beowulf* can often be illustrated directly by the
Scandinavian antiquities of the period."[24] To have foreign wooers was undoubtedly a feather in *Beowulf*'s cap and an incentive to Englishmen to
bring the poem home.

The exciting news from Sutton Hoo kept students of *Beowulf* busy for
years composing supplements, appendices, and addenda to earlier work.
Even a historical novel like Gisela Reichel's 1962 *Hakon's Song: A Story
about the Writer of the Beowulf Poem* seemed incomplete to the author
without a postscript on Sutton Hoo.[25] Frederick Klaeber in the 1941 supplement to his edition of the poem had time only to note cautiously that
"a burial ship apparently dating from the 7th century has been dug up in
East Suffolk."[26] The upbeat mood of Wrenn's 1959 supplement to R. W.
Chambers's *Beowulf* is more typical. It is not so much a critical overview
as a eulogy, an epithalamium in honor of the new couple in town. Here
are his opening words:

> By far the greatest single event in *Beowulf* studies in the period un-
> der review was the excavating of the East Anglian king's ship-ceno-
> taph with its treasures almost intact in the summer of 1939. Indeed
> this may well seem the most important happening since the Ice-
> lander Jón Grímur Thorkelin made his transcripts of the *Beowulf*
> MS. and from them published the first edition of the poem. For by
> the recognition of the significance of the Sutton Hoo finds has come
> about the illumination in a truly revolutionary manner of the whole
> background of the poem—historical, archaeological and folkloristic
> —as well as to some extent the means towards the reassessment of the
> problem of its genesis. By study of the actual parallels from the Sutton
> Hoo treasures . . . has been established a historical basis in reality for
> that loving connoisseurship of material art which used to astonish the
> critics of this "Dark Age" poem. The swords and helmets, the royal
> standards, the precious drinking-bowls of *Beowulf* and its harp, have
> become suddenly vitally related to actual history. The seemingly am-
> bivalent relationships of pagan Germanic and Christian elements in
> *Beowulf* have become natural and intelligible through their material
> parallels at Sutton Hoo. The so puzzling and basic position of the
> Swedes and the Geats of southern Sweden in the poem has become
> convincingly historical. *Beowulf* is seen, as a result of the Sutton Hoo
> finds . . . , to be the product of a civilization of the highest then known
> cultivation, centuries in advance of the rest of Western Europe. The fu-

neral departure of Scyld Scefing . . . , the hoard of ancient treasures in the dragon's mound . . . , and the account of Beowulf's own funeral rites, all these now may be seen to contain memories of factual traditions not far from living recollection when the poem was composed.[27]

Wrenn covers all the bases. Sutton Hoo was, is, and will be the answer to *Beowulf*'s dreams and prayers. No red-blooded poem or Englishman could want more. But when we look back, from the perspective of this golden anniversary, to see what a half-century of togetherness with Sutton Hoo has actually done for *Beowulf*, it is hard not to be disappointed.

Happy relationships are supposed to make you look younger. Life with Sutton Hoo, however, did nothing to retard the aging of *Beowulf*; indeed, it had the opposite effect. The discovery at once lent support to the traditional dating of the poem, thought in 1939 to have been composed in the late seventh or very early eighth century. In the 1920s, Liebermann, Cook, and Lawrence had dated *Beowulf* to 675-725 and decided it was Northumbrian.[28] The poem aged a bit more in the 1930s, when Girvan proposed 700 as the latest possible date and raised the possibility of East Anglian origins.[29] A seventh-century East Anglian ship burial and a seventh-century East Anglian *Beowulf* was a match made in heaven. In her 1945 lectures, written even before the objects of Sutton Hoo could be viewed, Elizabeth Martin-Clarke noted the perfect convergence: "It is of remarkable interest that scholars . . . do ascribe *Beowulf* to a non-West-Saxon area and allocate its production to a period of time not later than the middle of the eighth century and probably as early as, if not earlier than, the middle of the seventh century."[30] Bruce-Mitford in 1947 saw the poem as just a bit younger than the burial: "It is generally accepted that *Beowulf* was composed in England about the year A.D. 700, that is, some forty-five years after the burial of the Sutton Hoo ship" (at that time thought to have occurred between 650-670).[31] Lindqvist in 1948 did not hesitate to place the poem in East Anglia and its composition in 700, within living memory of those who had witnessed the construction of Mound 1.[32]

Sutton Hoo has, over the years, been not so much a brake on successive attempts to rejuvenate its younger partner as a yo-yo string; it lets *Beowulf* fall forward, naturally, propelled by the gravity of the moment, before yanking the poem back, into its grasp again. Wrenn, for example, started out in 1950 with a firm date of circa 700 but, three years later, moved to a somewhat less firm date of "before 750."[33] In between, Dorothy Whitelock had singlehandedly advanced the terminus ad quem of *Beowulf* from 700 to 825, halting before the Viking incursions of mid-century.[34] Wrenn fought against her late dating of *Beowulf* with Sutton Hoo as his chief weapon, arguing in 1959, for example, that "the seemingly vivid memories of the Sutton Hoo ship-burial which lie behind the accounts of the passing of Scyld Scefing and of the hero's own funeral rites in the poem, would point rather to an earlier date for its composition."[35] And again: "The Sutton Hoo discoveries . . . have furnished new evidence bearing on the date and genesis of *Beowulf*, clearing away obstacles to the early dating of the poem."[36] It is now generally acknowledged that neither an East Anglian origin for *Beowulf* nor a date of composition anywhere near the date of the burial is demonstrable, but so strong are the bonds between the poem and its "significant other" that, though frayed, they seem unable to be severed.

A number of studies published over the last twenty-five years have explored a possible late-ninth- or tenth-century date for the poem.[37] But the yo-yo trick, that silent "Come back, little *Beowulf*" flick of the wrist, is still at work. "There is a close link," insists Hilda Ellis Davidson in 1968, "between objects and funeral practices as described in *Beowulf* and archaeological evidence from the sixth and seventh centuries A.D. . . . Links with the royal ship burial of Sutton Hoo are particularly detailed and impressive. . . . There are no allusions in the poem to objects or practices which must be dated later than the seventh century."[38] Eric John, arguing in 1973 against an early-tenth-century date, is also convinced that "the archaeological evidence certainly suggests a much earlier date, nearer the traditional date."[39] "Aspects of the poem's 'archaeology,' " Patrick Wormald confirms in 1978, " . . . point towards an earlier rather than a post-Viking date."[40] "In an English context," states John Hines in 1984, "the archaeological horizon of *Beowulf* reflects the late 6th and 7th centuries with a striking consistency." For it is, he explains, "material of the later sixth and seventh centuries that corresponds most closely to the objects mentioned in the poem."[41]

Back in 1957, before any of these claims were made, Rosemary Cramp observed wisely if too optimistically that "today one would hesitate even more than Stjerna did [in 1912] to rely on archaeological evidence for dating *Beowulf*; gaps in the material evidence after the cessation of heathen burials are still too immense."[42] Despite her warning, archaeology is still being used, subtly, to age *Beowulf*. The corselet or coat of mail found at Sutton Hoo (and matched by chain mail in Swedish seventh- and eighth-century boat graves) shows, we are told, how accurately the *Beowulf* poet described his warriors' byrnies, the iron circles " 'hard and hand-locked,' ringing as the wearer walked (322-3) and acting as a 'woven breast-net' against attack (551-3)."[43] The accuracy of this description has, of course, no bearing on the date of the poem, and not only because chain mail, like pattern-welded sword blades, continued in use into the tenth century. *Beowulf* is, above all, a work of the imagination. A poet who tells us in loving if bloody detail precisely what happens when dragon fangs wrap themselves around a warrior's neck was certainly able to represent the sounds and texture of a mail coat without having handled one himself. For the material culture of *Beowulf* is the conventional apparatus of heroic poetry. Old Norse skalds from the tenth to thirteenth centuries allude in terms almost identical to those of the *Beowulf* poet to the clattering, interlocked rings of byrnies they call "ring-woven," "ring-sark," "iron-sark," and "ring-shirt."[44] The so-called archaeological horizon of *Beowulf* is remarkably wide, stretching from late Roman times to the Norman Conquest. No linguistic, historical, or archaeological fact compels us to anchor *Beowulf* within reach of Sutton Hoo. If we do so it is more from our emotional commitment to their association than from hard evidence.

It is also because a grateful *Beowulf* is loath to leave Sutton Hoo's side. Mound 1 has served the poem well and faithfully these fifty years. It is largely thanks to the ship burial that the poet's golden hero remains in the mind's eye, not as a shapeless hulk, cloaked Grendel-like in mist, but as a well-turned-out knight in shining armor. From the top of his head to the tips of his spears he is heavy metal. The Beowulf whose footsteps we hear departing Denmark — the poet says, with deliberate metrical weighting, "guðrinc goldwlanc græsmoldan træd" (the gold-adorned warrior trod the greensward, line 1881) — cannot be traveling lightly: our imagination puts a crested helmet with garnet-eyed boar images on his head, a pair of clasps with garnet and enamel cloisonné on his shoulders, on his arm a shield shining gilt bronze, at his waist a great gold buckle, a gold-framed purse, a gold and jewelled sword pommel above a gold-embossed scabbard, and spilling all over him a splendid confusion of golden hinges, clasps, mounts, and ornamental studs. Sutton Hoo casts light on *Beowulf* because our memory lets its "things" do duty for the poet's words. When the shape of an item, such as the helmet or harp, changes, the poem graciously adjusts. The revised helmet with its new lifesaving features was an easy substitution. More embarrassing was the 1970 transformation of the harp into a Germanic round lyre, for *Beowulf* scholars had already made much of the 1948 reconstruction.[45] Lexicography, however, came swiftly to the rescue, murmuring that it was the word, not the thing, that we had earlier got wrong: the *hearpe* that once in Heorot sung was not what we now think of as a harp but was, instead, a "lyre."[46]

Sutton Hoo's power over *Beowulf* can be traced in the Old English dictionaries produced over the last fifty years. Entries for words that name objects in the burial deposit have become progressively more precise, and not always to the advantage of the poetry. One term apparently "solved" with Sutton Hoo's help is the notorious *wala* (MS *walan*), the feature that the *Beowulf* poet focuses on when describing a helmet given to his hero. This *wala* is "wound about with wires" that go "around the roof of the helmet" (lines 1030-34). In 1898 *wala* was defined as "some part of a helmet"; in 1912, as "guard, bulge, a part of the helmet"; in 1931, as "ridge, rib, comb" (of helmet).[47] In 1952, Bruce-Mitford, on the basis of the first reconstruction of the Sutton Hoo helmet, confirmed what Knut Stjerna in 1912 and Elizabeth Martin-Clarke in 1945 had suggested with regard to a detached comb found with a helmet in Boat Grave 1 at Vendel. The *wala* was the nose-to-nape band of the late Roman parade helmet, the thick tubular iron crest or comb running up over the crown.[48] The Sutton Hoo helmet crest, he declared, "has enabled the meaning of the unique word *wala* to be established precisely for the first time."[49] Typical post–Sutton Hoo dictionary entries gloss *wala* as "metal ridge on top of helmet, like that on Sutton Hoo helmet at *Beowulf* 1031," and as "ridge or comb inlaid with wires running on top of helmet from front to back," with the definition referring the reader to Rupert Bruce-Mitford's 1952 statement.[50] These definitions of *wala* give a special sense to its use in *Beowulf*, a sense that fits the immediate context. Elsewhere in Old English, when the word occurs in charter bounds it apparently means "ridge" (of land); when the term refers, four times, to man-made objects it seems to have the general sense "raised band or strip."[51] In three of these four occurrences, including *Beowulf*, *wala* is found in conjunction with the word *wir* (Mod. E. "wire," OE "metal ornament, thread"), and in all four, *wala* appears to refer to some kind of raised ornamentation, whether the decorative ribbing on the walls of a Roman building or, in an Old Testament gloss, the ornamental brass work that Hiram of Tyre designed for Solomon, specifically the two rows of striated ornamentation about the edge of a cast bronze piece. Giving *wala* in *Beowulf* a special meaning, defining it as the comb on a Sutton Hoo type helmet, is not wrong, but it has the unfortunate effect of ironing out the figurative language. If the Old English poet had wanted to use a technical term, the gloss word *camb*, "comb" of a helmet, was ready and waiting,[52] but he used *wala*, instead, in a generalizing, metaphorical way, as part of his overall architectural imagery. In conjunction with the other shelter words in the passage, *wala* suggests a vault, an overhanging, protecting roof that shielded the man within from the showers raining down upon him.[53] The Sutton Hoo helmet gives us an idea of what such a protuberance may have looked like; the poem explores its essence.

Perhaps the quickest way to gauge the influence of Sutton Hoo on *Beowulf* is to pick up any post-1939 translation of the poem, such as the excellent one by Howell D. Chickering that many of us assign year after year to our students.[54] Most noticeable is a drastic increase in the gold and silver content of the verse. In line 37, in a passage describing burial treasure from far-off lands, the translator's words "bright gold and silver" and "gems" are an interpretation of the Old English term *frætwa*, meaning "ornaments, treasure, armour." The translation fits Sutton Hoo with its forty-five individual pieces of gold jewelry (forty-five not counting the coins and blank ingots) and its sixteen pieces of late antique silver, but it is alien to *Beowulf*, which never once mentions the lesser metal. In line 2761 of the poem, the Old English words *fyrnmanna fatu*, "cups of ancient men," have been similarly transmuted into "golden beakers" (as have *bunan*, "cups," in line 2775), while the descriptive phrase in line 2762, *hyrstum behrorene*, "deprived of adornments," is refined into "its garnets broken." Garnets, like silver, are never mentioned in *Beowulf*, but the Sutton Hoo burial deposit contains four thousand of them, estimated to represent a year's gem-cutting for a workshop of seventeen men.[55] Apparently, as far as students of *Beowulf* are concerned, the riches of Sutton Hoo belong equally to its long-term partner, their poem.

The presence of Sutton Hoo in translations of *Beowulf* is largely unconscious, the result of years of seeing each in the other. The same subtle interaction may have affected the Old English text of the poem. Before 1939, the last two words of line 3157a read *on [h]liðe* (on a hill, cliff); now, in almost all editions of the poem, they are *on hoe* (on a promontory). Although *hoh* is the Old English word from which modern Hoo (as in Sutton) developed, it was in the year before the excavation that the manuscript page was photographed under ultraviolet light, producing the new reading.[56] Klaeber, in his 1941 supplementary notes, rejected *hoe* because, he argued, "the noun *hoh* in the sense of 'promontory' occurs nowhere else in Old English poetry,"[57] and Holthausen in 1948, reluctant to alter his edition, convinced himself that the photographs showed *liðe* rather than *hoe*.[58] But many more editors, beginning in 1940, were delighted with the change, and Wrenn explains why: "If my reading of ll. 3156-8 is correct, Beowulf, it may be worth noticing, was given his funeral barrow on just such a headland as has given us the name Sutton Hoo."[59] And although a number of the 1938 ultraviolet readings have been ignored, challenged, or modified in the last half-century, there has not since 1948 been a whisper of discontent with *hoe*. The silence is surprising. Not only is the meaning "promontory" otherwise restricted to prose, as Klaeber noted, but the form *hoe* rather than *ho* should have raised, if not a hue and cry, at least a few scholarly eyebrows: the dative singular ending *-oe* does not occur in prose until the reign of Edgar in the late tenth century, and is never found in verse.[60] Yet *hoe* sits still, lofty and solitary, in our editions, and we nod approvingly. Burying Beowulf on a hoo is a good thing, since it allows Sutton Hoo once again to shed its lovely light over our poem.

"But what light," asked Michael Wallace-Hadrill, "does *Beowulf* cast upon Sutton Hoo?" "Not very much," was his answer.[61] What the poem has shed, and that liberally, upon the ship burial seems to have been its Scandinavian, regal, and pagan color. From the start, the apparent Swedish connections of Sutton Hoo recalled the geography of *Beowulf*, the poet's almost exclusive concern with one corner of Scandinavia. By 1948, the East Anglian royal line of the Wuffings had been found to include two names similar to two in *Beowulf*: English Wuffings became Wylfings, who although not Swedish were vaguely Baltic, while Wehha of the East Anglian king list became Weohstan, father of Wiglaf and kinsman of Beowulf, not Swedish perhaps but at least near neighbors. The goal of these onomastic mergers was to suggest that *Beowulf* was composed in honor of the Sutton Hoo Wuffings, "who were in origin Swedes," said Lindqvist, "a branch of the Royal House of Uppsala and descendants of

Wiglaf."[62] So because there is a Swedish element at Sutton Hoo and in *Beowulf*, there is a Swedish element in the East Anglian genealogies, and because there is a Swedish element in the East Anglian genealogies, there is a Swedish element in Sutton Hoo and *Beowulf*. The argument is perfectly circular and apparently irresistible, since it is still widely accepted as fact.[63] The first step—dyeing Sutton Hoo Nordic blonde—was taken by Rupert Bruce-Mitford in the 1940s and repeated by him in every decade thereafter: "It may be taken as certain," he wrote in 1949, "that in the Sutton Hoo grave we meet pure Scandinavian elements in the East Anglian milieu, as we meet them in *Beowulf*."[64] And again: "It is the unique nature of the Swedish connection revealed at Sutton Hoo that seems to open up the possibility of a direct connection between the poem and the burial."[65]

Yet this "Swedish connection," though much invoked, is still unproven. There are parallels between the burial deposits at Sutton Hoo, Vendel, and Valsgärde, but the usual biological explanation, the positing of a common royal ancestor, is at the very least contestable. It is far from certain that the treasures of Sutton Hoo are heirlooms, handed down from father to son like Weohstan's helmet, mail coat, and sword in *Beowulf*. Similarities between the East Anglian and East Scandinavian material may have more to do with the mobility of Dark Age artisans, a shared North Sea/Baltic trade in luxury items, and the desire of two wealthy fringe groups to adopt locally all the status symbols of the Franks. The Sutton Hoo articles crying out for a link with Sweden are few, chiefly the shield (and here there are suggestive Langobardic analogues) and, to a lesser extent, the helmet.[66] *Beowulf*, with its Danish, Swedish, and Geatish cast of characters and its focus on the shores of the Kattegat, is far more exclusively Scandinavian. The garnet- and goldwork of the ship burial hint at a Kentish pedigree;[67] the Coptic dish, the ten silver bowls, the Greek-inscribed spoons, the silver ladle, and the Anastasius Dish are east Mediterranean in origin; the combs are from Saxony; the great cauldron, the chain, the hanging bowls, the millefiori inlays, the naturalistic stag, even the singular dinner bell discovered in 1970 point to the Romano-British world; while the thirty-seven Merovingian gold coins and the congruence of the gold buckle and purse-lid designs with known Frankish objects recall East Anglia's powerful overseas neighbor.[68] The objects of Sutton Hoo, even those most often called barbaric, belong less to the *Beowulf* poet's retrospective Germania than to a European maritime culture that had for centuries imitated Roman ways.

Beowulf tells of treasure-bestowing pagan kings, and once the unparalleled richness of Mound 1 was known, scholars wasted no time in declaring the burial "royal" and "pagan." H. M. Chadwick in 1940 declared it "impossible to believe that in the times with which we are concerned a treasure of such amount and value can have belonged to anyone except a king," and he cited in support the passage in *Beowulf* in which the hero on his return home presents to his king all the treasures he had been given in Denmark.[69] The bronze stag now topping Sutton Hoo's ceremonial whetstone called to mind the Danish royal hall in *Beowulf*, Heorot or "hart," so named, suggests one writer, possibly thinking of the whetstone, because of the "stags' heads . . . displayed over the door."[70] Another scholar is so eager to have the iron stand of Sutton Hoo resemble the golden standards of *Beowulf*'s kings that he invents for the former a gold-embroidered banner, concluding, "Indeed the royal standard — though of course the gold embroidery of the Sutton Hoo exemplar has left no trace — . . . is a marked feature alike at Sutton Hoo and in *Beowulf*."[71] (Unfortunately for this parallel, the one thing we can be sure about in connection with the iron stand of Mound 1 is that there never were any gold threads associated with it.)[72] The splendor of the burial deposit at Sutton Hoo is unmatched in the sixth-and seventh-century North and may well indicate the grave of a king, though it is salutary to recall that the graves at Vendel and Valsgärde were once interpreted as royal, but are now regarded as the tombs of great landowners.[73] But if a king, how big a king? Without other royal graves to compare with Mound 1, we have no way to judge the relative status and wealth of the man commemorated,[74] or his religion. Because the poet of *Beowulf* tells of the doings and deaths of noble heathen, his accounts of cremations, auguries, buried gold, and funeral boats have been used to color Sutton Hoo pagan. We keep trying to find in Mound 1 the heathen remains that the nineteenth century long sought in the words of *Beowulf*, with a similar lack of success. For although the Christian objects buried at Sutton Hoo do not prove that the deceased was Christian, there is nothing in the deposit that could not have been owned by a Christian. The desire to uncover leafy pagan beliefs at Sutton Hoo seems to be behind the notion that the Sutton Hoo harp was shattered at the graveside in an act of ritual destruction.[75] Numismatists, weighing the possible supernatural uses to which the gold coins and blanks might have been put, attribute their own paganizing imagination to the poet's audience: "Perhaps," suggests one, "the first hearers of *Beowulf* envisaged ghostly oarsmen taking over the conduct of Scyld's funeral ship once it was out of sight of land."[76] Another writer, identifying the iron stand with Scyld's golden banner, confidently reports that "the standard of the Wuffings was placed in the howe of Sutton Hoo to accompany its dweller as he sailed into the realm of the dead."[77] Sutton Hoo is so malleable, so full of possibilities, that *Beowulf*, the speaking partner, is able to shape the mound in its own image. What resistance could a poor little rich dig offer? There was no other role model on the horizon, no other mirror to look in and be seen, no other constant guide and helpmate. Like any marriage, that of *Beowulf* and Sutton Hoo has limited, for better or worse, the couple's options, preventing each from wandering wherever curiosity and natural inclination led.

By the late 1950s, *Beowulf* and Sutton Hoo were so inseparable that, in study after study, the appearance of one inevitably and automatically evoked the other. If *Beowulf* came on stage first, Sutton Hoo was swiftly brought in to illustrate how closely seventh-century reality resembled what the poet depicted; if Sutton Hoo performed first, *Beowulf* followed close behind to give voice to the former's dumb evidence. And just as, after years of living together, husband and wife or man and dog start to look and sound alike, so now — fifty years down the road — the two at moments seem to merge, to become interchangeable. Because the Danish king in *Beowulf* picks at a stringed instrument, we are informed that the king buried at Sutton Hoo was an accomplished performer on the harp;[78] because the golden standard of Beowulf's dragon kicked around for some time before ending up in his den, we are asked to believe that the iron stand at Sutton Hoo was "already ancient when buried."[79] Men boast over mead cups in *Beowulf,* and we are quickly assured that the impressive drinking horns of Mound 1 were "intended for just such occasions."[80] And when Beowulf dies, we are consoled with the thought that "his grave must have been much like the ship burial discovered in our own generation at Sutton Hoo"[81] (give or take a few rivets, I suppose). In plotting the *Beowulf*/Sutton Hoo story, a half-century of scholarship has lingered over scenes of discovery and reconciliation, of harmony and consonance, destining the pair to live happily ever after. For, as Byron's *Don Juan* says:

> All tragedies are finished by a death,
> All comedies are ended by a marriage.
> (canto 3, stanza 9)

The only sour note in all this sweetness comes from after-dinner speakers who imagine themselves called upon, even at this late hour, to lament, as if they were dealing with a realistic novel, the triumph of arbitrary plot over probability, of pictorial convenience over consistency of characterization. Such killjoys may even try to tell you that a temporary separation, perhaps a creative divorce, would be productive for both parties. But don't worry. Neither *Beowulf* nor Sutton Hoo is about to throw over fifty years of shared learning and experience, at least not until a more likely prospect comes along.

Notes

1. Robert T. Farrell, "*Beowulf,* Swedes, and Geats," *Saga-Book of the Viking Society* 18 (1972): 281.

2. Eric Stanley, "The Date of *Beowulf*: Some Doubts and No Conclusions," in *The Dating of Beowulf,* ed. Colin Chase (Toronto, 1981), p. 205.

3. W. H. Auden, *A Certain World: A Commonplace Book* (New York, 1970), p. 248.

4. The definitive account is Rupert Bruce-Mitford, *The Sutton Hoo Ship-Burial*, with contributions by Paul Ashbee et al., 3 vols. in 4 (London, 1975-83), 1:718-31.

5. Sune Lindqvist, "Sutton Hoo och *Beowulf*," *Fornvännen* 43 (1948): 94-110; English translation by R. L. S. Bruce-Mitford, "Sutton Hoo and *Beowulf*," *Antiquity* 22 (1948): 131.

6. Lindqvist,"Sutton Hoo and *Beowulf*," p. 140.

7. C. L. Wrenn, "Sutton Hoo and Beowulf," in *Mélanges de linguistique et de philologie: Fernand Mossé in memoriam* (Paris, 1959), pp. 495-507; reprinted in *An Anthology of Beowulf Criticism*, comp. Lewis E. Nicholson (Notre Dame, Ind., 1963), p. 313.

8. C. L. Wrenn, "Recent Work on *Beowulf* to 1958: Chapter I, Sutton Hoo and *Beowulf*" in *Beowulf: An Introduction to the Study of the Poem*, R. W. Chambers, 3rd ed. (Cambridge, 1959; repr. 1963), p. 510.

9. C. W. Phillips, cited in Bruce-Mitford, *The Sutton Hoo Ship-Burial* 1:722.

10. C. W. Phillips, "The Excavation of the Sutton Hoo Ship-Burial," *Antiquaries Journal* 20 (1940): 182; and H. M. Chadwick, "The Sutton Hoo Ship Burial," *Antiquity* 14 (1940): 87.

11. Rupert Bruce-Mitford, *The Sutton Hoo Ship-Burial: A Provisional Guide* (London, 1947), p. 41.

12. The phrase is from Eric Stanley's preliminary statement (1979) to the Toronto conference on the date of *Beowulf* (20-23 April 1980).

13. John Mitchell Kemble, *The Anglo-Saxon Poems of Beowulf, The Travellers Song, and The Battle of Finnesburh* (London, 1833 [100 copies]; 2nd ed., vol. 1, 1835; vol. 2, *A Translation of the Anglo-Saxon Poem of "Beowulf," with a Copious Glossary, Preface, and Philological Notes* (London, 1837).

14. William J. Thoms, *The Primeval Antiquities of Denmark. Translated and Applied to the Illustration of Similar Remains in England* (London, 1849), cited in Bateman (see note 19), pp. 32-33. Three years earlier, Thoms had introduced the term "folklore" into the English language, replacing with "a good Saxon compound" what had previously been called "popular antiquities" or "popular literature" (*Athenaeum*, no. 982 [22 August 1846], p. 862).

15. Charles Roach Smith, *Collectanea antiqua* . . . (London, 1852), 2:241. I am deeply grateful to Professor E. G. Stanley who, with fortitude and humor, tracked down this volume for me at the Bodleian Library, where it had languished misshelved and unread for over a century.

16. John Yonge Akerman, *Remains of Pagan Saxondom* (London, 1855), pp. xvff.

17. Charles Roach Smith, "Introduction," in *Inventorum sepulchrale: An account* . . . by the Rev. Bryan Faussett of Heppington (London, 1856), p. xxxv.

18. Faussett excavated about seven hundred graves in all. See C. J. Arnold, *An Archaeology of the Early Anglo-Saxon Kingdoms* (London, 1988), p. 3.

19. Thomas Bateman, *Ten Years' Diggings* . . . (London, 1861; repr. 1978), p. x. Boat burial had been mentioned in Scandinavian literature since the late seventeenth century. Michael Müller-Wille, "Boat Graves in Northern Europe," *International Journal of Nautical Archaeology and Underwater Exploration* 3.2 (1974): 187-204, estimates about three hundred locations with more than 420 boat graves. In 1874, Thomas Wright, *The Celt, the Roman, and the Saxon: A History of the Early Inhabitants of Britain* (London, 1874), pp. 465-504, was still citing the *Collectanea* and included the usual excerpts (now nine in number) from *Beowulf*.

20. *The British Museum Guide to Anglo-Saxon Antiquities* (1923), p. 48.

21. See esp. H. M. Chadwick, *The Origin of the English Nation* (Cambridge, 1907), and idem, *The Heroic Age* (Cambridge, 1912). He was impressed, too, with the relevance to Old English verse of what was being dug up in Scandinavia: "The evidence of these deposits then fully bears out the statements of the poems. So numerous were the articles found that it is possible to reconstruct from them with certainty the whole dress and equipment of the warriors of those days" (*The Origin*, p. 187).

22. Ritchie Girvan, *Beowulf and the Seventh Century* (London, 1935; 2nd ed., with a new chapter by R. L. S. Bruce-Mitford, 1971).

23. J. R. R. Tolkien, "*Beowulf*: The Monsters and the Critics," *Proceedings of the British Academy* 22 (1936): 245-95, as reprinted in *An Anthology of Beowulf Criticism*, ed. Nicholson, pp. 51-103, at p. 69.

24. Haakon Shetelig and Hjalmar Falk, *Scandinavian Archaeology*, trans. E. V. Gordon (Oxford, 1937), p. 265.

25. Gisela Reichel, *Hakons Lied: Ein Roman um den Schreiber des Beowulf-Epos* (Leipzig, 1962), Sutton Hoo postscript, pp. 261-64.

26. Frederick Klaeber, *Beowulf and the Fight at Finnsburg* (Boston, 1922; London, 1923; 3rd ed. with supplement, 1941), p. 453.

27. C. L. Wrenn, "Recent Work on *Beowulf*," p. 508.

28. Felix Liebermann, "Ort und Zeit der Beowulfdichtung," in *Nachrichten von der königl. Gesellschaft der Wissenschaften zu Göttingen*, phil-hist. Klasse (1920), pp. 253-76; A. S. Cook, "The Possible Begetter of the Old English *Beowulf* and *Widsith*," *Transactions of the Connecticut Academy of Arts and Sciences* 25 (1922): 281-346; and William W. Lawrence, *Beowulf and Epic Tradition* (Cambridge, Mass., 1930), pp. 244-91.

29. Girvan, *Beowulf and the Seventh Century*.

30. Elizabeth Martin-Clarke, *Culture in Early Anglo-Saxon England* (Baltimore, Md., 1947), p. 56.

31. Bruce-Mitford, *The Sutton Hoo Ship-Burial: A Provisional Guide*, p. 39.

32. Lindqvist, "Sutton Hoo and *Beowulf*," p. 131.

33. John R. Clark Hall, trans., *Beowulf and the Finnesburg Fragment*, rev. ed. with notes and intro. by C. L. Wrenn (London, 1950); Charles L. Wrenn, ed., *Beowulf with the Finnesburg Fragment* (London, 1953), pp. 32-37.

34. Dorothy Whitelock, *The Audience of Beowulf* (Oxford, 1951), p. 25.

35. Wrenn, "Sutton Hoo and *Beowulf*," in *An Anthology of Beowulf Criticism*, comp. Nicholson, p. 328.

36. Wrenn, "Sutton Hoo and *Beowulf*," in Chambers, *Beowulf*, p. 523.

37. See Colin Chase, "Opinions on the Date of *Beowulf*, 1815-1980," in *The Dating of Beowulf*, ed. Chase, pp. 5-7, and articles in that volume by Kiernan, Goffart, Murray, Page, Frank, and Stanley.

38. Hilda Ellis Davidson, "Archaeology and *Beowulf*," in *Beowulf and Its Analogues*, ed. G. Norman Garmonsway and Jacqueline Simpson (London, 1968), p. 359.

39. Eric John, "*Beowulf* and the Margins of Literacy," *Bulletin of the John Rylands University Library of Manchester* 56 (1973-74): 392.

40. Patrick Wormald, "Bede, *Beowulf*, and the Conversion of the Anglo-Saxon Aristocracy," in *Bede and Anglo-Saxon England: Papers in Honour of the 1300th Anniversary of the Birth of Bede . . .* , ed. Robert T. Farrell, British Archaeological Reports 46 (Oxford, 1978), p. 94.

41. John Hines, *The Scandinavian Character of Anglian England in the Pre-Viking Period*, British Archaeological Reports, British Series 124 (Oxford, 1984), pp. 296-97.

42. Rosemary Cramp, "*Beowulf* and Archaeology," *Medieval Archaeology* 1 (1957), reprinted in *The Beowulf Poet: A Collection of Critical Essays*, ed. Donald K. Fry (Englewood Cliffs, N.J., 1968), p. 117.

43. Ellis Davidson, "Archaeology and *Beowulf*," p. 353.

44. See Finnur Jónsson, *Lexicon poeticum antiquae linguae septentrionalis . . . af Sveinbjörn Egilsson*, 2nd ed. (Copenhagen, 1931; repr. 1966), s.v. *hringofinn, hringkofl, hringserkr, jarnserkr, hringskyrta*, etc.

45. See J. B. Bessinger, "*Beowulf* and the Harp at Sutton Hoo," *University of Toronto Quarterly* 27 (1957): 148-68. The current reconstruction of the *hearpe* is explained in Rupert and Myrtle Bruce-Mitford, "The Sutton Hoo Lyre, *Beowulf*, and the Origins of the Frame Harp," *Antiquity* 44 (1970): 7-13, reprinted in R. L. S. Bruce-Mitford, *Aspects of Anglo-Saxon Archaeology* (London, 1974), pp. 188-97.

46. *Hearpe,* "Lyre," quickly found its way into textbook glossaries; it appeared the very next year, e.g., in *Bright's Old English Grammar and Reader,* ed. Frederic G. Cassidy and Richard N. Ringler (New York, 1971), p. 434.

47. See s.v. *wal, wala,* and *walu,* respectively, in Joseph Bosworth and T. Northcote Toller, *An Anglo-Saxon Dictionary . . .* (1882-98; repr. Oxford, 1983); Christian W. M. Grein, *Sprachschatz der angelsächsischen Dichter* (Cassel, 1861-64; rev. ed. by J. Köhler, with the help of F. Holthausen, Heidelberg, 1912-14); and John R. Clark Hall, *A Concise Anglo-Saxon Dictionary for the Use of Students* (London, 1894; 3rd ed., rev. and enlarged, 1931).

48. See note 21 in Bruce-Mitford's appendix on "The Sutton Hoo Ship-Burial," in *A History of the Anglo-Saxons,* Robert H. Hodgkin, 2 vols. (Oxford, 1935; 3rd ed., 1952), 2:752-54, reprinted as chapter 9, "A Note on the Word *Wala* in *Beowulf,"* in Bruce-Mitford, *Aspects of Anglo-Saxon Archaeology,* pp. 210-13. Also Knut Stjerna, *Essays on Questions Connected with the Old English Poem of "Beowulf",* trans. and ed. by John R. Clark Hall (Coventry, 1912), p. 14; and Martin-Clarke, *Culture in Early Anglo-Saxon England,* pp. 63 and 76.

49. Bruce-Mitford, "The Sutton Hoo Helmet," *British Museum Quarterly* 36 (Autumn 1972), reprinted in Bruce-Mitford, *Aspects of Anglo-Saxon Archaeology,* p. 204.

50. Herbert D. Meritt, supplement to *A Concise Anglo-Saxon Dictionary,* John R. Clark Hall, 4th ed. (Cambridge, 1960), s.v. *walu;* and Alistair Campbell, *Enlarged Addenda and Corrigenda to the Supplement by T. Northcote Toller to an Anglo-Saxon Dictionary Based on the Manuscript Collections of Joseph Bosworth* (Oxford, 1972), s.v. *wala.*

51. See examples and discussion in Herbert Meritt, "Three Studies in Old English," *American Journal of Philology* 62 (1941): 334-38. Outside of *Beowulf, wala* occurs in verse only as the second element of a compound: *weallwalan wirum* (*Ruin,* line 20). Unless otherwise stated, editions and abbreviations used are those cited in *A Microfiche Concordance to Old English: The Lists of Texts and Index of Editions,* ed. Richard L. Venezky and Antonette diPaolo Healey, Publications of the *Dictionary of Old English* 1 (Toronto, 1980).

52. See *Fascicle C* of *The Dictionary of Old English,* ed. Ashley C. Amos and Antonette diPaolo Healey et al. (Toronto, 1988), s.v. *camb* 2b.

53. In lines 1030-34, e.g., the poet has the *wala,* said to provide *heafodbeorg* (head-protection) around the helmet's *hrof* (roof), deflecting swords described as *scurheard* (shower-hard); cf. *scurbeorg* (roof), *Ruin,* line 5.

54. Howell D. Chickering, *Beowulf: A Dual Language Edition* (New York, 1977).

55. See Edward James, *The Franks* (Oxford, 1988), p. 204, following Birgit Arrhenius, *Merovingian Garnet Jewellery: Emergence and Social Implications* (Stockholm, 1985).

56. A. Hugh Smith, "The Photography of Manuscripts," *London Mediaeval Studies* 1 (1938): 179-207. Smith gives *lide* (visual) but *hoe* (photograph). The upper part of what looks like *d* in the manuscript disappears under ultraviolet light. The photographs read *hleo* before *on hoe,* but both John C. Pope (*The Rhythm of Beowulf,* [New Haven, 1942], pp. 232-34) and Norman Davis (in *Beowulf,* ed. Julius Zupitza, 2nd ed., Early English Text Society 245 [London, 1959], p. xi) reject *hleo* in favor of the "almost inevitable" *hlæw.*

57. Klaeber, *Beowulf and the Fight at Finnsburg,* p. 459.

58. Ferdinand Holthausen, *Beowulf nebst dem Finnsburg-Bruchstück,* 2 vols. (Heidelberg, 1905-6; 8th ed. 1948), p. 126.

59. Wrenn, "Sutton Hoo and *Beowulf"* in Chambers, *Beowulf,* p. 514. The first editor to accept *hoe* as the MS reading is Else von Schaubert, 15th rev. ed. (Paderborn, 1940) of *Beowulf. Mit ausführlichem Glossar,* ed. Moritz Heyne (Paderborn, 1863).

60. The earliest *hoe* spelling in the Toronto *Microfiche Concordance* is the place-name *on Wirtroneshoe* in a Somerset charter from 973 (Sawyer 791 [Birch 1294], 8); the spelling (*fram micle*) *hohe* occurs two years earlier, in a 971 charter from County Lincoln (Sawyer 782 [Birch 1270], 5). Under the year 654, *Chronicle A* (tenth century) spells the East Anglian place-name *æt Icanho; Chronicle E* (twelfth century), under the year 653, has *æt Icanhoe.* Of the 54 OE spellings ending in *-oe,* only one, *Noe* (Noah), a foreign proper name, occurs in

verse. I am indebted to the late Ashley Crandell Amos, coeditor of the *Dictionary of Old English*, for a list of these spellings.

61. J. M. Wallace-Hadrill, "The Grave of Kings," *Studi Medievali*, 3rd ser., 1, i (1960): 177-94, reprinted with additions in J. M. Wallace-Hadrill, *Early Medieval History* (Oxford, 1975), p. 41.

62. Lindqvist, "Sutton Hoo and *Beowulf*," p. 140. In the same volume of *Fornvännen*, Birger Nerman, "Sutton Hoo: en svensk kunga-eller hövdinggrav," pp. 65-93, argued that the man commemorated was a Swede. Two years earlier, Herbert Maryon, "The Sutton Hoo Shield," *Antiquity* 20 (1946): 21-30, suggested that all the treasures, jewelry included, were Swedish imports. The question posed by N. E. Lee's title, "The Sutton Hoo Ship Built in Sweden?" (*Antiquity* 31 [1957]: 40-41), was answered in the affirmative. Norah K. Chadwick, "The Monsters and *Beowulf*," in *The Anglo-Saxons: Studies in Some Aspects of Their History and Culture Presented to Bruce Dickens*, ed. Peter Clemoes (London, 1959), p. 202, observed, tentatively, that just as *Wehha* was a possible diminutive for *Weohstan*, "*Wuffa* is a possible Anglo-Saxon diminutive for *Beo-wulf*." Cf. R. L. S. Bruce-Mitford, *The Sutton Hoo Ship-Burial: A Handbook* (British Museum, 1968), p. 70: "The most likely explanation [for the Swedish pieces at Sutton Hoo] seems to be that the dynasty of the Wulfingas was Swedish in its origin, and that probably Wehha, said to be the first of the family to rule over the Angles in Britain, was a Swede." J. L. N. O'Loughlin, "Sutton Hoo — the Evidence of the Documents," *Medieval Archaeology* 8 (1964): 1-19, held that the Wuffings/Wylfings were Geats, who had won in battle against the Swedes the heirlooms buried at Sutton Hoo. See Farrell, "*Beowulf*, Swedes, and Geats," p. 273, on the weaknesses of both these opposed solutions.

63. See, e.g., J. M. Wallace-Hadrill, *Bede's "Ecclesiastical History of the English People": A Historical Commentary* (Oxford, 1988), p. 190 (lines 13-19; II, 15): "Wuffing connections with their homeland, Sweden, seem to have been less active than those they enjoyed with Francia." James Campbell in *The Anglo-Saxons*, ed. James Campbell (Oxford, 1982), p. 67, is more tentative: "Wuffa, perhaps the Swedish founder of the line. . . . " Henry Mayr-Harting, *The Coming of Christianity to Anglo-Saxon England* (London, 1972), p. 17, follows O'Loughlin rather than Lindqvist: his Wuffings are Geats.

64. Rupert Bruce-Mitford, "The Sutton Hoo Ship Burial: Recent Theories and Comments on General Interpretation," *Proceedings of the Suffolk Institute of Archaeology and Natural History* 25 (1949): 1-78, reprinted in *Aspects of Anglo-Saxon Archaeology*, p. 52. On the Swedish question, see esp. pp. 43-72.

65. R. L. S. Bruce-Mitford, "Sutton Hoo and the Background to the Poem," added chapter in Girvan, *Beowulf and the Seventh Century* (1971), pp. 85-98, reprinted as "Sutton Hoo and the Background to *Beowulf*," in Bruce-Mitford, *Aspects of Anglo-Saxon Archaeology*, p. 259. Bruce-Mitford still regards the Swedish connection as dominant: see "The Sutton Hoo Ship-Burial: Some Foreign Connections," in *Settimane di studio del Centro italiano sull'alto medioevo 32: Angli e Sassoni al di qua e al di là del mare 1* (Spoleto, 1986): 195-207.

66. Bruce-Mitford, *The Sutton Hoo Ship-Burial* 2:91-99 and 205-25; and Joachim Werner, "Ein langobardischer Schild von Ischl an der Alz," *Bayerische Vorgeschichtsblätter* 18 (1952): 45-58. Doubts concerning the overriding influence of eastern Sweden are expressed by Werner, "Das Schiffsgrab von Sutton Hoo: Forschungsgeschichte und Informationsstand zwischen 1939 und 1980," *Germania* 60 (1982): 193-228; and by David M. Wilson, "Sweden — England," in *Vendel Period Studies*, ed. J. P. Lamm and H.-A. Nordström (Stockholm, 1983), pp. 163-66.

67. Martin Carver, "Sutton Hoo in Context," in *Angli e Sassoni*, pp. 106-7.

68. On the gold buckle as reliquary, see Werner, "Das Schiffsgrab von Sutton Hoo," pp. 198-201; contra Bruce-Mitford, "The Sutton Hoo Ship-Burial: Some Foreign Connections," pp. 80-87. On the combs, see Bruce-Mitford, *The Sutton Hoo Ship-Burial* 3:827-30. I am much indebted to Ian Wood for a preview of his article concerning the Merovingian presence in Mound 1; see "The Franks and Sutton Hoo," in *People and Places in Northern Eu-*

rope, 500-1600: Essays in Honour of Peter Hayes Sawyer, ed. Ian Wood and Niels Lund (Woodbridge, 1991), pp. 1-14.

69. H. M. Chadwick, "The Sutton Hoo Ship Burial," *Antiquity* 14 (1940): 77.

70. Michael Wood, *In Search of the Dark Ages* (London, 1981), p. 69. Also William A. Chaney, *The Cult of Kingship in Anglo-Saxon England: The Transition from Paganism to Christianity* (Berkeley, 1970), p. 132.

71. Wrenn, "Sutton Hoo and *Beowulf,*" in *An Anthology of Beowulf Criticism,* comp. Nicholson, pp. 316-17.

72. Bruce-Mitford, "Sutton Hoo and the Background to the Poem," in Girvan, *Beowulf and the Seventh Century* (1971), p. 93, reprinted in Bruce-Mitford *Aspects of Anglo-Saxon Archaeology,* p. 257.

73. See Björn Ambrosiani, "Background to the Boat-Graves of the Mälaren Valley," in *Vendel Period Studies,* ed. Lamm and Nordström, pp. 17-18.

74. This point was made in 1960 by Wallace-Hadrill, "The Graves of Kings," esp. pp. 41-47.

75. Chaney, *The Cult of Kingship,* p. 98.

76. Philip Grierson, "The Purpose of the Sutton Hoo Coins," *Antiquity* 44 (1970): 17, cited in E. G. Stanley, "Some Doubts and No Conclusions," in *The Dating of Beowulf,* ed. Chase, p. 204.

77. Chaney, *The Cult of Kingship,* p. 144.

78. C. L. Wrenn, *A Study of Old English Literature* (London, 1967), p. 140.

79. Wrenn, "Sutton Hoo and Beowulf," in *An Anthology of Beowulf Criticism,* comp. Nicholson, p. 318; in his chapter of the same name in Chambers, *Beowulf,* p. 520, Wrenn assigns the standard "in all probability" an early sixth-century date.

80. Ellis Davidson, "Archaeology and *Beowulf,*" p. 352.

81. Kenneth Rexroth, "Classics Revisited—IV: *Beowulf,*" *Saturday Review* 10 April 1965, p. 27, reprinted in *The Beowulf Poet: A Collection of Critical Essays,* ed. Fry, p. 169.

✛

CHAPTER 5

Sutton Hoo and the Recording of *Beowulf*

Robert Payson Creed

I n this chapter I suggest and offer some support for a new approach to prehistoric Germanic oral traditions. The approach is through *Beowulf*, considered not as the work of a writer, but as the work, composed in performance, of a continuator of traditions many generations old. The approach depends upon a reading of the strata preserved in the performance: the uppermost stratum is that of the particular performance; the next lower stratum is that of the formulas and other traditional compositional devices. The second stratum has been explored by many scholars for forty years, beginning with Albert B. Lord's doctoral dissertation at Harvard in 1949, "The Singer of Tales." My work on the prosody of *Beowulf* has taken me to a stratum below the formula, to what I call the "Ideal Structures" that form the core of the many verse lines of the poem.[1] These structures consist of pairs (or sets of interlocking pairs) of words containing sound-linked stems of words that encapsulate the ideas and ideals of prehistoric speakers of Germanic. This stratum puts us in touch with prehistoric Germanic "Memorable Speech."[2]

The analysis of the text of *Beowulf* into three strata has implications for the relationship between archaeology and recorded early oral traditions. I sketch some of these relationships in this chapter, which is structured around my 1977-78 recording of *Beowulf* accompanied by the reconstructed Sutton Hoo lyre.[3]

The Recording

Sutton Hoo played a role in one recording of *Beowulf*. This recording was made in 1977-78 in New York City, not in seventh-century East Anglia. A reconstruction of the Sutton Hoo musical instrument accompanied my performance of parts of *Beowulf* for a pair of radio broadcasts. Although the twentieth-century recording was designed for contemporary audiences, it was also intended to be as authentic as possible. So the producer, Charles Potter; the technical director, David Rapkin; and I were delighted when Rupert Bruce-Mitford, then Keeper of Medieval and Later Antiquities in the British Museum, lent us a working copy of the second reconstruction of the Sutton Hoo instrument. Mary Remnant, a musician-musicologist who teaches at the Royal College of Music in London, accompanied me with several simple pentatonic melodies that give some indication of what the range of the original instrument might have been.

At the time of the recording it seemed reasonable to have an early Anglo-Saxon instrument accompany a performance of *Beowulf*. The date most scholars accepted for the composition of *Beowulf* lay within a century and a half of the deposition at Sutton Hoo, even assuming that date to be in the 620s. The justification for performing with an instrumental accompaniment came both from the poem and from the work of certain modern prosodists, in particular, John C. Pope of Yale University and myself. In the poem, the *Beowulf* poet has both a *scop* and a king sing tales to the accompaniment of a musical instrument. Pope and I had argued for a rhythm in which rests in certain measures of the verse suggest the need for accompaniment. Pope's analysis of the normal verses of the poem into isochronous measures appeared in 1942.[4] My comparison of measures and an attempt to reduce them to basic types appeared in 1966.[5] By 1977 I had been performing *Beowulf* and other Old English poems to audiences at colleges and meetings of learned societies for more than twenty years and had even made a recording for Folkways Records.[6] During this time I had also acquired some acting experience. So it seemed that archaeological reconstruction of the instrument and work on the prosody and the performance of the poem might join with Remnant's musicological reconstruction to produce a recording with some claim to authenticity.

Dating *Beowulf*

In the years that have passed since that recording there have been several developments that affect the question of its authenticity. First, some scholars now argue for a date that would place the composition of *Beowulf* not only much later than Sutton Hoo but into the time when a different kind of instrument had made its appearance in Anglo-Saxon England. Second, my work on Beowulfian prosody has gone significantly beyond not only Pope's 1942 analysis but also my own modifications of that analysis in 1966. Yet I argue that the recording can still claim a degree of authenticity.

The date of *Beowulf* is still in doubt. We have little evidence about the time, the place, and the circumstances of the composition. A symposium at the University of Toronto in 1980 failed to produce a consensus on the date of the poem.[7] Some scholars at the symposium argued for a very late date, as late as the generally accepted date of the making of the single surviving manuscript of the poem, that is, between 975 and 1025. Such a date would effectively sever any relationship between Sutton Hoo and *Beowulf*. By that time there is evidence for the existence in England of the true harp, possibly in addition to, possibly replacing, the round lyre that the Sutton Hoo instrument seems to have been.

The true harp is characterized by its triangular shape, a design that accommodates strings of different lengths. The round lyre, referred to in some medieval documents as *cythara teutonica*, seems to have been a flat, bilaterally symmetrical instrument with strings of roughly the same length, though probably not of the same thickness. The strings run across a resonance chamber formed by the hollowing out of the thin lower part of the instrument and, in the case of the Sutton Hoo instrument, most of the arms that support the yoke. This instrument is represented in several early Anglo-Saxon paintings. Representations of triangular harps appear toward the end of the Anglo-Saxon period. It has been conjectured that the word *harp* (Old English *hearpe*) was transferred to the triangular instrument after referring to the symmetrical instrument.

It is not my purpose to deal here with all the arguments about the dating of *Beowulf*. The late-daters — and others — have their say in the volume that came out of the Toronto symposium. I do not agree with the late-daters. My reasons for disagreeing will become apparent in the course of this chapter.

When we made the recording in 1977 I believed that my work on Beowulfian prosody would soon be concluded. I was wrong. It took another nine years to complete and several more to find a publisher. This work suggests an early date for the composition and thus, I think, for the recording of *Beowulf*. My study of the prosody thus suggests that *Beowulf* belongs, after all, to the same world as Sutton Hoo.

Beowulf and Archaeology

I do not think, however, that *Beowulf* and Sutton Hoo are related in the rather simple way that some archaeologists suggest. It is true that the description of certain weapons and armor in *Beowulf* may fit some of the artifacts unearthed at Sutton Hoo. It is true that the description of Heorot in *Beowulf* may fit some early Anglo-Saxon buildings for which evidence still survives elsewhere in England. But what is important is what the poet says happened in Heorot and in the Geatland of the poem. I do not mean the attacks by the Grendel-kind and the dragon, but rather the behavior of the men and women dealing with each other, the land, and the sea. If *Beowulf* is what I take it to be, it preserves — albeit somewhat cryptically — a record of behaviors acted out and memorialized in speech and in artifacts before the deposition at Sutton Hoo and even before the migration from the Continent to Britannia.

Beowulfian Prosody

I have come to this rather startling conclusion largely on the basis of my recent work on the prosody of *Beowulf*. A full account of this work is to be found in my *Reconstructing the Rhythm of Beowulf*. Here I can do little more than sketch the process that led to this conclusion. Very simply, every verse line of *Beowulf* consists of two kinds of syllable, sound-linked syllables and syllables that are not sound-linked. Sound-linked syllables that are the stems of content words form the core of the verse line. I give some examples.

In verse lines 861, 1209, and 1298 the sound-linked stem syllables at the core are *ric-*, from *rice*, meaning "authority, area in which authority is exercised, kingdom" or, as an adjective, "powerful," and *rond* (or *rand*), meaning "edge," but standing for "shield." Here are the lines as they occur in the MS:[8]

*rond*hæbbendra	*rice*s wyrðra	861
shield-bearers	of authority WORTHIER	
rice þeoden	he under *rande* gecranc	1209
powerful prince	HE UNDER shield fell	
*rice rand*wiga	þone ðe heo on ræste abreat	1298
powerful shield warrior	whom she ON REST killed	

A closer look at verse line 1209, for example, shows that the poet built that line around *rice* and *rand-*. We know this because the modern prosodist can only extract the verse line from the space-saving, prose-seeming lines of the manuscript by *listening* to the sound-linkage on *R* carried only by these two syllables. The prosodist divides the verse line into two halflines by working back from the last sound-linked syllable, *rand-*, and then adding to it the words *he under* to indicate a measure that begins with a rest. The poet, on the other hand, always worked forward. He thought of *rond* and *rice* together because in that way he could compose his poem rapidly and without writing.[9]

There can be no doubt that both words existed before the poet used them in these lines. I suggest that the poet and his audience heard them as a pair and heard meaning in the pair apart from the meaning they help to create in these lines. That meaning is the association of authority (*rice*) with a shield (*rond*)—a kingdom with defense.

The word *rice* did not necessarily call to mind *rond*. In fact, it sometimes evoked *ræd*, a word meaning "counsel, (good) advice." I list here the three verse lines that contain *rice* and *ræd*:

rice to rune	*ræd* eahtedon	172
powerful one TO council;	counsel they-considered	
*rice*s hyrde	and þæt *ræd* talað	2027
kingdom's HERDsman	AND THAT counsel considered	
*rice*s hyrde	*ræd* ænigne	3080
kingdom's HERDsman	counsel ANY	

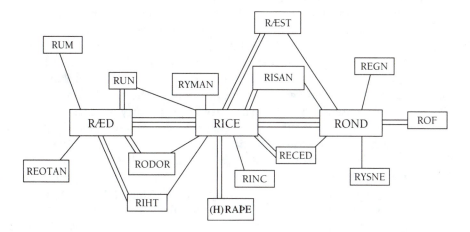

Figure 5.1. Word pairings in *Beowulf*. An example of verse-line-determining word pairings in *Beowulf*. Each line represents one use of the two linked words in the same verse line. Each such pair determines the sound-patterning (alliteration) of that verse line.

These lines neatly indicate a stratum between the sound-linked pair and the verse line. It is a stratum in which *rice* calls up a formula, *rices hyrde*, before continuing on to complete this sound-linked pair – and the verse line – with *ræd*.

Each word, *rond* or *rand* and *ræd*, occurs with *rice* three times in *Beowulf*, more often than either occurs with any other word, as Figure 5.1 shows. The two words *ræd* and *rond* do not occur in the same verse line; they are linked only by *rice*. For its part, *rice* occurs somewhat more frequently with *rond* and with *ræd* than with other words sound-linked on R with which it builds verse lines. The diagram displays all of the words with which *ræd*, *rice*, and *rond* build verse lines. The higher frequency of occurrence of *rice/ræd* and *rice/rond* suggests a degree of stability. I have already suggested the meaning of the pair *rice/rond*. The meaning of *rice/ ræd* associates power with good advice or counsel. The chiefs and the folk reminded themselves that kingly power – *rice* – should not only be a shield but should also seek good counsel – not a bad ideal for government at any period.

Ideal Structures of Memorable Speech

I call pairs like *rice/rond* and *rice/ræd* Ideal Structures because they build information into mnemonically constructed capsules that seem to convey the ideas and ideals of the people who constructed them and handed them on. These pairs form a stratum in *Beowulf* that seems to be even older than the formulas. I can give here only a few examples of Ideal Structures (ISs) in *Beowulf*, but my ongoing work indicates that at least every fifth verse line of *Beowulf* is built around an IS that occurs at least three times in the poem. In *"Beowulf on the Brink"* (see note 1) I deal more fully with the IS *dom/deaþ* "DOOM/DEATH," which suggests that one should act to achieve the good judgment (*dom*) of the folk before DEATH. An even more frequent IS in *Beowulf* survives into early Modern English as "SOOTH/SAY" (*soþ/secgan*) and is the subject of study by Cynthia Balcom.[10] Many ISs in *Beowulf* do not survive, or survive only in part, in Modern English. The first element of the IS *guþ/god*, "battle/GOOD, brave" has been completely lost, while the meaning "brave" for GOOD survives only in certain locutions (see the *OED*, s.v. "good" A.2). The *Beowulf* poet builds nine verse lines around the IS *guþ/god*. Both members of all three of these ISs have their roots in Indo-European times. There appear to be vestiges of ISs in the Homeric poems (cf. *epos/ergon*, "utterance/action," with OE *word/weorc* "WORD/WORK" — although only the second members are cognates) and in the Vedic Hymns (cf. *mad/madhu*, "rejoice/mead" — honey-sweet juice, soma, cognate with OE *meodo*). But these traditions, as they have come down to us, only occasionally build verse lines or significant parts of them around ISs, whereas the *Beowulf* poet regularly does so. Much work remains to be done on this stratum of the language of *Beowulf* and its relation to the thinking of earlier speakers of Indo-European.

The occurrence of a number of Ideal Structures in a poem that claims to be about the events that took place on the Continent before the migration to Britannia provides circumstantial evidence for an early date for the composition of *Beowulf*. I would date the poem to a time when a great traditional singer had been recently converted and had found a way to combine the best of the old ways with the new religion.[11] That, of course, might have been any time up to the end of the eighth century.

But perhaps it was not so late as the end of the eighth century. The *Beowulf* poet was not only a great composer of tales, he also knew and loved the old ways of the folk. For that reason I would place him closer to the times he sang about, the period when the folk still lived in Scandinavia. He was, of course, an Anglo-Saxon. But his poem suggests that he may not have been separated by many generations from the time of migration.

These are speculations. They are intended to suggest that what is needed is a new way of thinking about *Beowulf* by placing the poem in a wider historical and archaeological context. We can do that, I think, by attempting to formulate and test a hypothesis that takes into account the new knowledge of the strata of the poem. A colleague, Wade Tarzia, and I have formulated such a hypothesis.

Beowulf: A Hypothesis

Beowulf is what it proclaims itself to be: an example of a traditional Germanic "chiefdom tale" told by a Christian who was nevertheless heir to and continuator of an oral tradition developed by generations of speakers of early Germanic "Memorable Speech."

Tarzia and I have already begun to try to "read" *Beowulf* by the light of artifacts and concepts produced by the prehistoric archaeology of Scandinavia and northern Germany.[12] These readings are partly based on the Ideal Structures that seem to form an early stratum of the poem.

If we study *Beowulf* in this way we will find that it tells us what mattered most to those who fashioned the Germanic tradition. It does so by telling us something about the behaviors that were felt to be worthy of remembrance in those societies either because of their good effects or their bad. This view of *Beowulf* links Sutton Hoo and the poem in a new way. The old way saw a link between archaeological artifact and poetic description. The new way treats *Beowulf* and Sutton Hoo as joint heirs of prehistoric Germanic oral and technological traditions.

An Anglo-Saxon Recording Studio?

If, as I believe, the surviving text of *Beowulf* is a copy of a recording made early in the historical Anglo-Saxon period, one must ask when and how that recording could have been made. In *The Singer of Tales*, Albert Lord claims that "there is very little chance, if any, . . . that our written texts at any time were taken down during performance."[13] He suggests instead that "the singer was asked to dictate his song without singing, pausing after each verse to give the scribe time to write." A little earlier Lord writes of the possibility that a scribe might have used shorthand. He also speaks of the possibility of "a battery of two or more scribes taking down alternate lines or every third line, depending on the number of scribes employed." But he continues, "There is no evidence to my knowledge that this means has been used at any time in the past."[14]

Lord, who has spent many seasons collecting by various means from traditional singers in the field, is the foremost authority on these questions. It may have been, as he suggests, that the *Beowulf* poet slowly dictated the poem to a scribe, pausing after each line to allow the scribe time to write. Indeed, the excellence of *Beowulf* may partly be the result of the slowing down of the process of composition, since, Lord notes, "dictation . . . may be instrumental in producing the finest and longest of songs."[15]

Yet I cannot help pointing out that a painting made in Canterbury between 730 and 740, a painting that was useful to the Bruce-Mitfords in reconstructing the round lyre from the Sutton Hoo fragments, shows a battery – a pair – of scribes flanking the biblical King David as he com-

Figure 5.2. The "David page" of the Canterbury Psalter, British Library Cotton Vespasianus A. 1, folio 30 verso. (By permission of the British Library.)

poses the Psalms.[16] (See Figure 5.2.) The interpretation of the scene as depicting the act of composition is not only mine but also Carl Nordenfalk's.[17]

If the scene depicts an Anglo-Saxon recording studio, that "studio" would have been a difficult place for scribes to work in. Two dancers clap their hands as they step out. Four musicians blow as many horns. No wonder that the scribe to David's left looks rather desperate. Since he is wielding a stylus on a wax tablet, it seems to be up to him to get down David's words as fast as the king speaks. By contrast, the scribe writing on the scroll seems very calm.

But this is probably too realistic an interpretation of this early medieval painting. The painting is more likely to be somewhat allegorical: the dancers are there to show both the joy of the occasion and—perhaps—the rhythm of David's composition. I am not sure what the horn blowers represent, but clearly four horns would drown out the round lyre David seems to be playing. The two scribes are, to me, the most interesting figures in the painting.

The scribes suggest to me the following. First, on some occasion in Anglo-Saxon England around or before 730 a battery of scribes *was* employed to take down a performance in writing. That is the reason the painting shows more than one scribe. Second, both—or all—of the scribes used what the right-hand scribe uses in the painting, wax tablets, and styli. Third, the scribes later transferred to parchment what they had taken down on wax, as the left-hand scribe shows.

A number of paintings of King David survive from this period and before. At least one other I know of contains a scribe, but only one. The painter of the Canterbury Vespasian Psalter David is unusual if not unique in depicting a pair of scribes. The existence of a pair of scribes suggests to me that the painter knew of a remarkable occasion when a singer not of psalms but of tales had come to the attention of some wealthy patron who supplied scribes and materials to take down one of his performances.

Who was this wealthy patron? The fact that this painting was made in Canterbury suggests that it was someone associated with that episcopal city. The fact that a traditional performance of some sort was translated into writing suggests that it was someone who heard the traditional singing of Anglo-Saxons with the ears of a foreigner. Lord offers sound arguments to suggest that the traditional singer and his group "would not have had any reason . . . for wanting these . . . songs . . . written down."[18] We may never know who the sponsor of this—supposed—recording studio was, but it is unlikely that he was an Anglo-Saxon.

If the painting does indeed represent some local knowledge of the recording of traditional singing, we must ask who the singer might have been. Caedmon comes first to mind, although Bede never actually says that the miraculously inspired cowherd sang for or dictated to scribes. Besides, both Bede and Caedmon were from the North, and the painting is so close to the time of Bede's writing about Caedmon that the story might not have had the chance to travel as far south as Canterbury. The composer of the Old English Psalms in the so-called *Paris Psalter* might seem to be a good candidate. He was, after all, translating King David's poems. But his poetry seems to me so lame that it can only be the work of a writer of small or poorly remembered training in traditional verse making. And a writer would have no need of scribes.

Was it, then, the *Beowulf* poet who sat and sang to the accompaniment of the round lyre as scribes incised his words on wax tablets? I would like to think so, but we have no way of telling.

At the very least, the painting tells us that round lyres existed or at least were known in southeastern England in the first half of the eighth century and that they were used — or thought to be used — to accompany psalm singing. The two scribes in the painting *may* suggest the idea and even the existence of an Anglo-Saxon recording studio. But again, we cannot be sure.

Conclusion

We cannot be sure of any direct connection between *Beowulf* and Sutton Hoo. In fact, we can be sure of very little about *Beowulf*. But I think the circumstantial evidence suggests an early rather than a late date for the composition of the poem. A date toward the end of the Anglo-Saxon period might mean that a more authentic accompaniment would require a harp rather than a lyre. But we cannot be sure that the lyre disappeared simply because the harp had appeared. Beowulfian prosody, as I sketch it here on the basis of many years of study, indicates that certain verse lines of *Beowulf* consist of at least three strata, the deepest of which may be many generations older than the deposition at Sutton Hoo. So Sutton Hoo and *Beowulf* are linked indirectly: both belong to the same world of ideas and ideals memorialized in traditions and artifacts that look back to the Continental home of makers and speakers alike.

Notes

1. Robert Payson Creed, *Reconstructing the Rhythm of Beowulf* (Columbia, Mo., 1990); and idem, "*Beowulf* on the Brink: Information Theory as Key to the Origins of the Poem," in *Comparative Research on Oral Traditions: A Memorial for Milman Parry*, ed. John Miles Foley (Columbus, Ohio, 1987), pp. 139-60.

2. See Robert Payson Creed, "A Student of Oral Traditions Looks at the Origins of Language," in *Studies in Language Origins*, ed. Jan Wind et al. (Amsterdam, 1989), 1:43-52.

3. Originally produced for WNYC-FM as a two-part series (available on cassette from RadioArts, Inc., 838 West End Avenue, No. 6D, New York, NY 10025).

4. John C. Pope, *The Rhythm of Beowulf* (New Haven, Conn., 1942).

5. Robert Payson Creed, "A New Approach to the Rhythm of Beowulf," *PMLA* 81 (1966): 23-33.

6. *Lyrics from the Old English*, Robert P. Creed and Burton Raffel, Folkways FL9858 (1964).

7. Colin Chase, ed., *The Dating of Beowulf* (Toronto, 1981).

8. All quotations of the text of *Beowulf* are cited from Zupitza, supplemented by Thorkelin A. Zupitza indicates the photographs (not the transliteration) of the manuscript in *Beowulf . . . in Facsimile with a Transliteration and Notes by Julius Zupitza*, 2nd ed., containing a new reproduction of the manuscript with an introductory note by Norman

Davis, Early English Text Society 245 (London, 1959). Thorkelin A indicates the photographs on pp. 1-99 of *The Thorkelin Transcripts of Beowulf in Facsimile,* ed. Kemp Malone (Copenhagen, 1957). The text has been divided into words and compounds and then divided into verse lines and halflines on the basis of procedures discussed in Creed, *Reconstructing the Rhythm of Beowulf.* Certain manuscript characters — *yogh* (the flat-topped g), crossed thorn (= THAT), and runic *wynn* — have been replaced in these quotations by g, þæt, and w, respectively. Verse line numbers are those in modern edited texts such as that of Frederick Klaeber, *Beowulf and the Fight at Finnsburg,* 3rd ed. with first and second supplements (Lexington, Mass., 1950). Modern English reflexes of Old English words appear in capital letters in the accompanying translations.

9. I use the masculine pronoun to refer to the *Beowulf* poet for the following reasons: Two of the three performers of poetry presented *within* the poem are clearly men, and the third is probably a man; Beowulf, in his report to King Hygelac, describes King Hrothgar as a singer at lines 2105f.; the poet characterizes the singer on horseback who celebrates Beowulf's defeat of Grendel in masculine nouns and pronouns — *cyninges thegn* (line 867), *guma* (line 868), *secg* (line 871), and *he* (line 875). No pronouns reveal the sex of Hrothgar's *scop* (line 1066), who sings the so-called Finnesburg Episode (lines 1063-1160a), but this song is called a *gleomannes gyd* (line 1160), a "GLEEMAN'S lay." The only vernacular poets whose names come down to us are masculine: Caedmon and Cynewulf. While these facts do not prove that the *Beowulf* poet was a man, they accord with modern observations made in at least one recently traditional society in the rural towns and villages of Yugoslavia of the 1930s, 1940s, and 1950s. In those years in such areas men performed long ("epic") tales and women generally performed shorter verse genres such as laments, charms, and recipes. For the latter, see Joel M. Halpern, *A Serbian Village* (New York, 1967), especially chaps. 8 and 9. For the recording of "epic" genres from men during the 1930s and 1940s, see Albert B. Lord, *The Singer of Tales* (Cambridge, 1960).

10. Cynthia A. Balcom, "Ideal Structures in Hrothgar's Ræd" (Ph.D. diss., University of Massachusetts at Amherst, 1989).

11. See Robert Payson Creed, "The Remaking of *Beowulf,*" in *Oral Tradition in Literature,* ed. John Miles Foley (Columbia, Mo., 1986), pp. 136-46.

12. Wade Tarzia, "The Hoarding Ritual in Germanic Epic Tradition," *Journal of Folklore Research* 26.2 (1989): 99-121. See also R. P. Creed, "*Beowulf* and the Language of Hoarding," in *Medieval Archaeology,* Charles L. Redman, ed. (Binghamton, N.Y., 1989), pp. 155-67. (A corrected copy of the latter article is available from the author.)

13. Albert B. Lord, *The Singer of Tales* (Cambridge, Mass., 1960), p. 126.

14. Ibid., pp. 125-26.

15. Ibid., p. 128.

16. See Myrtle and Rupert Bruce-Mitford, "The Sutton Hoo Lyre, 'Beowulf' and the Origins of the Frame Harp," in *Aspects of Anglo-Saxon Archaeology: Sutton Hoo and Other Discoveries* (New York, 1974), pp. 188-97.

17. Carl Nordenfalk, *Celtic and Anglo-Saxon Painting: Book Illumination in the British Isles, 600-800* (New York, 1977). The David page is pl. 32, facing p. 95; Nordenfalk's discussion is on p. 95.

18. Lord, *Singer of Tales,* p. 156.

PART III

✣

Sutton Hoo and Anglo-Saxon History

CHAPTER 6

✣

The Impact of the Sutton Hoo Discovery on the Study of Anglo-Saxon History

James Campbell

The story of the effort to recover the reality of the early Anglo-Saxon past is in large measure one of a dialogue between archaeology and history. This dialogue got off to a good start in the work of the founder of modern Anglo-Saxon studies, John M. Kemble.[1] For example, he made key observations on the similarities between funerary pottery in Germany and in England. For many years his pioneering work seemed in vain. Thus William Stubbs in his *Constitutional History*, for some decades from the 1870s a determinative work for the study of early England, made no use of archaeology, except once, and then it was to put forward a most extraordinary, indeed indefensible, claim. He wrote of the German settlers in England, "The cattle of their native land were it would appear imported too: the store they set by their native breeds is proved by researches into the grave places of the nations."[2] A statement of Charles Oman's is representative of the attitude of the textbook writers of the late nineteenth and early twentieth centuries. "The spade, so useful in the Roman period, helps us little here."[3] John Richard Green was something of an exception. Thus in *The Making of England* (1882) he showed a realization that burial grounds may sometimes mark boundaries, though his exceedingly lively imagination could carry him miles away from fact, as when he said, "The armour of such a freeman [sc. the free warrior] has been preserved for us in the grave-mounds which are scattered over the face of England."[4]

The real impact of archaeology on the main literature begins a generation later with Hector Munro Chadwick's *Origin of the English Nation*[5] and with Edward Thurlow Leeds's first work on the archaeology of the Anglo-Saxon settlements.[6] Chadwick was truly learned. His is the first modern book that is still indispensable for the student of Sutton Hoo. It is the only book written before 1939 that could have enabled its readers to be less astonished by the discovery than they seem to have been. For example, he emphasized the wealth of parts of the German world;[7] he first drew attention to the importance of the appearance of Merovingian trientes in England and got their date about right;[8] he first emphasized the importance of the slave trade;[9] he mentioned, as few historians have done since, the possible importance of *Widsith*;[10] he discussed early Dark

Age helmets and their likely Roman origin,[11] reminded his readers that we do not know the boundaries of early East Anglia,[12] drew attention to the significance of ceremonies involving ploughs:[13] I could go on.

Leeds's first book marked a fundamental advance in the analysis of Anglo-Saxon cemeteries and the amazing quantity of artifacts that survives from them.[14] Although the tradition of study that he founded has been one of the most fruitful in English archaeology, it is in important ways no more than tangential to Sutton Hoo, because its thrust has been in large measure toward the use of typological analysis to study the history of Anglo-Saxon invasion and settlement. It was this approach that dominated the first general work on early English history into which the new archaeological learning was fully integrated: Nowell Myres's section of the first volume of the *Oxford History of England*,[15] an astonishing achievement for a man aged thirty-three; it is in some ways as gripping as a historical novel. It was essentially the Leeds/Myres approach that dominated university historians' attitudes toward Anglo-Saxon archaeology up to at least the sixties. "Can the archaeological record of the settlement of early Wessex be reconciled with that of the *Chronicle?*" is the sort of question we were set when I was an undergraduate more than thirty years ago. If we were asked a question about Sutton Hoo, it was general: "What, in your opinion, is the significance of the Sutton Hoo discovery?" or the like. Such generality was an indication that the learned world had not really got its teeth into the subject. But there was a routine of discourse on the matter. We all knew we had to comment on the interest and significance of there being no body in the grave. We all knew that the expertise of numismatists had proved nugatory Chadwick's attempt to link the burial to Rædwald, for the coins could not be earlier than circa 650.[16] Considerable ingenuity was used in reconciling this late date with the written evidence. Thus Frank M. Stenton, though plainly uneasy about a late date, suggested in a carefully imaginative manner that the Sutton Hoo burial was a memorial to Æthelhere, the king of the East Angles who perished at the battle on the Winwæd in 655.[17]

The history of the publication of the Sutton Hoo finds is a little complicated. The war, and other circumstances, delayed the beginning of the definitive publication until 1975. Notwithstanding the appearance from the 1940s of a considerable periodical literature, the ordinary reader, indeed the ordinary nonspecialist scholarly reader, who wished to know about Sutton Hoo had for some years little to turn to except the successive editions of the British Museum *Provisional Guide*, the *Handbook*, the admirable appendix that Rupert Bruce-Mitford contributed to the third edition of Robert Howard Hodgkin's *History of the Anglo-Saxons*,[18] and the catena of preliminary studies published in *Antiquity* in 1940. There was no monograph on Sutton Hoo until Charles Green's seriously useful publication in 1963.[19]

Indeed, until quite recently few monographs on Anglo-Saxon history of any kind were published. The impact of the discovery is thus largely to be traced through textbooks. Let us begin with the most influential of these, that published by Stenton in 1943. At that time he accepted an early date for the coins, the absence of a body, and a likely association with Rædwald (mentioning the Rendlesham link).[20] The discovery provides us, he says, with a new perspective. It shows that historians have "underestimated or at least understressed [Stenton was a *very* cautious man] the moveable wealth available to a great seventh-century English king." It enlarges our idea of the range of contacts available at this time and suggests "peaceful if sporadic influence between England and the eastern Mediterranean." The mail and textile fragments provide important evidence of "the development of the in-dustrial arts." One feature of Stenton's account has been repeated in that of almost every textbook since. It is essentially self-contained. Remove it from the book and there would be no visible scar. If, as Stenton says, Sutton Hoo provides a new perspective, it is not one that seems to have altered his view of any aspect of early England discussed elsewhere in his famous book. Five years later appeared George Osborne Sayles's *Medieval Foundations of England*, a most influential textbook in its day.[21] Leeds's arguments on the origins of Wessex were the aspect of archaeology that most engaged Sayles's attention. He deals with Sutton Hoo very briskly. He duly emphasizes the wealth displayed, duly says that it must lead us drastically to revise our con-ceptions, and duly fails to display any sign at all that his conceptions have been revised, except to the extent that he says they have been.[22] His account differs from that of Stenton in two regards: first, he mentions the Swedish connection; second, the Bretwaldic theory makes its first appearance in a textbook. Bede, he says, "hailed: Rædwald as 'Bretwalda.' "[23] (Bede did not, in fact, use this term; but never mind.) If the Sutton Hoo treasure was Rædwald's, then "there would seem to be every justification for such a ti-tle."[24] I like "every justification": the interest of this loose language (charac-teristic of the rhetoric that haunts Sutton Hoo studies) lies in its reliance on a strongly intuitive and unargued conviction.

The late Peter Hunter Blair's *Anglo-Saxon England* (1956)[25] marks something of a new departure. He still, of course, has the circa 650 date. He has more to say about the Swedish connection, carefully expressed in the evasive prose that has to be part of the Dark Age historian's stock-in-trade: " ... *has been claimed as* Swedish" (my italics).[26] Hunter Blair, first of the textbook writers, comments on the whetstone and the "stan-dard." In those days, of course, the stag rode the "standard" and not the whetstone. These objects, he says (again displaying a good command of Dark Age prose), "can most readily be interpreted" as "emblems of sover-eignty." He tells his readers, again first among textbook writers in this, that elsewhere in southeast England are found luxuries from, probably, Egypt: bronze vessels, cowrie shells, and amethysts.[27]

By this time the pattern of textbook descriptions of Sutton Hoo was established, to be modified chiefly by the redating of the coins in the early sixties. One or two things strike the eye in the accounts from the sixties and seventies, for example, Sir David (as he now is) Wilson's use of the imperative style in his book of 1960. Sutton Hoo "*must* be considered as a cenotaph"; the king commemorated there "*must* be seen as the peer of any Germanic or Saxon king in western Europe" (my italics).[28] It is interesting to observe points that have become commonplace about Sutton Hoo making their first appearance in print. For example, it was Dorothy Whitelock who in *The Foundations of English Society* (1952) seems first to have made (by implication) the point that one important effect of Sutton Hoo was to give much more of an air of realism to descriptions of treasures in what was believed to be early poetry[29] (a suggestion admirably developed by Rosemary Cramp).[30]

Something of a watershed in Sutton Hoo studies was marked by a firecracker article published by Christopher Hawkes in 1964.[31] He drew attention to the significance of Lafaurie's redating of seventh-century Merovingian coins, and he lamented, perhaps somewhat more in sorrow than in anger, that the finds had not as yet received more than interim publication. In 1975 his wishes were answered by the appearance of the first of the four great British Museum volumes.[32] This work has not indeed passed altogether uncriticized: disagreements with some of Bruce-Mitford's views are expressed later in this chapter. Uncertainty is inevitable in Dark Age studies, and disagreements are therefore intrinsic to them. But the magnitude of the achievement of Bruce-Mitford and his colleagues should be beyond debate. Their most learned and detailed work forms the foundation for all later studies on Sutton Hoo.

Bruce-Mitford's powerfully marshaled case on the identity of the man commemorated by Mound 1 at Sutton Hoo is as follows.[33] The burial must be that of a king. This is demonstrated not only by its outstanding wealth and magnificence, but also by the presence of objects, above all the whetstone, identifiable as "regalia." The coins prove that it must be later than circa 625; the non-Christian elements in the burial put it before circa 640. In principle there are three or four East Anglian kings who might have been buried within the period indicated. But the overwhelming likelihood is that the man concerned is Rædwald. Bruce-Mitford sometimes puts his case in a nuanced way, but he is often categorical, and very much so. Thus he states that it seems "beyond all doubt"[34] that the burial is that of a king and that a terminus ad quem of circa 640 "can be absolutely relied upon."[35] In 1986 he summed up the position as he saw it by stating that what we have in Sutton Hoo, Mound 1, "is now held for sound reasons, to be the burial of king Rædwald."[36]

Most other writers have adopted Bruce-Mitford's position, though generally with some circumspection. Thus Angela Care Evans in her excellent book published by the British Museum employs the useful expression "thought to be." "It is thought to be the grave of one of the seventh-century kings of East Anglia, perhaps Rædwald"; "the symbols of power in the Sutton Hoo ship burial are thought to be contained within two enigmatic objects. . . . " She has doubts about how precisely the term *regalia* can be used: " . . . four major works of art that can be loosely termed as regalia."[37] She is uneasy about the association with Rædwald because the estimated date of the latest coins is uncomfortably close to the date of the king's death, but all the same she accepts that the burial must be that of one of four kings of East Anglia and that of these, Rædwald is the best candidate.[38] Barbara Green writes similarly in her revision of Charles Green's book. Her tone is some-what more agnostic than that of Care Evans; for example, "If one accepts that these pieces are regalia belonging to a king. . . . " But for all her intima-tions of caution, the general impression and conclusions are essentially Bruce-Mitford's. "Many feel that Rædwald is the most likely candidate for this great burial."[39] There are exceptions to the widespread, albeit tempered, acceptance in the general literature of the "royal and Rædwald" view. Thus in his textbook Herbert Finberg was briskly agnostic; the burial was, he said, "seemingly intended as a memorial to some seventh-century king or chief-tain."[40] But in nearly all the nonspecialized literature (as of course in much that is specialized), the picture that is presented is Bruce-Mitford's, framed in greater or lesser expressions of reserve.

A second characteristic of that literature is the way in which some au-thors tend to gallop past Sutton Hoo. An extreme case is that of Peter Sawyer, in one of the best of recent textbooks. His sole reference is as fol-lows: "To the East of the Mercians lay the East Angles, who, despite the astonishing richness of the royal ship-burial, remain one of the most ob-scure of the early Anglo-Saxon kingdoms."[41] Only one scholar writing a textbook has gone beyond repeating what have become banalities about Sutton Hoo. That is Henry R. Loyn, in his interesting suggestion that aspects of Sutton Hoo exemplify ways in which the English seventh cen-tury, "in contact through Gaul with the Mediterranean, gold-loving, ca-pable of producing the luxury of Sutton Hoo," contrasted with the eighth, "whose main external efforts were directed east rather than south."[42]

The most important single contribution made by a historian to the study of Sutton Hoo was that of the late Michael Wallace-Hadrill in his article of 1960, "The Graves of Kings: An Historical Note on Some Archaeological Evidence."[43] It was consciously and provocatively icono-clastic and was directed against the emergent British Museum–led con-sensus. Wallace-Hadrill made three principal points. First, our evidence is such that anything approaching dogmatism about what may define a burial as royal is unjustifiable. Second, the evidence for the great wealth in treasures and bullion of the Merovingians might make one pause before allowing oneself to be bowled over by the magnificence of the contents of Mound 1. Third (by implication), much else may be learned about Sutton Hoo by putting it in a Merovingian context.

All three arguments hold. First, it is obvious that we do not have enough evidence to establish a full archaeological context for the study of royal graves. Bruce-Mitford's views on regalia are open to the suspicion of anachronism. There is no doubt that, in the Middle Ages, in some European kingdoms, certain objects were intrinsic to the ceremonies of power and so to power itself. The crown, orb, and scepter deployed at the last medieval coronation ceremony (1952) had a long and strange historic significance. Such objects are what we normally mean by regalia. The question is: were there objects in the seventh century that had the same quite definite and specific significance? Could there have been objects in the seventh century that corresponded to, let us say, the crown of St. Stephen, the symbols, almost the sacramental symbols, of a state or of a particular kind of power? Bruce-Mitford seems to assume that this was so. He could be right; sketchy evidence can contain many possibilities. Perhaps there were definite objects exclusively linked to a particular kind of authority. If so, it is not easy to know what they were. Bruce-Mitford's strongest case, as he puts it, is for the whetstone. What, then, do we make, for example, of the miniature whetstone found in a child's grave at Sancton?[44] We do not have to take it for granted that this infant was somehow royal and equipped with a miniature scepter. Though a whetstone may indeed have been a numinous object, that is not to say that it was specifically royal. Rather, a rich potentate might own, or be buried with, a very fine and big one just as a child from a poorer family might be buried with a less elaborate miniature one. At the very least the question "Were there regalia in the medieval sense in the seventh century?" has to be open. It follows that the presence of "regalia" cannot be used as a means of categorizing the burial in Mound 1 as "royal." A passage in Gregory of Tours may provide an insight into the relationship between kingship and treasures that is distinct from, if to an extent related to, that of "regalia." Gregory tells us that when he visited king Chilperic at Nogent, the king showed him a salver weighing fifty pounds that he had had made of gems and gold and said, "This have I had made for the glory and ennoblement of the Frankish race. And much more shall yet be done if life remain to me."[45] The suggestion is that it is not so much the specific nature of the object as its grandeur that gives it an almost national, almost ideological, weight. If the treasures of Sutton Hoo denote kingship, it may be more by their magnificence than because of their specific nature.

"If" is the most important word here. Wallace-Hadrill was right in maintaining that there is no known way in which the Sutton Hoo Mound 1 burial can be proved to be that of a king. Even if it is accepted as distinctly likely that it is in some sense royal, it does not by any means follow that it has to be that of one of the kings of the East Anglians whom Bede mentions as having reigned in the appropriate period. It could be that of any important member of the royal family. We do not know how power and wealth were divided within that family, and the "it must be one of Bede's kings" argument relies partly on the assumption that we do. We know of one king's brother in the seventh century for whom a wergeld corresponding to that of a king was paid.[46] It is a large assumption indeed that we have the means of distinguishing the grave of such a man from that of a king. Indeed our use of the very word "king" has to be moderated by a consciousness that our vocabulary and assumptions about kingliness are not those of the seventh century.

A principal argument in the "royal and Rædwald" case depends on the scale and splendor of the burial deposit. Here Wallace-Hadrill's second main point bears. He uses Continental evidence to emphasize the extent to which English scholars could have been mistakenly impressed by the very scale of the treasures of Sutton Hoo. He was, importantly, the first to draw attention in this context to the vast scale of the treasures stated to have existed in Merovingian Gaul and Visigothic Spain. He mentions, as examples, the fifty wagons of treasure that Chilperic was said to have sent off with his daughter when she went to marry in Spain, the forty thousand pounds of gold alleged as the fortune of the Ostrogothic princess Amalesuntha, the five-hundred-pound gold dish that the Visigothic king Sisenand was said to have sent to Dagobert, or the great treasures that Dagobert gave to St. Denis.[47] This argument, which could be very much expanded and fortified, Wallace-Hadrill somewhat later half withdrew, pusillanimously, so it seems to me. In a postscript to his article as re-printed in 1980 he said that he had rather overlooked the extent to which the East Anglian kingdom was what he described as a "one horse show" in which the richness of the Sutton Hoo deposit was more extraordinary than he had previously suggested.[48] This retraction is unimpressive. Our evidence for early East Anglia is extremely scanty; how other than by the vain deployment of argument, not from the silence of evidence but from its absence, are we to seek to show how many a horse show East Anglia was?

Two outstanding objections arise among those which can be raised against Wallace-Hadrill's argument that Sutton Hoo should be considered in a context of Merovingian wealth and that, as a result, we should be less sure of its "royal" status than leading authorities would have us be. First, may not the descriptions of Merovingian wealth and treasures in the written sources be hyperbolically inflated? Second, even if they are not, can we be at all sure that wealth comparable to that of the Merovingian world was to be found in contemporary England in general and in East Anglia in particular?

First, the evidence for the wealth of the Merovingians. It is of more kinds than one. Some of the descriptions of treasures are of a kind that suggests they were unlikely to have been mere rhetoric. Here may be mentioned in particular Gregory of Tours's eyewitness description of the treasures that Chilperic showed him at Nogent. They included not only the great gold and jeweled salver mentioned above, but also solidi weighing a pound each. These must have been what numismatists call medallions, giant coins, though none of those that survive weigh, I believe, as much as a pound.[49] Second, we have incontrovertible evidence of great seventh-century treasures. Particularly striking here is the battered little strip from the gold and cloisonné garnet "cross of St. Eloi," which was, until the Revolution, one of the treasures of St. Denis. It is a miserable fragment, but, thanks to the chance of the cross's appearing in a fifteenth-century picture, we know it to have been a part of an object far larger than anything else known in gold and garnet: it must have been at least three feet high.[50] Third, we have some details on the scale of the Byzantine subsidies to the Merovingians.[51] Gregory of Tours says the emperor Maurice sent Childebert fifty thousand solidi. The Byzantine chronicler Menander says that in 577 Tiberius sent thirty thousand gold pieces to Francia.[52] It is beyond doubt that in Merovingian Gaul there were abundant supplies of bullion and objects of staggering richness. Did we depend solely on the archaeological evidence we could be sadly misled, almost certainly as to the scale of the wealth, undeniably as to the nature and grandeur of many of the treasures; what survives is demonstrably by no means a fair sample, in either size or type, of what once existed. The same could be true of England.

But circumstances in Gaul are not necessarily a guide to those of England. For English treasures a good starting point is the marvelous book by Charles R. Dodwell, *Anglo-Saxon Art: A New Perspective.*[53] The novelty of his approach lies in his main evidence coming not from surviving objects, but from texts. Thus, in considering late Anglo-Saxon art, instead of stewing away on the trifles, which, manuscripts and ivories apart, are all that survive, he reminds us that we have evidence for life-size statues of saints covered in gold and silver plates, gold crosses half the height of a man, and so on.[54] What concerns us in relation to Sutton Hoo is the earlier period. Here our texts, relatively few though they are, describe many treasures. Caution is needed: for example, we may notice that a line in Alcuin's poem on *The Bishops, Saints and Kings of York* that tells us of a golden horse-bit is probably a literary reminiscence.[55] Some of the most glowing descriptions of treasures in Æthelwulf's *De Abbatibus* appear in a dream sequence.[56] All allowances made, there is still clear evidence that there were treasures in eighth-century England of kinds and on a scale that do not survive, or do not survive in England. Thus, when Alcuin tells us that Offa had an altar at York adorned with silver, gems, and gold, it is not unreasonable to suppose that the reference may be to something not unlike the famous (ninth-century) golden altar at San Ambrogio in Milan.[57] Some of the most compelling evidence comes from seventh-, eighth-, and ninth-century charters. From time to time charters specify a quid pro quo for land in terms of rich objects, not infrequently of stated weights. Here we have the descriptions that relate to a business transaction, so there can be no question in these instances of rhetorical exaggeration. Thus a charter of 823 refers to a vessel of gold and silver weighing five and a half pounds. That would have made the Tassilo chalice seem pretty small beer. References to arm-rings (*annuli*, *braciolæ*, and *armillæ*) are of special interest. We have references from eighth- and ninth-century charters to such, weighing 23, 30, 31, 75, and 100 mancuses of gold.[58] (At about four grams to the mancus the last one would have had about as much gold as the Sutton Hoo buckle.) I dwell on arm-rings in particular because our literary references suggest that they are, so to speak, a standard rich object.[59] Their absence from the archaeological record may have several explanations: the most likely is that their absence is indicative of how grossly inadequate, as a sample, our rich graves are, or, alternatively, of how far conventions about burial may limit any of our attempts to use graves as an index of the goods of the wealthy. It could be argued that the written evidence cited is too late to be demonstrably relevant to Sutton Hoo. It should, however, be noted that references to rich objects begin with our very earliest charters. Thus a Medeshamstede memorandum of the late seventh century contains a reference to what seems to be a golden brooch, such that no example survives.[60]

We have another means of seeking to put the Sutton Hoo treasure grave goods into a context of English seventh-century wealth and values: that is, by using the evidence of the early laws. I had hopes of being to an extent original in this. But on hearing the contribution of Jana Schulman and Edward Schoenfeld to the Minneapolis conference on Sutton Hoo I realized that I was bringing coals to Newcastle, for they have gone more thoroughly into the relationship between the fines and equivalences of the early laws and the contents of the Sutton Hoo burial than I have done. However, the conclusions I would draw are somewhat the opposite of theirs.

It is generally accepted that the shilling of the laws is what the Dark Age West called a solidus, that is to say a gold tremissis, or its weight in gold.[61] The figures for fines and compensations in the seventh-century laws seem high in terms of gold (or its equivalents). The lowest penalty indicated is 10 sceattas, that is to say, half a shilling, the compensation specified in the laws of Æthelberht for the nail of any toe other than the big toe.[62] The highest sum indicated is the 1,200-shilling wergeld of the nobleman.[63] Fines or compensations of 30, 60, or 120 shillings are common.[64] Quite minor offenses seem to cost a lot. Thus in Æthelberht's code the penalty for striking a man on the nose with one's fist was 3 shillings.[65] In the laws of Ine, fighting in the house of a *gebur* involved a range of payments including a payment of 6 shillings to the *gebur*.[66]

Beside the range of penalties and compensations can be set some equivalents for various items given in shillings and pence. The value of a slave is indicated as 50, 60, or 70 shillings,[67] a ewe with her lamb a shilling until a fortnight after Easter, a fleece 2 pence (that is to say half a West Saxon shilling).[68] The cost of maintaining a child for a year is put at 6 shillings or more.[69] One particular equivalent is very striking: it is stated in the laws of Ine that each 100 shillings of wergeld could include (it presumably means comprise) a slave, a coat of mail, and a sword.[70] Many problems arise in the consideration of these equivalents. It could be that they are archaic and not truly applicable to seventh-century circumstances. The absence of contemporary or near-contemporary manuscripts for the early laws can raise the opposite suspicion, that the fines and equivalents were altered later. Neither line of doubt appears to be justified. Supporting evidence comes from other texts and areas. The early eighth-century *Penitential* of Theodore says that a bishop should determine cases up to 50 solidi, but a king those involving a larger sum; it suggests that classes below the highest were involved in cases involving more than the equivalent of the contents of the Sutton Hoo purse. True, this provision might reflect non-English circumstances, but the *Penitential* in general seems to show strong awareness of contemporary English conditions. Continental laws from the sixth century onward have fines and equivalents of roughly the same orders of magnitude as those in the early English laws.[71] Near-contemporary references of a nonlegal kind convey the same impression of a relatively low value for gold. Thus in a letter of Pope Zacharias to Boniface of 751 advising him on what the appropriate rate was for *census ecclesium*, the pope says that it should be a solidus per *cassata*.[72] (Of course, the context is a German one, and it by no means follows that the idea was that an actual gold coin should be handed over.)

Let us suppose that the equivalents of the laws do really give us some insight into seventh-century values. The coins in the Sutton Hoo purse would not have sufficed to buy one slave. They would have sufficed to provide compensation for the removal of no more than eighty early seventh-century Kentish toenails from toes other than the big toe. The gold in the great brooch weighs 44.5 grams. It is therefore the equivalent of about 30 shillings as the term is used in the laws; that is, its gold would not have sufficed on the assumptions I am making to pay for more than thirty ewes, admittedly with their lambs. There was not enough gold in the Sutton Hoo burial to have paid the wergeld of one West Saxon or Kentish ceorl.

An objection that can be raised here is that even if the value of the Sutton Hoo objects was not very high in terms of sheep or the like, that is not to say that these treasures, even considered just as bullion, did not represent a considerable concentration of scarce metals. It is, of course, true that one cannot possibly use the endless mention of coin in the early laws as more than vaguely and inconclusively indicative evidence either for its abundance or for the abundance of bullion of any kind. It is clear that what was expressed in shillings or solidi could be and often doubtless was paid in goods other than bullion. Some general considerations are relevant here. First, all the gold and silver of the Romans (perhaps more than all when allowance is made for Byzantine subsidies) was probably still around in western Europe, and there is no obvious reason why the conquerors and predators of Britain should not have had their good share. Second, the relatively low values of animals and goods when expressed in terms of bullion in the laws would be more consonant with its being relatively abundant than relatively scarce.

Third, while the question of how far deduction from the statistical consideration of die-linkages can lead us to believe in seventh- and eighth-century coinages of millions of coins is controversial, there is little doubt that these coinages *could* possibly stand for tons, and maybe many tons, of silver.[73] Fourth, the finds of gold coin suggest there was a lot of it about in sixth-and seventh-century England. Stuart Rigold's list of finds is an impressive one and seems constantly added to.[74] A significant feature of his list is the extent to which unmounted gold of the period has appeared as casual finds. (It would be interesting to have a list of comparable finds of Roman gold in England.)

It may be contended that to consider such treasures as those of Sutton Hoo simply in terms of their gold content is exceedingly misleading. What about the workmanship, which must mark them out as objects of the greatest rarity and worth? The workmanship of the jewelry, above all of the gold and garnet cloisonné objects, is indeed marvelous. A question of immediate relevance here is that of how much such jewelry there was. Here the recent studies of Birgit Arrhenius, Mavis Bimson, Katherine East, N. D. Meeks, and R. Holmes are most important.[75] One of the most interesting discoveries to emerge from these is that jewelry such as that of Sutton Hoo was produced with the aid of mechanized techniques. First, Bimson has shown that in given pieces or groups of pieces of jewelry, the garnet slices had been ground to an exactly uniform thickness. The most likely way for this to have been done would have been by attaching the raw garnet slices to a surface with the aid of some temporary adhesive and then grinding them with an abrasive roller. Something like a machine would have been required. The likelihood that the garnets were often cut by a water-powered wheel has been strongly argued by Arrhenius, who maintains that much of the manufacture of garnet cloisonné jewelry was done at specialized centers, one might almost say factories, not improbably near Trier.[76] Some of the most interesting work has been on the gold foil that backs the garnet in most cloisonné jewelry. It is this foil that gives their appearance a particularly lively quality. Usually, as at Sutton Hoo, the foil has a pattern stamped on it. What is amazing is that the patterns are exceedingly regular and exceedingly small. Thus the Sutton Hoo garnets are backed by foils embossed with perfectly regular patterns of parallel lines, so close that there can be several lines to the millimeter. It seems impossible that the dies that stamped those patterns could have been cut by simple manual methods. Either some exceedingly ingenious process involving the use of textiles to make dies reproducing close-woven patterns was used (as Arrhenius suggests)[77] or (as Meeks and Holmes suggest) some machine of a jiglike kind was employed, a machine such as otherwise is not known to have existed until the seventeenth century.

The elements of mechanization and centralization in the production of the jewelry suggest that it was of a type more common than might otherwise be supposed. In saying this I do not wish to imply that the surpassingly high quality of the Sutton Hoo jewelry was common, but rather that if one asks the question "How many pieces of cloisonné gold and garnet work were there?" the best guess at an answer is one of many thousands, indeed tens of thousands, rather than hundreds.[78] With recognition of this possibility must go that of the very considerable difficulty of identifying the place, or places, of manufacture of jewelry such as that of Sutton Hoo. There is no obvious case for associating place of manufacture and place of find. One used to think of the "Sutton Hoo smith," chipping away with myopic obsession in Rendlesham or thereabouts. But there seems no necessary reason for believing the cloisonné work to have been made in East Anglia. Perhaps it was not. Perhaps it had been bought in a shop in Paris, such as Gregory of Tours mentions in an episode of circa 583. Here we meet Count Leudast (on what was to prove a very bad day for him) visiting *domus negutiantum*, examining the *species* and *ornamenta*, having the silver weighed, wondering what to buy.[79] Or perhaps the Sutton Hoo jewels were bought from a traveling salesman, such a *transmarinus negotiator*, as is mentioned in the Visigothic *Liber Iudicorum*, bringing gold, silver, garments, and *ornamenta*.[80]

There is other evidence besides that already put forward that demonstrates that a burial on such a scale would have been well within other than royal means. Bruce-Mitford refers to Chadwick's maintaining "that in the times with which we are concerned wealth was concentrated in the hands of kings."[81] Our best evidence for what a seventh-century nobleman could afford comes from Northumbria, and is to the contrary. The case is that of Benedict Biscop. As Bede describes him, what a Mæcenas was he. His twin stone monasteries, his several trips to the Mediterranean, his purchase (*pius emptor*) of abundant spiritual merchandise, the range of Bede's references that prove the scale and scope of one part of that merchandise – the manuscripts in the monastic library – all these things demonstrate very great wealth.[82] Suppose Biscop had wished to provide his father with a really lavish, old-fashioned burial. Could he have spared a ship, silver plate, fine weapons, splendid personal ornaments, an enigmatic whetstone, cauldron, and so forth? The likelihood is that they would hardly have dented his resources.

Not the least of Wallace-Hadrill's services in "The Graves of the Kings" lay in his drawing attention to the importance of Merovingian Gaul in relation to Sutton Hoo. Of course, the coins alone suffice to demonstrate that there is a Merovingian dimension to be reckoned with. But those who have considered and interpreted Sutton Hoo have tended to look east and north, rather than south and west, for their parallels and connections. There are two reasons for this, one particular, one general. First, Bruce-Mitford early recognized the great importance of the Swedish connection with Sutton Hoo. Although there has been argument about how much weight should be attached to this connection and how it should be interpreted, it is not easy to see how, one way or another, the Swedish link can be less than important.[83] Second, the tradition of Anglo-Saxon studies has been one that has looked to Germany and Scandinavia rather than to Gaul and the Mediterranean. This orientation is easily explicable: that Old English is a Germanic language must in itself be enough to wed the study of early England to that of Germany and Scandinavia. Furthermore, the nature of most of what is dug up and the history of the intellectual tradition of trying to make sense of it create a complementary bond. In the days when Sir Frank Stenton and Dorothy Whitelock were determinative influences, "Germanism" was dominant in Anglo-Saxon studies. It was above all Wallace-Hadrill who started to redress the balance.

A most important example of the relatively new recognition of the significance of Gaul, and of the Mediterranean world beyond, for the understanding of early England is the remarkable publication by Wallace-Hadrill's pupil Ian Wood, *The Merovingian North Sea*. Wood brings out some of the connections between Merovingian Gaul and Britain, including the possibility of Merovingian overlordship over parts of England.[84] He suggests that a factor in these may have been Merovingian control over the Frisian coastline for a substantial period. This could, of course, have had important significance in relation to East Anglia and raises important questions about Frankish sea power.[85] He makes characteristically interesting suggestions about the origin of the Byzantine plate at Sutton Hoo: that is to say, that it had come via Francia. The Anastasius dish would, he suggests, have been a perfect gift from Byzantium to Clovis or one of his descendants. Perhaps, he says, it was passed on to Sigberht (who Bede tells us was an exile in Gaul before he became king of the East Angles ca. 630) in the 620s or 630s when Eligius was reworking the royal plate in a new style.[86]

The particular point is, of course, highly speculative. The general one is of great importance and can be developed further. It is certain that valuable goods came from the Eastern Empire to England in the early seventh century. Among the Sutton Hoo finds, the nest of silver bowls, which appear to have been manufactured not earlier than circa 600, is demonstrably more significant in this connection than the Anastasius dish.[87] Other goods that came from the eastern Mediterranean at about the same time are "Coptic" bronze vessels, amethysts, and ivory, probably all from Egypt.[88] An intriguing discovery is the recent one of a lead seal, probably a baling seal, of a sixth-century Byzantine prefect, Phocas, found on the Thames shore at Putney.[89] A mile or so from Sutton Hoo a large Byzantine vessel has recently been found. Of copper alloy and inscribed with scenes of hunting, it bears a Greek inscription, in lettering that suggests a sixth-century date. It is one of eight examples known, probably from the same workshop, perhaps situated in Antioch. One of its siblings has been found in England, another seems to have been a gift to a church in Mesopotamia.[90] How did such objects come to England? A very safe answer would be by trade, exchange, or gift: yes indeed. We can do a little better than that insofar as we know that some rich Byzantine objects came to Gaul as diplomatic gifts or were brought back by the Frankish pretender Gundovald after his exile in Byzantium.[91] Could such gifts have come directly from an emperor to an English ruler? If Procopius was right in saying that Justinian's extravagant subsidies extended to Britain, then plate could have accompanied the solidi of which Byzantine subsidies were composed.[92] Procopius is not necessarily reliable, but it is worth noticing Rigold's observations on sixth-century gold solidi found in England: "On the evidence of the small available sample, it would appear that, in the generation or two before Saint Augustine's mission, say from ca. 530-40, . . . there was a very considerable influx of gold coin [into Kent]."[93] We can be on more certain ground in believing Procopius when he says that Angles accompanied a Frankish mission to Byzantium in circa 550.[94] In the later sixth and early seventh centuries Frankish diplomatic intercourse with Byzantium was frequent;[95] Anglo-Saxons could easily have gone with other missions than that which Procopius mentions. Sutton Hoo belongs to a world in which the Mediterranean was still largely a Christian lake. Alexandria did not fall to Islam till 641, Carthage not till 697. The papacy for long periods of the seventh century was very much a Byzantine affair. Involvement with Byzantium could bring about involvement with other parts of the Mediterranean world. Thus a Merovingian embassy could go to Byzantium via Carthage. On the one occasion when we know this route to have been taken (in 589), we learn (thanks to Gregory of Tours) of a way in which Mediterranean goods could come north, other than as diplomatic presents. Some members of the ambassadors' entourage stole a rich object (*speciem*) from a merchant. They murdered him when he protested, and this started a chain of events that caused a major diplomatic incident.[96] The ambassadorial party seems to have been a large one. It is extravagantly speculative, but not ridiculous, to point out that the man commemorated at Sutton Hoo could have been a member of it.

What is not merely speculative is the significance of the Roman, Byzantine, and Mediterranean connection that Sutton Hoo demonstrates. (By "significance" I do not, of course, mean precise significance.) Another example is this: While it has long been realized that the Sutton Hoo helmet's ancestry can be traced back to grand Sassanian military headgear imitated by the Romans from about the time of Constantine, it had not, until quite recently, been realized that the "dancing warriors" that appear on some of the decorative plates of the helmet are not, as in ignorance one might have guessed, shamans or something of the kind. Far otherwise: the kimono-like garments they are wearing are those of Sassanian warriors.[97] Bertil Almgren's reasonable guess is that such dress may have been adopted as uniform by some smart fourth-century Roman regiment. Then either the dress itself or depictions of it would have been imitated in the North. In this context it is worth bearing in mind that Sidonius's famous description of the Frank Sigismer's procession to his wedding strongly suggests that a barbarian comitatus could wear something like a uniform or livery.[98]

There are, of course, important distinctions to be drawn. Symptoms of southern or eastern influence such as those just described could derive from relationships that had nothing to do with the more immediate circumstances of the seventh century. In this they present a contrast with objects at least fairly near to the date of the burial, such as the nest of silver bowls. But they bring home to one a crucial thing about the contribution that Sutton Hoo makes to our knowledge. The more the objects found there are studied, and the more our knowledge of the early Dark Ages grows, the greater are the complexities and the more numerous the possibilities that emerge. Recent work has suggested considerable Byzantine influence on late sixth-century Gaul, in particular on fashions.[99] There are indications that such influences appear in England also.[100] How directly or indirectly they were mediated there seems no means of saying, but there is, in considering the possibilities, a risk in adopting "minimalist" assumptions that preclude recognition of the full range of possibilities. Thus Martin Carver in commenting on his map showing the range of "contacts" indicated by the finds at Sutton Hoo emphasizes that "this map does *not* imply [his italics] that seventh-century East Anglian merchants were in direct contact with Syria or Byzantium."[101] Surely all that one can say of such evidence is what it need not, rather than what it does not, imply. The question of the density (or lack of it) and nature of relations between England and the Mediterranean has a special interest in relation to the Gregorian mission. If we really knew what was going on in Gregory the Great's mind when he dispatched Augustine, we might find that realpolitik had played a part beside pastoral zeal. Christian English kingdoms, and more particularly, a Christian Kent, may have seemed to him to have a useful part to play in a web of relationships and connections, main threads in which were the need to contain the Lombards and reaction to the policies of the emperor Maurice.

A major point of convergence between arguments of Bruce-Mitford and those of younger archaeologists, whose emphases differ from his, has to do with the relative wealth of the Sutton Hoo burial. In replying to the arguments of Wallace-Hadrill, Bruce-Mitford reasonably emphasizes that comparison of the wealth of the grave goods at Sutton Hoo with descriptions of, for example, a Merovingian dowry is not to compare like with like. It is the wealth of the Sutton Hoo deposit compared with that of *other graves* that matters most and that, as he sees it, strongly indicates that it is royal.[102] In this emphasis on comparison he joins those archaeologists who have used comprehensive comparative analysis of the evidence of grave goods to illuminate social change in general and state formation in particular. The rich graves of the later sixth and early seventh centuries are very important in such inquiries.[103]

These scholars suggest that there is a connection between the appearance of rich burials, such as those at Sutton Hoo, and the appearance of (arguably new) kingdoms such as that of East Anglia. Thus the wealth of Sutton Hoo would be the product of new extensive authority and, put beside the argued absence of similar evidence for earlier periods and some other areas, would be indicative of state formation. In such arguments, as in those of Bruce-Mitford on the royal status of Sutton Hoo, certain assumptions have to be made (even though these may be accompanied by the formal admission of other possibilities). First, that the survival of rich burials has been such that it would in principle be possible to know where to place Sutton Hoo and other rich burials on the scale of rich burials that once existed. Second, to the extent that such burials survive, that enough of them have been excavated and with sufficient skill to make such calibration an effective rather than a hypothetical possibility. Third, that burial practices in a given period were sufficiently uniform to ensure that funeral deposits can be correlated with the distribution of power in a more than merely episodic manner.

The first assumption has to beg basic questions about the destruction and plundering of rich burials in the past thirteen or fourteen centuries. We know that some barrows (possibly containing Anglo-Saxon burials) had been broken into before 1066.[104] Very many may have been. An important (if entirely hypothetical) possibility arises here. Let us assume that a group of barrows such as that at Sutton Hoo was royal. There it stood high above the Deben, a strongly visible statement of dynastic power and claim. What then might normally have happened if another dynasty had conquered a kingdom containing such a royal burial site? Would the conquerors have left untouched the vaunting barrows and buried treasures of a defeated house, every living member of which they would kill if they could? Might they not well have invaded the barrows and taken the treasures? If this were so, then the rich burials that survived into later centuries would not be a sample of all there once were, but rather of those of the most successful dynasties. And the survivals could create a partial illusion of association with state formation, and of concentration of rich burials in the later sixth and early seventh centuries, because, on this hypothesis, later burials would have had a better chance of survival. It is a large assumption that Anglo-Saxon conquerors respected the burials of their enemies. In any case, there is no doubt that barrow robbing was extensively practiced in later centuries. The only reason that the burial in Mound 1 remained to us is that would-be robbers of circa 1600 downed tools too soon. Indeed, granted that it has always been known that barrows contained treasures, it may be thought remarkable that any have remained unrobbed, though to this the answer may be that the majority were prehistoric and unrewarding. In any case the answer to the questions "Could there have been burials richer than Sutton Hoo and quite unknown to us?" and "Could there have been fairly numerous burials as rich as Sutton Hoo and quite unknown to us?" have to be answered with a troubling affirmative. It is at this point that the evidence suggesting the presence of good supplies of bullion and numerous treasures has a relevance not destroyed by Bruce-Mitford's argument against Wallace-Hadrill. For this evidence calls into question one superficially attractive rejoinder to the possibilities just put forward. This would be to allege that the resources available would have been insufficient to have permitted many Sutton Hoos or better-than-Sutton Hoos. A further point: the absence of golden arm-rings (see p. 87 above) in the archaeological record could be an indication of the inadequacy of our rich graves as a sample.

What of the assumption that burial practices were sufficiently uniform to enable rich burials to be used as an index of the distribution of power in the period of Sutton Hoo? If we consider Britain as a whole this cannot be so. It would be absurd to deploy the absence of rich burials from the areas under the authority of Celtic rulers as evidence for the absence of significant concentrations of authority in northern and western Britain. One might as well attempt to deploy funerary evidence for the power of Mr. Gladstone. So far as we know, Celtic rulers of this period were not buried with grave goods, though inquiry into this matter would be much assisted by the discovery of the burial of even one Celtic ruler. Thus there were two zones in Britain, one in the north and west in which funerary archaeology tells us nothing about the distribution of power, the other in the south and east where it must tell us something, but the question is: how much? To put it another way, is it safe to assume that, at least in most of the south and east, all or nearly all potentates of a status corresponding to that of the man who was commemorated by Mound 1 at Sutton Hoo would have been interred with approximately equivalent, and in principle discoverable, grandeur? Surely it is not safe so to argue. To maintain so much is not to rely crudely on what might be called the undiscovered murders principle, namely, that one can readily show that the proportion of undiscovered murders will never be known. First, we know that men of the status concerned were not buried with uniform rites: both inhumation and cremation were practiced. There is an element of funerary eclecticism in the period, which strengthens the possibility that there were other rites that would not have left the same kind of evidence. An obvious possibility here is that of ship burial at sea, which literary evidence indicates as a real possibility,[105] and there may have been other means of disposing of the dead that would have left inadequate traces.

A third assumption has still to be questioned, that is, the assumption that there has been sufficient excavation to provide a sample good enough to enable us safely to generalize about the distribution in time and space of rich burials of circa 550 to circa 650. How many burials fall into what one might call the "approximately equivalent to Taplow or better" class, setting the Sutton Hoo barrows on one side? While Taplow, Broomfield, Caenby, Cuddesdon, Benty Grange, Snape, and Asthall would almost certainly be included in such a list, few scholars would argue the number up much above twenty, if so high. How many men died in the areas and period concerned who might have had burials on this scale? These would be those whom our Latin sources, once we have them, call *reges, subreguli, principes, duces,* and the like,[106] and possibly other members of powerful families who did not have the authority probably indicated by such descriptions, but still could have had extensive means. There could easily have been hundreds of these people in approximately the century involved. Even if one makes the *per impossibile* assumptions that burial practices were completely uniform and that every single relevant grave survives, it is singularly hard to see how the excavated evidence can be argued to provide anything resembling a representative sample. What we have is not, cannot be, the result of an orderly effort to search out the graves of the powerful. It is a random collection of chance discoveries. Arguments based on the hopeful assumption that it may be something more must have feet of clay.

To make such observations is not, I hope, to descend into a facile Pyrrhonism. Nor is it to undervalue the intense and intellectually creative activity of archaeologists. It is simply to say that the possibility of our current evidence relating to graves of very high status being irremediably skewed by variations in rite, chances of survival, and chances of discovery is so strong that attempts to use our present knowledge of such graves to calibrate the precise status of a burial such as that in Sutton Hoo, Mound 1, or to make deductions about the distribution of power can be no more than serious guesses, at best. But then, early Dark Age studies are the domain of the serious guess. Much of what we think we know about the period is a cat's cradle of hypotheses. A corpus of knowledge "meagre in extent and eccentric in distribution"[107] must in its nature breed speculation rather than provide assurance. Sutton Hoo and its study have contributed enormously to knowledge. But what we have learned is very largely about new possibilities. The study of the relationship of Sutton Hoo to social and political reality has to be in large measure not the establishment of new certainties, but the creation of new hypotheses, in a sense the creation of new uncertainties.

Notes

1. John Mitchell Kemble, "Burial and Cremation," *Archaeological Journal* 12 (1855): 309-37; Raymond A. Wiley, "Anglo-Saxon Kemble: The Life and Works of John Mitchell Kemble, 1807-57, Philologist, Historian, Archaeologist," *Anglo-Saxon Studies in Archaeology and History* (1979): 237-41.

2. William Stubbs, *The Constitutional History of England*, 3 vols. (Oxford, 1874-78), 1:64.

3. Charles Oman, *England before the Norman Conquest*, 4th ed. (London, 1919), pp. 187-88.

4. John Richard Green, *The Making of England* (New York, 1882), p. 165.

5. Hector Munro Chadwick, *Origin of the English Nation* (Cambridge, Eng., 1907).

6. Edward Thurlow Leeds, *The Archaeology of the Anglo-Saxon Settlements* (Oxford, 1913). Gerard Baldwin Brown, *Saxon Art and Industry in the Pagan Period*, 2 vols. (London, 1913), vols. 3 and 4 of his *The Arts in Early England*, 6 vols. in 7 (London, 1903-37), is more comprehensive and very learned, but does not seem to have had the same impact.

7. Chadwick, *Origin*, pp. 187-88.

8. Ibid. p. 17.

9. Ibid. p. 18.

10. Ibid. p. 113.

11. Ibid. p. 189.

12. Ibid. pp. 7, 11.

13. Ibid. pp. 238-39; cf. Martin O. H. Carver, "Anglo-Saxon Objectives at Sutton Hoo," *ASE* 15 (1986): 146-47.

14. Hubert Pierquin, *Les institutions et les coutumes des Anglo-Saxons* (Paris, 1913), is a little-read work and something of a historiographical curiosity in relying almost exclusively on works and texts published before 1840, but reveals in its Livre 2 a certain artefactual consciousness.

15. Robin George Collingwood and John Nowell Linton Myres, *Roman Britain and the English Settlements* (Oxford, 1936).

16. For the numismatic argument for a post-650 date, see Philip Grierson, "The Dating of the Sutton Hoo Coins," *Antiquity* 26 (1952): 83-86; and Rupert L. S. Bruce-Mitford, "Sutton Hoo — a Rejoinder," *Antiquity* 26 (1952): 76-82, in which the author drew on numismatic expertise to pulverize, as it appeared, Gordon Ward, who had suggested that the grave was that of Rædwald. At that period Bruce-Mitford was inclined to believe in a late date on other grounds also. "Purely archaeological considerations and particularly the gold jewelry with its affinities with the Book of Durrow, seem to me to suggest a later date than 625-6" (p. 82).

17. Frank Merry Stenton, "The East Anglian Kings of the Seventh Century," in *The Anglo Saxons: Studies in Some Aspects of Their History, Presented to Bruce Dickins*, ed. Peter Clemoes (London, 1959), p. 52.

18. Robert Howard Hodgkin, *A History of the Anglo-Saxons*, 2 vols., 3rd ed., (Oxford, 1952), 2:696-734. Francis P. Magoun, Jr., "The Sutton Hoo Ship Burial: A Chronological Bibliography," *Speculum* 29 (1954): 116-24, and its continuation by Jess B. Bessinger, Jr., *Speculum* 33 (1958): 515-22, list the literature available up to their publication dates.

19. Charles Green, *Sutton Hoo: The Excavation of a Royal Ship Burial* (London, 1963; new ed. rev. Barbara Green, 1988).

20. Frank Merry Stenton, *Anglo-Saxon England* (Oxford, 1943), pp. 50-52.

21. George Osborne Sayles, *The Medieval Foundations of England* (London, 1948).

22. Ibid. pp. 11, 27.

23. Ibid. p. 27.

24. Ibid. p. 27.

25. Peter Hunter Blair, *An Introduction to Anglo-Saxon England* (Cambridge, Eng., 1956).

26. Ibid. pp. 283-84.

27. Ibid. p. 204.

28. David Wilson, *The Anglo-Saxons* (London, 1960), pp. 46, 53.

29. Dorothy Whitelock, *The Foundations of English Society* (Harmondsworth, 1952), p. 49.

30. Rosemary Cramp, "Beowulf and Archaeology," *Medieval Archaeology* 1 (1957): 57-77.

31. Christopher Hawkes, "Sutton Hoo Twenty-Five Years After," *Antiquity* 38 (1964): 252-57.

32. Rupert Bruce-Mitford, *The Sutton Hoo Ship-Burial*, with contributions by Paul Ashbee et al., 3 vols. in 4 (London, 1975–83) [hereafter cited as Bruce-Mitford, *Sutton Hoo*].

33. The argument is laid out in Bruce-Mitford, *Sutton Hoo* 1:683-717.

34. Ibid., 1:690.

35. Ibid., 1:431.

36. Rupert Bruce-Mitford, "The Sutton Hoo Ship-Burial: Some Foreign Connections," *Settimane di studio del Centro italiano di studi sull'alto medioevo* 32, 2 vols. (1986), 1:143.

37. Angela Care Evans, *The Sutton Hoo Ship Burial* (London, 1986), pp. 9, 83.

38. Ibid. p. 110.

39. Green, *Sutton Hoo: Excavation,* 2nd. ed., pp. 97, 101.

40. Herbert P. R. Finberg, *The Formation of England, 550-1042* (London, 1974), p. 89. For, conversely, an uncritical taking for granted that the burial is a royal one, see James Campbell in *The Anglo-Saxons,* ed. James Campbell (Oxford, 1982), p. 32.

41. Peter H. Sawyer, *From Roman Britain to Anglo-Saxon England* (London, 1978), p. 40.

42. Henry R. Loyn, *Anglo-Saxon England and the Norman Conquest* (London, 1962), p. 72.

43. John Michael Wallace-Hadrill, "The Graves of Kings: An Historical Note on Some Archaeological Evidence," *Studi Medievali,* 3rd ser., 1 (1960): 177-94, reprinted with a new appendix in his *Early Medieval History* (Oxford, 1980), pp. 39-59.

44. Nicolas Reynolds, "The King's Whetstone, a Footnote," *Antiquity* 54 (1980): 232-36. For the argument that the whetstone must be a scepter, see Bruce-Mitford, *Sutton Hoo* 1:311-77.

45. *Ego hæc ad exornandam atque nobilitandam Francorum gentem feci. Sed et plurima adhuc, si vita comis fuerit faciam* (Gregory of Tours, *Libri Historiarum* 10, MGH, *Script. Rer. Mer.* 1 [1937], 6. 2). For treasures as something intrinsic to *regnum* and having a kind of suprapersonal significance, see Margarete Weidemann, *Kulturgeschichte der Merowingerzeit nach den Werken Gregors von Tours,* 2 vols. (Mainz, 1982), 1:18-20.

46. Thomas Charles-Edwards, "Early Medieval Kingship in the British Isles," in *The Origins of Anglo-Saxon Kingdoms,* ed. Steven Bassett (Leicester, 1989), p. 37.

47. Wallace-Hadrill, *Early Medieval History,* p. 41. For other descriptions of Merovingian treasures see Renée Doehaerd, "La richesse des Merovingiens," *Studi in onre di Gino Luzzatto,* 4 vols. (Milan, 1949-50), 1:30-46. For Visigothic wealth, see also P. D. King, *Law and Society in the Visigothic Kingdom* (Cambridge, Eng., 1972), pp. 190-92; note that even non-nobles seem sometimes to have been expected to pay six pounds of gold (King, *Law and Society,* pp. 184-85).

48. Wallace-Hadrill, *Early Medieval History,* pp. 53-56, esp. p. 54.

49. Gregory of Tours, *Libri Historiarum* 6.2; cf. John P. C. Kent and Kenneth Scott Painter, *The Wealth of the Roman World* (London, 1977), p. 160.

50. Erwin Panofsky, *Abbot Suger on the Abbey Church of St. Denis and Its Art Treasures,* 2nd ed., edited by by Gerda Panofsky-Soergel (Princeton, 1979), pp. 62-63 and 189, and pl. 19, 20, and 21. Another example of church treasure in gold and cloisonné garnet, far larger than anything at Sutton Hoo, which survives as an (in this case seventeenth-century) illustration is a chalice (also attributed to St. Eligius) from Chelles (Peter Lasko, *The Kingdom of the Franks* [London, 1971], fig. 89).

51. F. Goubert, *Byzance avant l'Islam,* 2 vols. (Paris, 1956), vol. 2 (part 1): *Byzance et les Francs,* pp. 23-26 and 107.

52. Gregory of Tours, *Libri Historiarum* 6. 42. Gregory may have been somewhat in error about the precise date and circumstances of the subsidy (Walter Goffart, "Byzantine Policy in the West under the Emperors Tiberius II and Maurice: The Pretenders Hermenigild and Gundovald," *Traditio* 13 [1957]: 110-11).

53. Charles R. Dodwell, *Anglo-Saxon Art: A New Perspective* (Manchester, 1982).

54. Ibid., chap. 7, esp. pp. 211-12.

55. Alcuin, *The Bishops, Saints and Kings of York,* ed. Peter Godman (Oxford, 1982), line 182.

56. Æthelwulf, *De Abbatibus*, ed. Alistair Campbell (Oxford, 1967), pp. 54-62; but references to treasures appear outside this section, e.g., in lines 449-50, 631, and 649-50. The editor suggested that the resemblances between what Æthelwulf describes and what Aldhelm describes in his poem on Bugge's church may bring the credibility of the passages concerned into question. The weight of this argument is diminished by the paradox that precisely the same evidence can be used to argue the opposite case.

57. Alcuin, *The Bishops, Saints and Kings of York*, lines 338-90. Dodwell, *Anglo-Saxon Art*, pp. 196, 198, 202, 203, and 205, collects seventh-and eighth-century references to ecclesiastical treasures; for altars, see p. 209, and for that of San Ambrogio, see Peter Lasko, *Ars Sacra, 800-1200* (Harmondsworth, 1972), pp. 50-54.

58. James Campbell, "The Sale of Land and the Economics of Power in Early England: Problems and Possibilities," *Haskins Society Journal* 1, ed. Robert Patterson (1989): 27. In the sentence occupying lines 20-22 ("Particularly striking . . . "), the words "and 100" should be omitted.

59. Dodwell, *Anglo-Saxon Art*, p. 189. The numerous references to rulers as "ring-givers" in *Beowulf* are strongly suggestive, although, as it stands, it is not contemporary evidence for our period.

60. Frank Merry Stenton, "Medeshamstede and Its Colonies," *Preparatory to Anglo-Saxon England* (Oxford, 1970), p. 182. The reference to the brooch runs as follows: "Fibulam auream cum iiii ex auro massiunculis arte artificiis compositis." Stenton suggested an attempt to describe a florid square-headed brooch. This transaction antedates 692.

61. Philip Grierson, "La fonction sociale de la monnaie en Angleterre aux VIIe-VIIIe siècles," *Settimane di studio del Centro italiano di studi sull'alto medioevo* 8 (1960): 344-47.

62. *The Laws of the Earliest English Kings*, ed. and trans. Frederick Levi Attenborough (Cambridge, Eng., 1922), p. 14 (Æthelberht 72:1).

63. Ibid., p. 58 (Ine 70).

64. E.g., ibid., pp. 4, 6, and 8 (Æthelberht 2, 5, 6, 21, 26, and 43); p. 20 (Hlothere 6 and Eadric 10); p. 24 (Wihtred 5); pp. 36, 38, 40, and 42 (Ine 2, 3, 6, 7, 8, 9, 10, 13, and 23).

65. Ibid., p. 10 (Æthelberht 57).

66. Ibid., p. 38 (Ine 6:3).

67. Ibid., pp. 30, 36, and 42 (Wihtred 27, Ine 3:2 and 23:3, 74).

68. Ibid., pp. 54 and 58 (Ine 55 and 69).

69. Ibid., p. 44 (Ine 26), cf. p. 48 (Ine 38).

70. Ibid., p. 54 (Ine 54:1).

71. See the data collected from the Frankish laws by Edward James, *The Franks* (Oxford, 1988), pp. 209-10 and 216-18.

72. *S. Bonifatii et Lulli Epistolæ* (MGH, Berlin, 1955), no. 87, p. 199.

73. D. Michael Metcalf, "How Large was the Anglo-Saxon 'Currency'?" *Economic History Review* 18 (1965): 475-82.

74. In Bruce-Mitford, *Sutton Hoo* 1:665-77. For recent discoveries in eastern England, see e.g., A. M. Burnett, "A Provençal Solidus from Hawkwell, Essex," *Numismatic Chronicle* 147 (1987): 182-83; and David Sorenson, "A Tremissis of Justin II Found at Southwold, Suffolk," *British Numismatic Journal* 53 (1983): 176.

75. Birgit Arrhenius, *Merovingian Garnet Jewellery: Emergence and Social Implications* (Stockholm, 1985); Mavis Bimson, "Dark Age Garnet Cutting," *Anglo-Saxon Studies in Archaeology and History* 4 (1985): 125-28; Katherine East, "Cross-Hatched Foils from Sutton Hoo," *Anglo-Saxon Studies in Archaeology and History* 4 (1985): 129-42; and N. D. Meeks and R. Holmes, "The Sutton Hoo Garnet Jewellery," *Anglo-Saxon Studies in Archaeology and History* 4 (1985): 143-58.

76. Arrhenius, *Merovingian Garnet Jewellery*, esp. chaps. 4 and 6.

77. Ibid., pp. 39-40.

78. Arrhenius lists over four hundred surviving pieces or fragments of such work from Europe (west of Hungary and Moravia) and Scandinavia, excluding the Sutton Hoo items (*Merovingian Garnet Jewellery*, pp. 208-19).

79. Gregory of Tours, *Libri Historiarum* 6. 32. The interest of this passage and of that next referred to was signaled by Renée Doehaerd, *Le haut moyen age occidental: Economies et sociétés* (Paris, 1971), p. 248.

80. *Lex Visigothorum*, MGH *Leges*. 1 (Hanover, 1902), p. 404.

81. Bruce-Mitford, *Sutton Hoo* 1:687.

82. Bede, *Opera Historica*, 2 vols. (Oxford, 1896), pp. 362-77, 389-93.

83. For Bruce-Mitford's most recently published views on the "Swedish connection," see his "Sutton Hoo Ship-Burial: Some Foreign Connections," *Settimane di studio del Centro italiano di studi sull'alto medioevo* 32, 2 vols. (1986), 1:143-210.

84. Ian N. Wood, *The Merovingian North Sea* (Alingsås, 1983).

85. On this little-considered subject, see also James, *The Franks*, pp. 103-4 and 171.

86. Wood, *The Merovingian North Sea*, p. 14.

87. Bruce-Mitford, *Sutton Hoo* 3:69-125.

88. J. W. Huggett, "Imported Grave Goods and the Early Anglo-Saxon Economy," *Medieval Archaeology* 32 (1988): 68-69, expresses doubts on the nature, and so the origin, of the ivory.

89. Martin Biddle, "A City in Transition: 400-800," in *The City of London from Prehistoric Times to ca. 1520*, ed. Mary D. Lobel, British Atlas of Historic Towns, vol. 3 (London, 1990) p. 21.

90. Marla M. Mango, Cyril Mango, Angela Care Evans, and Michael Hughes, "A Sixth-Century Mediterranean Bucket from Bromeswell Parish, Suffolk," *Antiquity* 63 (1989): 295-311.

91. Gregory of Tours, *Libri Historiarum* 6.24.

92. *Procopius*, ed. H. B. Dewing, 7 vols. (London, 1941-61), 6:233 (*Anecdota* 19, 13).

93. Bruce-Mitford, *Sutton Hoo* 1:662.

94. *Procopius*, ed. Dewing, 5: 254-55 (*History of the Wars* 8.20.10).

95. Goubert, *Byzance avant l'Islam* 2:passim.

96. Gregory of Tours, *Libri Historiarum* 10.2.

97. Bertil Almgren, "Helmets, Crowns and Warrior's Dress from the Roman Emperors to the Chieftains of Uppland," in *Vendel Period Studies: Transactions of the Boat-Grave Symposium in Stockholm, February 2-3, 1981*, ed. J. P. Lamm and H. Å. Nordström (Stockholm, 1983), pp. 14-16. The same garment appears in a presumably Byzantine relief in St. Mark's, Venice, said to show "Alexander the Great ascending to heaven" (Bernard Berenson, *The Passionate Sightseer* [London, 1960], illus. no. 38, p. 60).

98. Sidonius Apollinaris, *Epistolae*, ed. André Loyen, 2 vols. (Paris, 1970), 2: 155-56 (4.20).

99. M. Schulze, "Einflüsse byzantinischer Prunkgewänder auf die fränkische Frauentracht," *Archäologisches Korrespondenzblatt* 6 (1976): 149-61 (a reference that I owe to William Filmer-Sankey); and James, *The Franks*, p. 226. For the Scandinavian relationship with Byzantium, see especially Rudolph Zeitler, ed., *Les pays du nord et Byzance: Actes du colloque d'Upsal, 20-22 April 1979* (Uppsala, 1981).

100. William Filmer-Sankey, "On the Function and Status of Finger-Rings in the Early Medieval World" (D.Phil. thesis, Oxford University, 1989), vol. 1, esp. pp. 88-89, 133, and 212-15.

101. Martin Carver, "Sutton Hoo in Context," *Settimane di studio del Centro italiano di studi sull'alto medioevo* 32, 2 vols. (1986), 1:104.

102. Bruce-Mitford, *Sutton Hoo* 1:686-87.

103. Christopher J. Arnold, *The Archaeology of the Early Anglo-Saxon Kingdoms* (London, 1988), esp. pp. 163-93. Martin Carver, "Kingship and Material Culture in Early Medieval East Anglia," in *The Origins of Anglo-Saxon Kingdoms*, ed. Bassett, pp. 141-60, esp.

152-55, puts forward the case for supposing that Sutton Hoo may reflect the creation of the East Anglian kingdom through "a change of structure with a high-ranking peer group from local to regionalized independence" (p. 153). He also entertains, but expresses reservations about, the possibility that the wealth of Sutton Hoo may be indicative of an increasingly stratified society (pp. 141, 149, and 152-53).

104. John M. Kemble, *Horæ Ferales or Studies in the Archaeology of the Northern Nations* (London, 1863), p. 113.

105. David M. Wilson, "Sweden-England," in *Vendel Period Studies,* ed. Lamm and Nordström, p. 106. And some burials may have been made in such a way that they could not be found and robbed; cf. *Jordanis Romana et Getica, MGH, Auct. Antiquiss.* (Berlin, 1882), p. 99, chap. 30, for the extraordinary precautions said to have been taken to keep the tomb of Alaric safe for all time.

106. James Campbell, *Essays in Anglo-Saxon History* (London, 1986), pp. 85-98.

107. The expression is Carver's, "Kingship and Material Culture," p. 143.

CHAPTER 7

✣

Rædwald the Bretwalda

Simon Keynes

The favored candidate for identification as the person buried or commemorated in Mound 1 at Sutton Hoo has long been Rædwald, king of East Anglia in the first quarter of the seventh century. He features in Bede's *Ecclesiastical History*, notably as the fourth in the famous list of kings who held sway over all the kingdoms south of the river Humber; and as such, he is among those who were later accorded the title "Bretwalda," or "ruler of Britain." The case for regarding Rædwald as the Man in the Mound is certainly compelling, and represents such a happy conjunction of history and archaeology that it would prove difficult to dislodge from the public mind: the presence of objects with a "Christian" complexion in a burial spectacularly "heathen" in its conception seems appropriate for one who is known to have been broad-minded in his religious beliefs; the Merovingian coins in the purse seem to have been assembled at a time that is compatible with their deposit at the apparent date of Rædwald's death; and some of the items interpreted as regalia could be taken to imply that the person was rather more than an ordinary king.[1] The line of argument may be open to question, and an alternative case could be made for at least one other of the East Anglian kings,[2] but it would be pointless to pursue the matter any further until the place of Mound 1 in the context of the whole cemetery is clarified. All I wish to do, therefore, is look more closely at Rædwald himself, and in particular at the significance of his title "Bretwalda."

The sum total of historical knowledge about Rædwald could be written, without too much difficulty, on the back of the proverbial postage stamp. According to the venerable Bede, Rædwald "was the son of Tytil, whose father was Wuffa, from whom the kings of the East Angles are called Wuffingas"; but though noble by birth, he was "ignoble in his deeds."[3] Rædwald had been "initiated into the mysteries of the Christian faith in Kent, but in vain; for on his return home, he was seduced by his wife and by certain evil teachers and perverted from the sincerity of his faith, so that his last state was worse than his first." In this connection Bede alludes to the temple where Rædwald "had one altar for the Christian sacrifice and another small altar on which to offer victims to devils"; and it emerges that the temple in question was still to be seen in the 640s.[4] Rædwald apparently faced some internal opposition to his rule, to judge from the fact that his son's half-brother Sigeberht "had long been in exile in Gaul, while he was fleeing from the enmity of Rædwald."[5] And he is otherwise known to have given refuge to the Northumbrian prince Edwin when Edwin was being persecuted by King Æthelfrith: Rædwald first resisted and then yielded to Æthelfrith's bribery, promising to kill Edwin or hand him over to Æthelfrith's messengers; but then Rædwald's queen interceded on Edwin's behalf and persuaded her husband to change his mind, whereupon Rædwald raised a large army and defeated Æthelfrith "on the Mercian border on the east bank of the river Idle," thereby enabling Edwin to gain the Northumbrian throne.[6] It must have been at about this time that Rædwald's power was such as to earn him his place in Bede's list of Southumbrian overlords, but nothing is known of what it entailed.

One should like to be able to give firm dates for Rædwald's accession and death, but it has to be said that the chronology of East Anglian history in the first half of the seventh century is deeply obscure. Rædwald had been king for some time by 616, when Æthelberht of Kent died and when he helped Edwin to the Northumbrian throne; it is clear that he was dead by 633, since his son and successor Eorpwald was persuaded to accept Christianity by Edwin of Northumbria, who died in that year. For any greater precision one has to depend on information provided on quite uncertain authority by post-Conquest historians: for example, one could calculate from regnal and episcopal dates in the *Liber Eliensis* that the reign of Sigeberht of East Anglia began circa 630,[7] and since (on Bede's authority) Sigeberht came to the throne after a three-year pagan interlude following Eorpwald's death,[8] this calculation would have the effect of pushing Eorpwald's death back to circa 627, and Rædwald's to an indeterminate point before then; or one could turn to Roger of Wendover (writing at St. Albans toward the middle of the thirteenth century) and make hay of his categorical statement that Rædwald died in 624.[9] It is as well to remember, therefore, that there is a certain amount of flexibility in the date of Rædwald's death, depending on the quality of evidence that one is prepared to use: if one goes for Roger, Rædwald died in 624; if one chooses to trust the *Liber Eliensis*, he was dead by circa 627; but if one sticks with Bede, the date of his death cannot be expressed more accurately than sometime between 616 and 633.

Whatever the case, Rædwald's chief claim to fame depends on his inclusion in Bede's list of seven kings who held sway over all the kingdoms south of the river Humber, and it is to a consideration of this list that I must now turn. The reading is from the *Ecclesiastical History*, book 2, chapter 5:

> In the year of our Lord 616, the twenty-first year after Augustine and his companions had been sent to preach to the English nation, King Æthelberht of Kent, after ruling his temporal kingdom gloriously for fifty-six years, entered upon the eternal joys of the heavenly king-

dom. He was the third English king to rule (*imperauit*) over all the southern kingdoms, which are divided from the north by the river Humber and the surrounding territory; but he was the first to enter the kingdom of heaven. The first king to hold the like sovereignty (*imperium*) was Ælle, king of the South Saxons; the second was Cælin, king of the West Saxons, known in their own language as Ceawlin; the third, as we have said, was Æthelberht, king of the people of Kent; the fourth was Rædwald, king of the East Angles, who even during the lifetime of Æthelberht was gaining the leadership (*ducatus*) for his own race; the fifth was Edwin, king of the Northumbrians, the nation inhabiting the district north of the Humber. Edwin had still greater power and ruled over all the inhabitants of Britain, English and Britons alike, except for Kent only. He even brought under English rule (*Anglorum subiecit imperio*) the Mevanian islands [Anglesey and Man] which lie between England and Ireland and belong to the Britons. The sixth to rule (*regnum tenuit*) within the same bounds was Oswald, the most Christian king of the Northumbrians, while the seventh was his brother Oswiu who for a time held almost the same territory (*aequalibus pene terminis regnum nonnullo tempore cohercens*). The latter overwhelmed and made tributary even the tribes of the Picts and Irish who inhabit the northern parts of Britain; but of this more later.[10]

In this justly famous passage, Bede makes his most important and influential contribution to the understanding of Anglo-Saxon political history in the seventh century; indeed, it may be said that this passage has conditioned Anglo-Saxon historiography ever since. He appears to be recording the succession to some kind of *imperium*, or overlordship, associated in particular with rule over all the kingdoms south of the river Humber and held in turn by a series of kings whose power thus extended beyond the frontiers of their respective kingdoms. His list implies that this special degree of worldly power was enjoyed in the first instance by Ælle of Sussex (in the last quarter of the fifth century) and that there was then a period when no single king was regarded as being superior in power to his contemporaries, roughly coinciding with the first half of the sixth century (perhaps significantly a period that Gildas regarded, from a British point of view, as one of relative peace and calm after the British victory at *Mons Badonicus*).[11] It would appear that this special position was then reestablished by Ceawlin of Wessex, in the second half of the sixth century, and was held thereafter by Æthelberht of Kent, Rædwald of East Anglia, and finally by three successive kings of the Northumbrians, Edwin, Oswald, and Oswiu (implying that they controlled the kingdoms north *and* south of the river). In short, Bede is making a statement about shifts in the balance of power among the various kingdoms of early Anglo-Saxon England — a statement that seems to be of the utmost interest and importance.

Bede is normally the most pellucid of writers, and the text of his *History* is transmitted in early manuscripts that admit little possibility of contamination by careless copyists. But as luck would have it, the precise meaning of his one sentence about Rædwald in the list of seven kings is open to question. In Bede's words, "quartus Reduald rex Orientalium Anglorum, qui etiam uiuente Aedilbercto eidem suae genti ducatum praebebat, obtenuit." The traditional interpretation, common (in one form or another) to all the translations of Bede that are currently in use, is that Rædwald was already obtaining the overlordship of the southern English before Æthelberht's death in 616: even during Æthelberht's lifetime, he *praebebat* the *ducatum* to *eidem suae genti*, that is (I suppose) he was supplying the leadership to that same race of his; in other words (more loosely), he was obtaining it on their behalf.[12] One feels that this is what the sentence ought to mean, not least because *etiam* prepares us for something unexpected and contrary to Æthelberht's interest, but one has to admit that *ducatus* could be something more restricted in scope than the *imperium* mentioned earlier on and that the translation of *praebeo* is rather forced. The first of a series of three radical reinterpretations of Bede's intended meaning was propounded in 1971 by Hanna Vollrath-Reichelt. Proceeding from the assumption that Rædwald became overlord before Æthelberht's death, she construes the sentence to mean that Rædwald graciously allowed Æthelberht to retain control of Kent for the rest of his life: Rædwald *praebebat* the *ducatum suae genti* to *eidem*; that is, he offered the leadership over his people to the same man – in other words, he allowed Æthelberht to retain control of Kent.[13] This may make better sense of *praebeo* (to offer, supply) and *ducatus*, but it breaks up what appears to be the distinct phrase *eidem suae genti*, involves the strange construction *ducatum suae genti* (dative) for "leadership of his people," and takes the reflexive pronoun *suae* to refer not to Rædwald (who is the subject of the verb) but to Æthelberht. An alternative view, propounded more recently by Nicholas Brooks and others, depends to some extent on the same interpretation of the syntax, but starts from a different point and takes *suae* to refer to Rædwald. The assumption in this case is that Æthelberht held sway until his death, and the sentence is construed to mean that Rædwald conceded control of East Anglia to him: again, Rædwald *praebebat* the *ducatum suae genti* to *eidem*; that is, he offered the leadership over his people to the same man – in other words, he conceded control of East Anglia to Æthelberht.[14] This seems to make sense (and is certainly preferable to Vollrath-Reichelt's interpretation), but it may be thought that (like hers) it loses the natural force of *etiam*, since Rædwald could hardly give anything to Æthelberht at any time other than during Æthelberht's life. And so we come to the third radical reinterpretation (advocated by Thomas Charles-Edwards), which reverts to the syntax of the traditional view but produces a quite different result: Bede is saying that Æthelberht's supremacy began to crumble before his death, for while Æthelberht was still alive Rædwald *praebebat ducatum* for *eidem suae genti;* that is, he provided leadership for that same race of his — in other words, he managed to recover (or gain) control of the East Angles.[15] The implication here is that Æthelberht's supremacy gave him control of all the kingdoms under his sway but that he eventually lost control of East Anglia to Rædwald, who went on only after Æthelberht's death to achieve the wider supremacy.

It is as well to air these difficulties, because they serve as a salutary reminder of the distressing way in which our understanding of major matters of state can depend on the minutest details of Latin syntax.[16] My own preference would be for the traditional view, if only it were possible to find a convincing parallel for that use of *praebeo;* I would otherwise opt for the third of the radical reinterpretations, because (as Charles-Edwards shows) it has the support of other occurrences of the phrase *ducatum praebere* in Christian Latin. And in either case, my guess would be that Bede's remark was prompted by his desire to prepare his readers for what he intended to say later on, namely that before his accession, Edwin of Northumbria had found refuge at the court of Rædwald, who was sufficiently great a king to defeat King Æthelfrith in 616; for Bede's readers might have wondered how Rædwald could have achieved so much within so short a time of the death of Æthelberht of Kent, also in 616, unless it was clear that his star was by then already rising.

The question that now presents itself is whether Bede's list of seven kings is a true record of succession to some kind of recognized political office: does the selection of kings accord with one's general understanding of the changing balance of power in the seventh century, and was there any degree of uniformity in the nature and extent of the authority that each of the kings in the list successively enjoyed? The first two kings, Ælle of Sussex and Ceawlin of Wessex, stick out like a pair of sore thumbs from the rest, not least because Bede says nothing else about them. The exploits of both are well known from the *Anglo-Saxon Chronicle,* and the fact that Bede mentions them at all is evidence of their importance in the fifth and sixth centuries, respectively. It is frankly inconceivable, however, that either of them had anything approaching authority over all the Southumbrian kingdoms,[17] and one can only suppose that Bede included them to honor their memory and perhaps to carry a sense of political continuity way back into the fifth century. The third of Bede's kings is Æthelberht of Kent, of whom Bede says three times that his *imperium* or sway extended over all the English kingdoms south of the river Humber,[18] so he presumably believed it to be true. Yet he does not provide much by way of incidental and circumstantial evidence to indicate where Æthelberht's influence was felt outside Kent, beyond a statement that the king of Essex was under his power.[19] It is true to say, however, that there is a letter to Æthelberht in which Pope Gregory urges the king to instill knowledge of Christianity "into the kings and nations subject to you,"[20] but one is inclined to put this down to the excesses of papal hyperbole (not least because one of Gregory's successors made similar — and demonstrably untrue — remarks about all the peoples who were subject to Æthelberht's son and successor Eadbald),[21] and it may be that the letter itself determined Bede's conception of Æthelberht's power. The fourth king is Rædwald, and again one searches in vain for any clear indications that his rule really extended throughout England south of the Humber; in fact, the only suggestion of his power outside East Anglia is that he was able to defeat Æthelfrith of Northumbria in the battle on the banks of the river Idle (just south of the Humber),[22] but a military expedition to distant parts for a specific purpose does not necessarily amount to sustained political control.

The remaining three kings in Bede's list are the Northumbrians Edwin, Oswald, and Oswiu. Bede makes particularly extravagant claims for Edwin (616-33), stating (in the context of the list itself) that he ruled over all the inhabitants of Britain, English and Britons alike, except for Kent only (an exclusion that creates the impression that his sway in the South, however extensive, was not exercised by virtue of his holding a recognized office);[23] elsewhere Bede states that Edwin ruled over the whole of Britain,[24] seemingly forgetting the earlier exclusion of Kent, and he writes of the great peace in Britain, "wherever the *imperium* of King Edwin reached."[25] Edwin had sufficient power to conduct a military expedition into Wessex,[26] he was married to a Kentish princess,[27] and he was instrumental in persuading Eorpwald of East Anglia to embrace Christianity.[28] There is no doubt, in other words, that he was a force to be reckoned with south of the Humber, but in general one is left with the impression that the remarks about the great extent of his power had more to do with Bede's desire to show that a good Christian king prospered mightily in this world than with the realities of seventh-century politics. In the case of Oswald (634-42), we know from Adomnán's *Life of Columba* that after his great victory over Cadwallon in 634, Oswald was "ordained by God as emperor of the whole of Britain,"[29] a useful reminder of how such extravagant claims might arise. Bede himself can match the hyperbole: in the list, Oswald is said to have ruled within the same bounds (as Edwin), but later on Bede drools that he "gained from the one God who made heaven and earth greater earthly realms than any of his ancestors had possessed; in fact he held under his sway all the peoples and kingdoms of Britain."[30] Oswald was certainly on good terms with the king of Wessex (standing sponsor to him at his baptism and later marrying his daughter);[31] he is said to have ruled over the kingdom of Sussex;[32] and Edwin's widow did not think that her children were safe from him in Kent.[33] So he, too, had extensive influence south of the Humber, perhaps more so than Edwin; but one does suspect that Bede got carried away. Bede's seventh king was Oswiu (642-70), who *"for a time* held *almost* the same territory" as Oswald. The double qualification is important, since it shows that even Bede was careful not to imply that the Northumbrian supremacy was unbroken. In fact, he says elsewhere that Oswiu reigned for his twenty-eight years *laboriosissime*, with one hell of an effort, having to contend not only with the Mercians, but also with his son, his nephew, and with Oswine of Deira.[34] Indeed, it was only after Oswiu's victory over Penda of Mercia, at the battle of Winwæd in 655, that he came to the fore: "King Oswiu ruled over the Mercian race, as well as the rest of the southern kingdoms, for three years after King Penda was killed."[35] In other words, Oswiu's supremacy lasted from 655 to 658; before 655 it was Penda who was dominant south of the Humber,[36] and in 658 Penda's son Wulfhere became king of the Mercians and began to rebuild his kingdom's fortunes.[37] It would be mistaken, therefore, to regard the various indications of Oswiu's involvement in Southumbrian affairs as having had anything to do with his political power: when he promoted the interests of Christianity in the kingdoms of the Middle Angles and the East Saxons,[38] Penda was dominant in the South, and when he (allegedly) consulted with King Ecgberht of Kent about "the state of the English Church," in the mid-660s,[39] he had long since lost any supremacy that he might once have enjoyed.[40]

What, then, are we to make of Bede's Magnificent Seven? It is patently clear that if Bede's list is taken at face value, as a record of succession to a grand Southumbrian overlordship, the thing is a nonsense: it is simply impossible to believe, on the evidence available, that these kings were like unto each other, or that they exercised similar powers by virtue of holding a particular office; the extent of their sway varied, and one suspects that the nature of their royal authority was in each case quite different; and of course if the list is to be taken literally, then where are the Mercians? It strikes me, therefore, that the list of seven kings is far more likely to be the product of personal reflection on Bede's part and that in that sense it does not have any validity outside the context of the *Ecclesiastical History*. One should bear in mind that Bede was writing during the reign of Æthelbald of Mercia, whose claims to be regarded as a pan-Southumbrian overlord are a good deal stronger than any that could be entertained on behalf of Bede's seven kings;[41] it could have been Æthelbald's position that led him to believe that Southumbrian overlords were a fact of life and so encouraged him to project the position into the more distant past. One should also remember that unity in its various manifestations was one of Bede's main themes: he writes about the unity of the English church, and he tries to generate a sense of the unity of the English people, so it is not surprising that he should have wished to create impressions of political unity as well. In effect, the list of overlords provides a secular counterpart to the numerous passages where Bede is concerned to establish the order of succession to a particular episcopal see;[42] and most historians would sympathize with his desire in this way to create order out of chaos. One might even see the beginnings of a similar kind of list in the Whitby *Life of Gregory the Great*,[43] and since the prevailing view that Bede did not know the Whitby *Life* is wide open to question,[44] it is conceivable that Bede may actually have taken his cue from that work. Whatever the case, it would follow that the selection of names in Bede's list was entirely his own[45] and was determined by his desire to honor those kings whom he regarded as playing a particularly important role in his story: Ælle and Ceawlin, as heroes of the pre-Christian past; Æthelberht, in his capacity as the first king to "enter the kingdom of Heaven"; Rædwald, for his crucial role in bringing Edwin to the Northumbrian throne (or perhaps to bridge the transition of power from Kent to Northumbria); Edwin himself, as the first Christian king of Northumbria; Oswald, for his support of the Celtic missionaries; and Oswiu, for his victory over the wicked Penda of Mercia and for his example in promoting the interests of the church (notably at the Synod of Whitby). Perhaps this is all too rational, but to my mind it is a way to make sense of the list.[46] And if one then asks why the Mercians are not included in the list, it is quite simply because they have no place in what is essentially Bede's private scheme. Penda and Wulfhere were not "omitted" because Bede objected to the Mercians; they were left out because the question of their inclusion did not arise. And while one could attribute Æthelbald's "omission" to a wish on Bede's part to end with a Northumbrian chord or to his reluctance to come too close to the present, the readier explanation is again that the question of Æthelbald's inclusion never arose.[47]

The unknown person who translated Bede's *Ecclesiastical History* into English, toward the end of the ninth century, gives a simplified version of the list of seven kings;[48] one may pause to reflect on the fact that the translator, himself apparently a Mercian, refrained from inserting any reference to the Mercian overlords, but this should not occasion any surprise. A West Saxon chronicler, writing at about the same time, was rather more adventurous. Recording the various successes of King Ecgberht of Wessex in the first quarter of the ninth century, he brings the story to a climax in his annal for 829:

> In this year there was an eclipse of the moon on Christmas eve. And that year King Ecgberht conquered the kingdom of the Mercians, and everything south of the Humber; and he was the eighth king who was "Bretwalda." The first who had so great authority was Ælle, king of the South Saxons; the second was Ceawlin, king of the West Saxons; the third was Æthelberht, king of the people of Kent; the fourth was Rædwald, king of the East Angles; the fifth was Edwin, king of the Northumbrians; the sixth was Oswald who reigned after him; the seventh was Oswiu, Oswald's brother; the eighth was Ecgberht, king of the West Saxons.[49]

No one would doubt for a moment that this list is directly dependent on Bede's *Ecclesiastical History*, and no one would argue, therefore, that the chronicler could be said to corroborate Bede's testimony. The West Saxon chronicler was evidently eager to glorify the king who had founded West

Saxon political fortunes in the early ninth century, and chose for this purpose to resuscitate Bede's list of seven kings who held sway south of the river Humber, introducing it (quite correctly) *before* going on to describe how Ecgberht received the submission of the Northumbrians as well;[50] so with his copy of Bede open in front of him, he simply rattled off the list in book 2, chapter 5, ignoring all of Bede's explanatory comments, and then tacked the name of King Ecgberht on at the end.

In so doing, the chronicler did, however, make one further contribution that was to prove of the utmost significance, and he founded an academic industry at the same time. I refer, of course, to his statement that Ecgberht "was the eighth king who was 'Bretwalda.'" The word itself is made up of the elements *Bret-*, "Briton," and *-walda*, "ruler or king" (from OE *wealdan*, "to rule, govern," whence modern English "to wield"), so it appears to mean nothing less than "Briton-ruler," or "ruler of Britain." But while *Bretwalda* is the form in the earliest manuscript of the *Chronicle* (and if only for that reason is the one generally preferred by modern historians), the other manuscripts have different forms that may in fact represent a different word or words: *brytenwalda* or *brytenwealda* (MSS BDE) and *bretenanwealda* (MS C). The element *bryten* certainly could in these cases be the noun meaning "Britain," in which case *brytenwealda* would mean precisely "ruler of Britain"; the form in C, with *-anwealda*, would then give the meaning "sole ruler of Britain." On the other hand, the first element might be the adjective *bryten* (from the verb *breotan*, meaning "to break, disperse"), often used in poetic compounds to denote the wide or general dispersion of the noun that it qualifies;[51] so that just as *bryten-rice* means an extensive kingdom, and *bryten-grund* the wide expanse of the earth, so too does *bryten-cyning* mean a king whose authority was widely extended. On these analogies, *brytenwealda* would mean simply "wide ruler," without any necessary implication that his rule was regarded as extending throughout Britain.[52] Unfortunately, it seems impossible to decide which form of the word was originally intended by the chronicler: the Parker manuscript may be the oldest surviving manuscript, but it is not the original, and its readings are not always the best.[53] The chronicler may have given the (ambiguous) form *brytenwealda*, knowing what he intended, but leaving his readers to guess whether he meant "ruler of Britain" or "wide ruler," and one early copyist, understanding it in the former sense, may have written it as *bretwalda*. Or the chronicler may have given the (unambiguous) *bretwalda*, meaning "ruler of Britain," which another early copyist turned into *brytenwealda*, meaning the same thing, leaving his readers to divine whether he actually intended that, or "wide ruler." And if the earliest translators of the *Chronicle* into Latin clearly understood the word to signify a ruler of Britain,[54] the draftsman of a charter purportedly issued by King Æthelstan used it in a way that can only mean "wide ruler."[55]

So, what are we to make of the chronicler's list? There can be no doubt that King Ecgberht himself had a very good claim to be regarded as an overlord of all England south of the river Humber: he had defeated Beornwulf of Mercia at the battle of Ellendun in 825, thereby breaking Mercian control of the southeastern provinces and precipitating the submission to Ecgberht of Kent, Surrey, Sussex, and Essex; and he received the submission of East Anglia soon afterward, so that when from that position of strength he "conquered the kingdom of the Mercians," in 829, his political mastery south of the Humber was indeed complete.[56] It was a notable achievement, and one can well imagine that in this connection the chronicler suddenly remembered Bede's list of seven Southumbrian overlords (which of course he would have accepted at face value) and decided to add Ecgberht to their number, with the further explanation that he was "the eighth king who was Bretwalda." I do find it peculiar, however, that the copyists should have made such heavy weather of the chronicler's term, whatever it was, and no less peculiar that the term does not occur in any other source (apart from the spurious charter of King Æthelstan just mentioned—the begetter of which probably lifted it straight from the *Chronicle*); and I am inclined to infer that the term was not generally familiar to the Anglo-Saxons outside the context of this particular annal in the *Chronicle*. Indeed, I suspect that it may even have been coined by the chronicler himself, as his way of expressing in the vernacular what he understood to have been the position enjoyed by the kings in Bede's list, and that while, not unnaturally, he chose a term answering to Bede's conception of Edwin and Oswald (kings of Britain by virtue of combining the Southumbrian overlordship with their own Northumbrian sway), it was a term hardly appropriate to the earlier kings in the list and one unlikely to have had any currency among their own peoples. I should add that by tacking Ecgberht on to the end of Bede's list, the chronicler has in fact done Ecgberht a disservice: for Ecgberht represented not the *last* of Bede's series of overlords, whose credentials as such are questionable, but the *first* of a quite different line—the West Saxon kings, whose collective achievement would prove to be the political unification of England.

One need hardly say that by jumping directly from Oswiu, in the middle of the seventh century, to Ecgberht, in the first half of the ninth, the West Saxon chronicler seems to be cocking a snook at the succession of Mercian overlords in the intervening period: Wulfhere, Æthelbald, Offa, and Cenwulf. Æthelbald, for one, had been styled *rex Britanniae* in at least one of his charters,[57] and Offa had been described as *rex et decus Britanniae*;[58] it could be argued, on this evidence, that these eighth-century Mercian overlords were known to their contemporaries as kings of Britain and might even have been hailed in the mead-halls as Bretwaldas. The omission of the Mercian "Bretwaldas" might then be attributed to anti-Mercian bias on the part of the West Saxon chronicler or written off as the "mistake of an unintelligent annalist."[59] Yet neither explanation is satisfactory, for "anti-Mercian bias" is not something we should necessarily expect to find at the court of Alfred the Great,[60] and the chronicler himself was certainly no fool. One might prefer to argue, therefore, that the supremacy of the eighth-and early ninth-century Mercian kings, though undoubtedly more tangible than anything seen before, was deemed to be unlike that exercised by Bede's overlords,[61] or not as wide-ranging as that established by Ecgberht. It would, however, be a good deal more convincing to explain the "omission" of the Mercians in simpler terms. It was not that they were being deliberately omitted, as if they had a right to be included in the first place. Rather, the chronicler was honoring the achievements of his own West Saxon hero and to that end appropriated Bede's list of Southumbrian overlords: it was an act of literary plagiarism, not a considered historical statement, and as such the question of the inclusion or omission of the Mercian overlords never arose.

It was, however, a long time before the concept of the Bretwalda began to make a significant impression on the historiography of Anglo-Saxon England. Henry of Huntingdon, in the early twelfth century, was one of several medieval historians who picked up the list of kings from Bede and the *Chronicle*, and he stands out among those who did so by adding two more to their number, namely Alfred and Edgar;[62] but the chronicler's term "Bretwalda" (or "Brytenwealda") found no takers at this stage, and Henry himself seems to have been more interested in expounding his own quite independent vision of early Anglo-Saxon history in terms of the seven kingdoms of Kent, Wessex, Essex, Sussex, East Anglia, Mercia, and Northumbria,[63] thereby introducing the concept of political organization that in one form or another was to dominate subsequent historiography[64] and that by the end of the sixteenth century had come to be known as the Heptarchy.[65] The concept developed into one of seven kingdoms, each with its own political hierarchy but governed collectively by a "General Assembly," where matters of common interest were decided and where from time to time (as need arose) a single king from among the seven was elected to lead them all;[66] so when the term "Bretwalda" was introduced into common historical parlance,[67] apparently toward the end of the eighteenth century, it was greeted by an impressive constitutional apparatus derived from an essentially different (and wholly specious) historiographical tradition.

The term itself was generally understood by historians to mean nothing less than "ruler of Britain," and, removed from its proper context in the *Chronicle*, it began to take control of their minds. The term seems at once to crystallize, to institutionalize, and to extend the rather general formulation found in Bede (that these kings held an *imperium* that involved authority over the kingdoms south of the Humber). Moreover, when thus interpreted as a title, it seems also to imply that the position was a recognized office among the Anglo-Saxons, which existed independently of those who held it: the form of the chronicler's list, shorn of any explanatory comments, creates the impression that it represented a record of the succession to the office in question, and the fact that the office existed could be taken to imply that the Anglo-Saxons aspired to reconstitute the unity of Britain and watched as their kings vied with one another to gain the appointment. In short, the trap had been laid.

Initially, it was suggested (by Sharon Turner) that the Bretwalda was the leader of the Anglo-Saxon kingdoms against the Britons, "a species of Agamemnon against the common enemy," with little said about the nature or origin of the position.[68] It was not long, however, before Sir Francis Palgrave propounded the notion that the Bretwalda represented nothing less than the imitation of Roman imperial authority in Britain, the idea being that he was elected at the General Assembly of the seven kings of the Heptarchy to hold office as emperor of Britain, was then invested with the imperial decorations of the Roman state, and thereafter strutted around like a latter-day Julius Caesar.[69] The great Anglo-Saxonist, John Mitchell Kemble, rose to the challenge, arguing at length that the supremacy of the so-called Bretwalda was "a mere fluctuating superiority," "a mere accidental predominance": he put it down to the "ingenuity of modern scholars" and declared that "the development of all the Anglo-Saxon kingdoms was of far too independent and fortuitous a character for us to assume any general concert among them."[70] Kemble was, however, a voice in the wilderness, and a belief in Bretwaldas was soon reaffirmed by Edward Augustus Freeman: for him, the "Bretwaldadom" was "a real supremacy of some kind," but "something of purely English growth, something in no way connected with, or derived from, any older Welsh or Roman dominion."[71]

For a while at least, this heartfelt appeal to the Englishness of our national institutions found favor in high quarters. H. M. Chadwick judiciously refrained from making any capital out of the title Bretwalda, but he was inclined nonetheless to give credence to the supremacy implicit in Bede's list of seven kings: he imagined that what he calls "such a project as the invasion of Britain" was carried out by confederations of different peoples under a supreme king, and when the supremacy that thus originated in the Heroic Age of the migrations emerged into the historical period, it was "a far more tangible thing than has generally been supposed," conveying upon its holders certain rights over the lands of dependent kingdoms, including the taking of tribute and hostages.[72] Sir Frank Stenton's position was fundamentally the same, though he was bold enough to bring back the Bretwalda as "the English title applied to these outstanding kings." The term was not, in his view, "a formal style, accurately expressing the position of the bearer"; rather, "it belongs to the sphere of encomiastic poetry, and its origin should be sought in the hall of some early king, like Ælle or Ceawlin, whose victories entitled him, in that uncritical atmosphere, to be regarded as lord of Britain." What it conveyed was "clearly a defiance of British chiefs rather than the assertion of a claim to lordship over them," harking back to a time when the head of a confederacy of the southern English peoples had been "overrunning southern Britain in the years before the battle of Mons Badonicus."[73] More recently, Eric John has suggested that *brytenwealda* (in its sense "wide ruler") was the title of an office conceived by the earliest Anglo-Saxons in their desire not to be outdone by the aspirations of their Celtic neighbors to revive the imperial prestige of Roman Britain, and that when Bede restricted his list of such English overlords to just seven of their number, he did so as an intended *riposte* to an indigenous tradition of seven British emperors, later to surface in the *Historia Brittonum*.[74] But others have preferred to push the other way. In her survey of the vocabulary of Anglo-Saxon overlordship, Barbara Yorke has rightly emphasized how slight is the evidence that "either *bretwalda* or *brytenwalda* was commonly applied in the ninth century to those who controlled all the kingdoms south of the Humber,"[75] and Patrick Wormald has challenged the view, which appears to be implicit in the writings of Stenton and others, that the overlordships created in the early Anglo-Saxon period in some sense prepared the way for the political unification of England, tracing the origins of English unity back to quite different roots.[76] Both are moving in the right direction, but to my mind neither goes quite far enough: in the one case, it is not the reality of the Southumbrian overlordship that is under attack, but simply the terminology used to describe it, and in the other, it is not the existence of Bretwaldas that is called into question (indeed, their number is increased by the addition of the Mercian overlords), but the precise nature of their power and their particular role in relation to a grand historical issue.[77] Perhaps the time has come to Ban the Bretwalda altogether, though I know one would have about as much hope of success as those who would Ban the Bomb.

I have dwelt on the fortunes of the Bretwalda in modern historiography in the belief that it is always helpful to trace the views that have shaped received traditions and assumptions, and also in the belief that to describe the variety of interpretations is in this case the most effective way of exposing the slender foundations on which they all depend. I would argue that Bede's list of seven kings who held *imperium* over the Southumbrian kingdoms arose from the exercise of his own judgment as a historian and has little validity outside the context of his *Ecclesiastical History*; all of the kings may have been important figures in their different ways, and they were certainly important to Bede, but I cannot help feeling that we are being asked to swallow too much. The Anglo-Saxon chronicler, in the late ninth century, was simply the first of many to take the list out of its proper context: he resuscitated it in his desire to give Ecgberht his due, but by suppressing all of Bede's careful qualifications, and above all by introducing the title Bretwalda, he effectively transformed Bede's list into something quite different from what it had originally been. The modern tendency has been to take the term "Bretwalda" out of *its* proper context in the *Anglo-Saxon Chronicle*, to apply it retroactively not only to the seven kings in Bede's list, but also to the other overlords whom Bede and the chronicler appeared to "omit," and then to interpret early Anglo-Saxon history in terms of kings vying for the Bretwaldaship or exercising the rights of the Bretwalda.[78] Of course, there could be no objection to a belief in overlords, of one kind or another, as long as one recognizes that the kings who successively managed to establish such overlordships did so by virtue of their own separate efforts and exercised their power in their own separate ways; what should be resisted is the use of such phrases as "Bede's list of Bretwaldas,"[79] when there was no such thing, and the assumption that the overlords had a collective identity as successive holders of a status or office that was recognized as such by their contemporaries, that existed independently of themselves, and that gave them particular powers and privileges. Yet through no fault of its own, it is Sutton Hoo that has given the Bretwalda a new lease of life: not only is Mound 1 regarded as the burial of Rædwald "the Bretwalda," and the whole deposit as a tangible demonstration of the Bretwalda's power, but the remarkable "scepter" is interpreted as the very "symbol of the Bretwaldaship," buried with Rædwald because it represented his personal achievement, which could not be transmitted to his successors in East Anglia.[80] But just as we should respect the integrity of Bede's *Ecclesiastical History* and just as we should pay heed to the natural sympathies of the West Saxon chronicler, so too should we allow Sutton Hoo to speak with its own most eloquent voice: if we should abandon the idea that the scepter was a Bretwalda's magic wand, it remains nonetheless "a unique, savage thing,"[81] which in its own way can suggest much about the nature of early Anglo-Saxon kingship.

Notes

1. See Rupert Bruce-Mitford, "Who Was He?," in *The Sutton Hoo Ship-Burial*, with contributions by Paul Ashbee et al., 3 vols. in 4 (London, 1975-83), 1:683-717 (hereafter cited as *SH*); the items regarded as regalia are discussed in 2:311-93 (the whetstone-scepter), 394-402 (the wood, bone, or ivory rod), 403-31 (the iron stand), and 432-625 (the gold jewelry).

2. The case for Sigeberht in particular is worth consideration; see Ian N. Wood, *The Merovingian North Sea*, Occasional Papers on Medieval Topics 1 (Alingsås, 1983), p. 14, and idem, "The Franks and Sutton Hoo," in *People and Places in Northern Europe, 500-1600*, ed. Ian Wood and Niels Lund (Woodbridge, 1991), pp. 1-14. Sigeberht's connections with Francia would readily account for the special selection of coins in the purse, and since the nature of a burial is testimony of the esteem in which the person buried was held by his subjects, as opposed to a reflection of the religious beliefs of the buried person himself, it is more to the point that Sigeberht died at the head of the East Anglian army than that he had previously retired to a monastery. See Bede, *Historia ecclesiastica gentis Anglorum* 3.18 (hereafter cited as *HE*), in *Bede's Ecclesiastical History of the English People*, ed. Bertram Colgrave and R. A. B. Mynors (Oxford, 1969), pp. 268-69.

3. *HE* 2.15, pp. 190-91. For discussion of the East Anglian dynasty, see F. M. Stenton, "The East Anglian Kings of the Seventh Century," reprinted in *Preparatory to Anglo-Saxon England, Being the Collected Papers of Frank Merry Stenton*, ed. Doris Mary Stenton (Ox-

ford, 1970), pp. 394-402; and *SH* 1:693-96. For its alleged Swedish connections, see J. L. N. O'Loughlin, "Sutton Hoo—The Evidence of the Documents," *Medieval Archaeology* 8 (1964): 1-19.

4. *HE* 2.15, pp. 190-91; see also J. M. Wallace-Hadrill, *Bede's "Ecclesiastical History of the English People": A Historical Commentary* (Oxford, 1988), pp. 75-77 (hereafter cited as *Commentary*).

5. *HE* 3.18, pp. 266-67; see also *HE* 2.15, pp. 190-91, from which it emerges that Sigeberht had remained in exile during the lifetime of Rædwald's son and successor Eorpwald and (perhaps) for three years following Eorpwald's death.

6. *HE* 2.12, pp. 174-81; see also Monk of Whitby, *Vita S. Gregorii* 16, in *The Earliest Life of Gregory the Great by an Anonymous Monk of Whitby*, ed. Bertram Colgrave (Lawrence, Kans., 1968), pp. 98-101.

7. See *SH* 1:696-98. Anna, king of the East Angles, is said to have died in the nineteenth year of his reign (*Liber Eliensis*, ed. E. O. Blake, Camden 3rd ser., 92 [London, 1962], 1.7, p. 18). It is apparent from Bede that Anna was dead by 655, when his successor Æthelhere fought on Penda's side at the battle of Winwæd (*HE* 3.24, pp. 290-91, and 5.24, pp. 564-65), and the compilers of the *Anglo-Saxon Chronicle* placed his death in 654 (see also *Liber Eliensis* 1.7, p. 18); so it would follow that Anna's accession is to be dated 636/37. Bishop Felix died in the twelfth year of Anna's reign (*Liber Eliensis* 1.6, p. 17), which on this reckoning would be 647/48, and since Felix was bishop for seventeen years (*HE* 2.15, pp. 190-91, and 3.20, pp. 276-77) and had apparently come to East Anglia at the time of Sigeberht's accession (*HE* 2.15, pp. 190-91, and 3.18, pp. 268-69), it would follow that Sigeberht's accession is to be dated 630/31.

8. *HE* 2.15, pp. 190-91.

9. Roger of Wendover, *Flores Historiarum*, in *Rogeri de Wendover Chronica, sive Flores Historiarum*, ed. H. O. Coxe, 4 vols. (London, 1841-44), 1:124. The date seems to be in accordance with the apparent date of Sigeberht's accession (see above, n. 7), but Roger's authority is undermined by the fact that the other information he provides about the chronology of seventh-century East Anglian kings is demonstrably unreliable.

10. *HE* 2.5, pp. 148-51.

11. Gildas, *De excidio Britanniae*, chaps. 25-26, in *Gildas: The Ruin of Britain and Other Works*, ed. and trans. Michael Winterbottom (Chichester, 1978), pp. 27-28 and 98-99. See also H. Munro Chadwick, *The Origin of the English Nation* (Cambridge, 1907), pp. 14-15; and David N. Dumville, "The Chronology of *De Excidio Britanniae*, Book I," in *Gildas: New Approaches*, ed. Michael Lapidge and David Dumville, Studies in Celtic History 5 (Woodbridge, 1984), pp. 61-84, at pp. 76-78.

12. See *Baedae Opera Historica*, ed. J. E. King, 2 vols., Loeb Classical Library (London, 1930), 1:225; *English Historical Documents, c. 500-1042*, ed. Dorothy Whitelock, 2nd ed., English Historical Documents 1 (London, 1979), no. 151, p. 663; *Bede: A History of the English Church and People*, trans. Leo Sherley-Price (Harmondsworth, 1955), p. 106, revised by R. E. Latham (Harmondsworth, 1968), p. 107; and Colgrave and Mynors, *Bede's Ecclesiastical History* (see above, n. 2), p. 149. The translation derives, perhaps, from the note in *Venerabilis Baedae Opera Historica*, ed. Charles Plummer, 2 vols. (Oxford, 1896), 2:86, but it is also found in John Mitchell Kemble, *The Saxons in England: A History of the English Commonwealth till the Period of the Norman Conquest*, 2 vols. (London, 1849), 2:16.

13. Hanna Vollrath-Reichelt, *Königsgedanke und Königtum bei den Angelsachsen bis zur Mitte des 9. Jahrhunderts* (Cologne and Vienna, 1971), pp. 80-88.

14. See Patrick Wormald, "Bede, the *Bretwaldas* and the Origins of the *Gens Anglorum*," in *Ideal and Reality in Frankish and Anglo-Saxon Society: Studies Presented to J. M. Wallace-Hadrill*, ed. Patrick Wormald with Donald Bullough and Roger Collins (Oxford, 1983), pp. 99-129, at p. 106 n. 30 (citing Brooks); Nicholas Brooks, *The Early History of the Church of Canterbury: Christ Church from 597 to 1066* (Leicester, 1984), pp. 63 and 341; and Wallace-Hadrill, *Commentary*, p. 59. This translation appears to have been foreshad-

owed in *The Venerable Bede's Ecclesiastical History of England*, ed. J. A. Giles, 2nd ed., Bohn's Antiquarian Library (London, 1849), p. 76.

15. Thomas Charles-Edwards, in Wallace-Hadrill, *Commentary*, pp. 220-22; see also J. M. Wallace-Hadrill, *Early Germanic Kingship in England and on the Continent* (Oxford, 1971), pp. 31-32. This translation is adopted in *Bede: Ecclesiastical History of the English People with Bede's Letter to Egbert and Cuthbert's Letter on the Death of Bede*, trans. Leo Sherley-Price, revised by R. E. Latham and D. H. Farmer (Harmondsworth, 1990), p. 111.

16. In much the same way, our understanding of the circumstances surrounding one of the major battles in the seventh century depends on whether a splotch in an early manuscript of Bede's *Ecclesiastical History* is a punctuation mark or a splotch; see J. O. Prestwich, "King Æthelhere and the Battle of Winwæd," *English Historical Review* 83 (1968): 89-95; and Wallace-Hadrill, *Commentary*, p. 121.

17. Cf. J. N. L. Myres, *Anglo-Saxon Pottery and the Settlement of England* (Oxford, 1969), pp. 112-15 (and Map 8) and 116-19 (and Map 9), for an attempt to find tangible support for the supremacies of Ælle and Ceawlin in the archaeological record.

18. *HE* 1.25, pp. 72-73; *HE* 2.3, pp. 142-43; and *HE* 2.5, pp. 148-49.

19. *HE* 2.3, pp. 142-43. Of course, Æthelberht was married to Bertha, a Frankish princess (*HE* 1.25, pp. 72-75), which gives some indication of his standing in the eyes of those across the channel; also, it was with Æthelberht's "help" (whatever that may mean) that Augustine summoned the British bishops to a meeting at "Augustine's Oak," on the borders of the Hwicce and the West Saxons, presumably somewhere in Gloucestershire (*HE* 2.2, pp. 134-35), and Rædwald himself is said to have been "initiated into the mysteries of the Christian faith in Kent," presumably at the instigation of King Æthelberht (*HE* 2.15, pp. 188-89). See also Wallace-Hadrill, *Commentary*, pp. 32-33, 34, 52, 54-55, and 63-64.

20. *HE* 1.32, pp. 112-13; the letter is addressed to Æthelberht as "rex Anglorum."

21. *HE* 2.8 (Boniface to Justus), pp. 160-61, and 2.10 (Boniface to King Edwin), pp. 168-69. For the suggestion that the "Adulualdus rex" mentioned in the first of these letters was not Eadbald of Kent, but an otherwise unrecorded king called Æthelwald, see Peter Hunter Blair, "The Letters of Pope Boniface V and the Mission of Paulinus to Northumbria," in *England before the Conquest: Studies in Primary Sources Presented to Dorothy Whitelock*, ed. Peter Clemoes and Kathleen Hughes (Cambridge, 1971), pp. 5-13, at pp. 7-8; but cf. Wallace-Hadrill (and Charles-Edwards), *Commentary*, pp. 64-65 and 222.

22. *HE* 2.12, pp. 180-81.

23. *HE* 2.5, pp. 148-51.

24. *HE* 2.9, pp. 162-63.

25. *HE* 2.16, pp. 192-93.

26. *HE* 2.9, pp. 164-67; according to the "northern recension" of the *Anglo-Saxon Chronicle* (represented by MS. E), Edwin's expedition took place in 626 and resulted in the overthrow of five kings.

27. *HE* 2.9, pp. 162-63, perhaps accounting for the exclusion of Kent from the orbit of his alleged sway.

28. *HE* 2.15, pp. 188-89.

29. Adomnán, *Vita S. Columbae* 1.1, in *Adomnan's "Life of Columba"*, ed. Alan Orr Anderson and Margorie Ogilvie Anderson (London, 1961), pp. 200-201: "totius Brittanniae imperator a deo ordinatus est." For further discussion, see Francis J. Byrne, *The Rise of the Uí Néill and the High Kingship of Ireland* (Dublin, 1969); and Máire Herbert, *Iona, Kells, and Derry* (Oxford, 1988), pp. 41-42 and 144-45.

30. *HE* 3.6, pp. 230-31; and Wallace-Hadrill, *Commentary*, pp. 96 and 230-31. See also *HE* 3.3, pp. 220-21, with allusion to "those kingdoms of the English over which Oswald reigned."

31. *HE* 3.7, pp. 232-33. The king of Wessex was Cynegisl, and (according to a twelfth-century *Life* of St. Oswald) the daughter was called Cyneburh (*Vita S. Oswaldi*, chap. 11, in *Symeonis Monachi Opera Omnia*, ed. Thomas Arnold, 2 vols., Rolls Series [London, 1882-

85], 1: 349). It should be noted that on this evidence the marriage of one king to the daughter of another king does not necessarily indicate the "inferior" status of the son-in-law. Bede goes on to say that Cynegisl *and* Oswald gave Dorchester to Bishop Birinus, which is often regarded as a reflection of Oswald's power; but see Wallace-Hadrill, *Commentary*, pp. 98 and 231.

32. *HE* 4.14, pp. 378-79; see Wallace-Hadrill, *Commentary*, p. 155.

33. *HE* 2.20, pp. 204-5. The remark is not, however, necessarily indicative of Oswald's power in Kent: Æthelburh may simply have feared that King Eadbald of Kent would dispose of the children in order to curry favor with him.

34. *HE* 3.14, pp. 254-55.

35. *HE* 3.24, pp. 292-95.

36. According to Bede (*HE* 3.24, pp. 290-91), thirty *duces regii* were on Penda's side at the battle of Winwæd, one of whom was Æthelhere, king of East Anglia. The identity of at least some of the others may be suggested by the (Mercian) "Tribal Hidage," which includes the names of the various peoples (nearly thirty in number) who were known more generally as the "Mercians" or "Middle Angles." See David Dumville, "Essex, Middle Anglia, and the Expansion of Mercia in the South-East Midlands," in *The Origins of Anglo-Saxon Kingdoms*, ed. Steven Bassett (Leicester, 1989), pp. 123-40, at p. 129, and idem, "The Tribal Hidage: An Introduction to Its Texts and Their History," ibid., pp. 225-30. It should be noted, incidentally, that the version of the "Tribal Hidage" printed by Sir Henry Spelman in 1626, designated "Recension B" (ibid., p. 230), had in fact been printed in editions of William Camden's *Britannia* published from 1600 onward and in John Speed's *The Theatre of the Empire of Great Britaine* (London, 1611).

37. *HE* 3.24, pp. 294-95. See also Stephanus, *Vita S. Wilfridi* 20, in *The Life of Bishop Wilfrid by Eddius Stephanus*, ed. Bertram Colgrave (Cambridge, 1927), pp. 42-43, to the effect that Wulfhere "roused all the southern nations against our kingdom, intent not merely on fighting but on compelling them to pay tribute in a slavish spirit"; *HE* 3.30, pp. 322-23, for Wulfhere's control of Essex; and P. H. Sawyer, *Anglo-Saxon Charters: An Annotated List and Bibliography*, Royal Historical Society Guides and Handbooks 8 (London, 1968), no. 1165 (trans. *English Historical Documents*, ed. Whitelock, no. 54), for other "subkings" under his control.

38. *HE* 3.21, pp. 278-79, and 3.22, pp. 280-83; see also Wallace-Hadrill, *Commentary*, p. 118.

39. *HE* 3.29, pp. 318-19 (and Colgrave's note, p. 318 n. 1).

40. See Brooks, *Early History of the Church of Canterbury*, pp. 69-70; and Wallace-Hadrill, *Commentary*, pp. 133-34.

41. See *HE* 5.23, pp. 558-59; see also F. M. Stenton, *Anglo-Saxon England*, 3rd ed. (Oxford, 1971), pp. 203-5; and Wallace-Hadrill, *Commentary*, pp. 199-200.

42. See, e.g., *HE* 3.20, pp. 276-79; 3.24, pp. 292-93; 4.5, pp. 352-55; and 4.12, pp. 368-71.

43. Monk of Whitby, *Vita S. Gregorii* 12, pp. 94-95.

44. The views expressed by Colgrave (*Earliest Life of Gregory*, pp. 56-59; see also "The Earliest Saints' Lives Written in England," *Proceedings of the British Academy* 44 [1958]: 35-60, at 49-51) remain influential, but the view that Bede did know the *Life*, expressed by Plummer (*Venerabilis Baedae Opera Historica* 2:389-91), among others, has been revived from time to time, most recently and effectively by Walter Goffart, *The Narrators of Barbarian History* (A.D. 550-800): *Jordanes, Gregory of Tours, Bede, and Paul the Deacon* (Princeton, 1988), pp. 264-67 and 303-6. Cf. Wallace-Hadrill, *Commentary*, p. 122.

45. Others would argue that the list of kings reached Bede from Canterbury: see Patrick Wormald, "The Age of Bede and Aethelbald," in *The Anglo-Saxons*, ed. James Campbell (Oxford, 1982), pp. 70-100, at pp. 99-100; Wood, *Merovingian North Sea*, p. 14; and Wallace-Hadrill, *Commentary*, pp. 58-59.

46. Bede's consciousness of the "hierarchies of kings and relativities of kingliness" is well demonstrated by James Campbell, "Bede's *Reges* and *Principes*," reprinted in his *Essays*

in Anglo-Saxon History (London, 1986), pp. 85-98, at pp. 90-92. There may be other ways of looking at the list. It has been suggested, for example, that the *imperium* that Bede credited to Edwin and Oswald (and to the other kings in the list) conveyed a sense of good rule and concern for a people's religion, contrasting the tyranny of the five rulers castigated by Gildas and the tyranny of Cadwallon as represented by Bede; see Thomas Charles-Edwards, "Bede, the Irish and the Britons," *Celtica* 15 (1983): 42-52. But on Bede's (apparently interchangeable) use of *regnum* and *imperium*, see B. A. E. Yorke, "The Vocabulary of Anglo-Saxon Overlordship," *Anglo-Saxon Studies in Archaeology and History* 2, British Archaeological Reports, British Series 92 (Oxford, 1981): 171-200, at 175-76; and Judith McClure, "Bede's Old Testament Kings," in *Ideal and Reality*, ed. Wormald, pp. 76-98, at pp. 97-98.

47. It might be thought that Bede restricted (or extended) his list to seven kings because he was conscious of the symbolic properties of the number seven in classical and in Christian tradition, but if so, it would have to be said that he did not make much of the point.

48. *HE* (OE) 2.5, in *The Old English Version of Bede's Ecclesiastical History of the English People*, ed. Thomas Miller, 4 parts, Early English Text Society, original series 95-96 and 110-11 (London, 1890-98), 1, part 1: 108-11.

49. *Anglo-Saxon Chronicle*, s.a. 827 (for 829); see *Two of the Saxon Chronicles Parallel*, ed. Charles Plummer, 2 vols. (Oxford, 1892-99), 1:60-61 (text); and *English Historical Documents*, ed. Whitelock, no. 1, p. 186 (translation).

50. Cf. Wormald, in *The Anglo-Saxons*, ed. Campbell, p. 139.

51. The derivation of *bryten* from the verb *breotan* was asserted by Kemble, *Saxons in England* 2:20-21; see also *An Anglo-Saxon Dictionary*, ed. T. Northcote Toller (Oxford, 1898), p. 131. But according to the (original) editors of the OED, "Kemble's conjectured derivation of *bryten* from *breotan* 'to break' is etymologically impossible; and there can be little doubt that, even in the poetic compounds, the word is simply a poetic use of *Bryten, Breoten, Britannia*" (*The Oxford English Dictionary*, 2nd ed., prepared by J. A. Simpson and E. S. C. Weiner, 20 vols. [Oxford, 1989], 2:532); see also F. Holthausen, *Altenglisches etymologisches Wörterbuch* (Heidelberg, 1934), p. 34.

52. It has been suggested that the phrase *bredun giwald* in the Old Saxon poem *Heliand*, used to describe the emperor Augustus's *imperium*, is cognate with *brytenwealda* and that the term, in the sense "wide ruler," was therefore "an ancient one in Germanic linguistic history" (see Eric John, *Orbis Britanniae and Other Studies* [Leicester, 1966], pp. 7-8), but D. H. Green advises me that there is no etymological or semantic connection between *bredun giwald* and *brytenwealda*.

53. See *The Anglo-Saxon Chronicle, MS. A*, ed. Janet M. Bately, vol. 3 of *The Anglo-Saxon Chronicle*, ed. David Dumville and Simon Keynes (Cambridge, 1986), p. cxvii n. 332; for further discussion of the form in the Parker manuscript, see D. N. Dumville, "The Terminology of Overkingship in Early Anglo-Saxon England" (forthcoming).

54. Æthelweard, *Chronicon* 3.3, in *The Chronicle of Æthelweard*, ed. A. Campbell (Edinburgh, 1962), p. 29: Ecgberht was "the eighth king who was masterful in his power in Britain" (*octauus rex qui in Brittannia fuerat pollens potestate*). See also *Anglo-Saxon Chronicle, MS. F*, in *Two Chronicles*, ed. Plummer, 1:61 n. 3: Ecgberht was "the eighth king who ruled Britain" (*octauus rex qui rexit Bryttanniam*). For the rulership of "Britain" in Anglo-Saxon England, see H. R. Loyn, *The "Matter of Britain": A Historian's Perspective*, Creighton Trust Lecture 1988 (London, 1989), pp. 2-3; see also Simon Keynes, "The Conception and Unification of Britain," *Times Higher Education Supplement*, 22 February 1985, p. 15.

55. Sawyer, *Anglo-Saxon Charters*, no. 427: King Æthelstan is styled (in the Latin text) "Angul Saxonum necnon et totius Brittanniæ rex" and (in the vernacular text) "Ongol Saxna cyning and bryten walda ealles þyses iglandæs."

56. A group of (spurious) charters preserved in the cartulary of the Old Minster, Winchester, are dated 826, in the twenty-fourth year of Ecgberht's reign and the fourteenth year of his *ducatus*, but it is quite uncertain what event, ca. 812, is implied by this formulation.

See Sawyer, *Anglo-Saxon Charters*, nos. 272, 275, and 276; see also Heather Edwards, *The Charters of the Early West Saxon Kingdom*, British Archaeological Reports, British Series 198 (Oxford, 1988), pp. 147-48.

57. Sawyer, *Anglo-Saxon Charters*, no. 89 (trans. *English Historical Documents*, ed. Whitelock, no. 67): Æthelbald is "king of the South English" in the text and "king of Britain" in the witness list. See F. M. Stenton, "The Supremacy of the Mercian Kings," in *Preparatory to Anglo-Saxon England*, ed. F. M. Stenton, pp. 48-66, at pp. 53-56, and idem, *Anglo-Saxon England*, 3rd ed. (Oxford, 1971), pp. 34 and 203 (where *rex Britanniae* is regarded as a "Latin rendering of the English title *Bretwalda*"). The combination of styles in the charter appears to support the notion that a Southumbrian overlord could be regarded as a ruler of Britain (and that the chronicler's use of "bretwalda" is thus not so inappropriate to the non-Northumbrians in the list), but it is more likely that, given an inch, the Mercian draftsman of the charter (in 736) has taken a mile, perhaps on a flight of fancy inspired by Bede (731). There is not sufficient evidence of the style "rex Britanniae" outside the context of this charter to suggest its general currency beside the normal "rex Merciorum."

58. Sawyer, *Anglo-Saxon Charters*, no. 155 (trans. *English Historical Documents*, ed. Whitelock, no. 80), a charter of Cenwulf of Mercia, preserved at Christ Church Canterbury. In a letter to Offa, Alcuin described him as the "glory of Britain" (*Epistolae Karolini Aevi* II, ed. Ernest Dümmler, *Monumenta Germaniae Historica, Epistolae* 4 [Berlin, 1895], no. 64; trans. *English Historical Documents*, ed. Whitelock, no. 195). In both cases, the terminology is perhaps no more than standard hyperbole.

59. See Stenton, "Supremacy of the Mercian Kings," pp. 48-49; see also Stenton, *Anglo-Saxon England*, p. 34.

60. See Simon Keynes, "King Alfred and the Mercians," in *Kings, Currency, and Alliances*, ed. Mark Blackburn and David Dumville (Woodbridge, 1991). It might be thought more difficult to explain why the chroniclers did not make a point of including the Mercians than to explain why they left them out.

61. H. R. Loyn, *The Governance of Anglo-Saxon England, 500-1087* (London, 1984), pp. 24-28, points out that eighth-century Mercian overlordship was quite different from the overlordships of the seventh century and suggests that the chronicler may have had this in mind when he excluded them from his own list.

62. Henry of Huntingdon, *Historia Anglorum* 2.23, in *Henrici Archidiaconi Huntendunensis Historia Anglorum*, ed. Thomas Arnold, Rolls Series (London, 1879), pp. 51-52 (introduced in connection with the accession of King Æthelberht).

63. *Historia Anglorum* 1.4, pp. 8-9: "Quando autem Saxones hanc terram sibi subjugaverunt, reges septem statuerunt, regnisque nomina pro libitu imposuerunt," naming the seven. See also *Historia Anglorum* 2.40, pp. 64-66. In Henry's scheme, the several kingdoms persisted until the time of Ecgberht of Wessex, who was "rex et monarcha Brittanniæ" (*Historia Anglorum* 4.30, pp. 133-34). Neither William of Malmesbury nor John of Worcester had seen early Anglo-Saxon history in terms of seven kingdoms. The former refers to the four powerful kingdoms of Kent, Wessex, Northumbria, and Mercia (*Gesta Regum*, Prol., in *Willelmi Malmesbiriensis Monachi De Gestis Regum Anglorum Libri Quinque*, 2 vols., ed. William Stubbs, Rolls Series [London, 1887-89], 1:2), until their consolidation into one by King Ecgberht. See also James Campbell, "Some Twelfth-Century Views of the Anglo-Saxon Past," reprinted in his *Essays on Anglo-Saxon History*, pp. 209-28, at p. 213.

64. A slightly different scheme occurs in the *Libellus de primo Saxonum vel Normannorum adventu, sive de eorundem regibus* (in *Symeonis Monachi Opera Omnia*, ed. Arnold, 2:365-84), tracing the descent of royal dynasties from the sons of Woden, treating the various kingdoms in turn (with no fixed sense of their number) and regarding Æthelstan as the first monarch of all England. A variant of this scheme is given by Roger of Wendover, *Flores Historiarum*, ed. Coxe, 1:345-49, in which Woden's "seven" sons gave rise to the dynasties of seven kingdoms (not, however, including the South Saxons) and in which King Alfred is seen as the first sole monarch (from 886). Roger's scheme was tidied up by Matthew

Paris and represented by him in diagrammatic form: see Suzanne Lewis, *The Art of Matthew Paris in the Chronica Majora* (London, 1987), pp. 166 (fig. 93) and 169 (fig. 96).

65. One of the first appearances of the term "Heptarchy" (in its Anglo-Saxon context) is in a (Latin) note accompanying a map of the seven kingdoms in William Lambarde's *Archaionomia* (London, 1568); an expanded version of the note (in English) accompanied a more elaborate form of the map in Lambarde's *A Perambulation of Kent* (London, 1576); see also Retha M. Warnicke, *William Lambarde: Elizabethan Antiquary, 1536-1601* (Chichester, 1973), plate 2, showing the map and the note in the autograph manuscript of the *Perambulation of Kent*. William Camden, *Britannia* (London, 1586), p. 48, cited Bede, *HE* 2.5, as evidence that in the Heptarchy there was always a Monarchy, and in his view, it was Ecgberht who "commanded by an Edict and Proclamation, that the Heptarchie which the Saxons held, should be called Englelond, that is, England" (*Britain* [London, 1610], p. 138).

66. See, e.g., Rapin de Thoyras, *The History of England*, trans. N. Tindal, 2 vols., 2nd ed. (London, 1732), 1:148 and 152-53. This work was first published in French (De Rapin Thoyras, *Histoire d'Angleterre*, 2 vols. [The Hague, 1724]), and it includes two relevant engravings: one depicting three Anglian kings rendering homage to King Ecgberht as head of the Heptarchy (1:277 in the French edition of 1724; 1:82 in the English edition of 1732), and the other depicting the council, or general assembly, of the Heptarchy (1:475 in the French edition; 1:147 in the English edition), in which (as Kemble put it) "the president, Monarch or Bretwalda, is very amusingly made larger and more ferocious than the rest, to express his superior dignity" (*Saxons in England* 2:10 n. 1).

67. The term had been avoided by the earliest editors and translators of the *Chronicle*, who rendered the operative phrase as follows: "regum autem qui Britannos devicerunt, octavus fuit" (Abraham Wheloc, 1643); "is autem fuit octavus Rex, qui toti Britanniæ imperavit" (Edmund Gibson, 1692); "being the eighth king who was sovereign of all the British dominions" (James Ingram, 1823). Thereafter, it was treated as a title: "and he was the eighth king who was Bret-walda" (Richard Price, 1848); "and he was the eighth king who was Brytenwalda" (Benjamin Thorpe, 1861).

68. Sharon Turner, *The History of the Anglo-Saxons, from the Earliest Period to the Norman Conquest*, 3 vols., 7th ed. (London, 1852; first published in 1799-1805), 1:283 and 326.

69. See Francis Palgrave, *The Rise and Progress of the English Commonwealth*, 2 vols. (London, 1832), 1:279, 429, 562-67, and 636; see also his *History of the Anglo-Saxons*, new ed. (London, 1876), pp. 63-83.

70. Kemble, *Saxons in England* 2:8-22.

71. Edward A. Freeman, *The History of the Norman Conquest of England, Its Causes and Its Results*, vol. 1, 2nd ed. (Oxford, 1870), pp. 542-47.

72. Chadwick, *Origin of the English Nation*, pp. 12-15 and 181-85.

73. Stenton, *Anglo-Saxon England*, pp. 33-35.

74. John, *Orbis Britanniae*, pp. 6-13, esp. pp. 12-13; for the Celtic tradition, see *Historia Brittonum* 20-27, in *Nennius, British History, and the Welsh Annals*, ed. and trans. John Morris (Chichester, 1980), pp. 64-65 and 23-25. Cf. Wallace-Hadrill, *Early Germanic Kingship*, pp. 22 and 109-10, and idem, *Commentary*, p. 58.

75. Yorke, "Vocabulary of Anglo-Saxon Overlordship," pp. 171-75 and 195-96.

76. Wormald, "Bede, the *Bretwaldas*, and the Origins of the *Gens Anglorum*," esp. pp. 104-19. Stenton said of the seventh-and eighth-century "confederacies" that "no other institution did so much to prepare the way for the ultimate unity of England" (*Anglo-Saxon England*, p. 36; see also pp. 202 and 211), but it is not clear how far he would have pressed the point.

77. For further reflections on Bretwaldas, see Wormald in *The Anglo-Saxons*, ed. Campbell, pp. 73, 99-100, 139, and 155.

78. See, e.g., Cyril Hart, "The Tribal Hidage," *Transactions of the Royal Historical Society*, 5th ser., 21 (1971), 133-57; and Henry Mayr-Harting, *The Coming of Christianity to Anglo-Saxon England* (London, 1972), pp. 18-21, 60-61, 64-65, and 99. I cannot forbear to

mention André Crépin's light-hearted attempt to render the list of Bretwaldas into Old English verse, beginning "Hwæt we Bretwealda" ("Bede and the Vernacular," *Famulus Christi: Essays in Commemoration of the Thirteenth Centenary of the Birth of the Venerable Bede,* ed. Gerald Bonner [London, 1976], pp. 170-92, at pp. 174-75).

79. See, e.g., Colgrave and Mynors, *Bede's Ecclesiastical Hisotry,* pp. 162 n. 1, and p. 322 n. 3; Wormald, in *The Anglo-Saxons,* ed. Campbell, pp. 99 and 139; and Wallace-Hadrill, *Commentary,* p. 10.

80. *SH* 1:689-90, 699-700, 715-17; *SH* 2:375-77. For further discussion, see, e.g., Michael J. Enright, "The Sutton Hoo Whetstone Sceptre: A Study in Iconography and Cultural Milieu," *Anglo-Saxon England* 11 (1983): 119-34; and Carol L. Neuman de Vegvar, "The Iconography of Kingship in Anglo-Saxon Archaeological Finds," in *Kings and Kingship,* ed. Joel Rosenthal, *Acta* 11 (1986 for 1984): 1-15. Angela Care Evans, *The Sutton Hoo Ship Burial* (London, 1986), pp. 83-93 and 107-10, is commendably restrained.

81. T. D. Kendrick, "Other Finds," in *British Museum Quarterly* 13 (1939): 128-31, at 128.

CHAPTER 8

✦

Sidereal Time in Anglo-Saxon England

Wesley M. Stevens

From the manuscripts and the fragmentary materials that survive, it is possible to recognize the active scientific labors of Scots of Ireland, Britons of Wales and Cornwall, Saxons of Wessex, and Angles of Northumbria. These evidences of intellectual activities show that they were not merely occasional concerns or literary allusions. They are arithmetical calculations, geometric models of heaven and earth, complicated *argumenta* about solar and lunar cycles. The study of natural phenomena and the reckoning of their relationships were necessary for the organized life and the social relations of Christians in the British Isles, and those studies have left many manuscripts from the Anglo-Saxon period, especially medical, computistical, and astronomical tracts and tables. In this discussion the emphasis will be upon *computus* and astronomy. [1]

Some of these scientific materials survive because of Benedict Biscop's five or six trips to the markets of Gaul and of Italy and his fortunate return each time with another load of books for libraries of Wearmouth and Jarrow.[2] Other works survive because quite a few Franks and Scots visited each others' schools and traveled to Angle and Saxon schoolmasters. Aldhelm and Bede each knew students who had traveled for study to Ireland,[3] and books certainly moved in both directions along the same routes and may have been exchanged by the same persons. Almost all of the computistical sources used by Bede have been identified, and they are extremely diverse and of no single origin.[4] These and many other computistical materials known and used from the seventh through the eleventh centuries in Anglo-Saxon schools will allow a broad assessment of scientific labors in all parts of England, from which the particular study of lunar and solar cycles will permit us to identify sidereal time as a new theoretical development in astronomy prior to introduction of the astrolabe.

Computus up to the Age of Bede

In England the reckoning of dates did not begin with Bede. He was taught the Scriptures by Trumberht and probably learned *computus* from Ceolfrith, whose letter about 706 to Nechtan IV, king of the Picts,[5] explained the new Easter reckoning that had been accepted in Northumbria—

gradually by some, grudgingly by others. There were at least four computistical systems represented in 664 at the famous Synod before King
Oswiu, his son Alchfrith, king of Deira, and their host the noble abbess
Hild of Streanæshalch (Whitby).[6] Spokesmen for the different Easter tables and *computi* were the Irish Colman, the Frank Acgilbert, and the Angle Wilfrid. When the teachings of each of the three learned men are put
into their particular contexts, a rather complicated picture of scientific
knowledge emerges for their several schools.

Colman was a monk of Iona before becoming bishop of Northumbria
(661?-64) with his seat on the Lindisfarne. At Whitby he presented the
case for a *Canon paschalis* that dated the series of Easter Sundays by not-
ing the full moon nearest vernal equinox within the limits of that
month's *luna* XIV-XX (the days of the lunar month were calculated from
the first appearance of the crescent of the new moon); and the equinox
was taken to be March 21, though earlier it had been March 25 therein, as
Bede detected. The *Canon* (referred to below as the "pseudo-Anatolian
system") elaborated a table of eighty-four years and was thought to be in
accord with teachings of Anatolius, supposed by Colman to have been a
disciple of the apostle John. The actual Anatolius had been a teacher in
Alexandria and became bishop of Laodicea (269-80).[7] Colman's practice
had been brought to Northumbria from Iona by Aidan and was known
also in parts of northern Ireland, Scotland, and Wales. Other Irish centers
nevertheless were using the Alexandrian or the relatively similar Victurian paschal tables.[8]

Another notable personage in the presence of King Oswiu, Alchfrith,
and Hild at Whitby was Acgilbert, who wielded considerable influence.
Acgilbert had been raised in a noble Frankish household in Gaul near
Soissons before coming about 635-40 to study in southern Ireland, possibly at Ráth Maélsigi. We lose track of him for ten years, but during some
part of the period from 650 to 664 he served as a bishop in Wessex (wandering without a seat?) and later as a bishop in Paris from 667/68 until his
death about 680. Though his life and pastoral concerns were completed in
Paris, this bishop helped his cousin Adon to found the abbey of Jouarre
near Fleury and Orléans about 635, and his sister Teodechildis was abbess
of Jouarre, where Acgilbert was buried. Furthermore, his cousin Adon or
Audoenus (St. Ouen) was bishop of Rouen, and his nephew Leuthere succeeded him as bishop of Wessex.[9] Many tracts and tables were available to
a Frankish bishop with such wide-ranging experience on the Continent,
southern Ireland, and southern England. But what Easter table did this
family and this bishop use?

It should be assumed that Acgilbert's Easter practices were in accord
with his circumstances, unless there is supporting evidence to the contrary. But what were these circumstances? During the sixth and seventh
centuries some Frankish bishops in council had accepted the explanations
and tables created about 457 by the calculator Victurius of Aquitaine,[10]

though by the eighth century several were trying out the Dionysian tables.[11] What the Frankish student could have studied at Ráth Maélsigi was the great diversity of computistical documents found in the Sirmond group of manuscripts, which contained many texts supporting the Alexandrian cycle and included selections from both Victurian and Dionysian applications of that nineteen-year cycle and their assumptions for coordinating lunar and solar cycles. But at the present there seems to be no evidence for Acgilbert's practice in any of the places he served. This is unfortunate, for it was he whom Oswiu addressed first and who deferred to Wilfrid at Whitby.

Wilfrid had been ordained priest by Acgilbert, and then after the Synod of Whitby he was sponsored by King Alchfrith of Deira, who sent him to Acgilbert for consecration as bishop of York, though he was never able to exercise that office. The views expressed by Wilfrid at Whitby on the dating of Easter had doubtless been rehearsed with Acgilbert before addressing the Synod. His argument was a good account of the basic Alexandrian terms of reference for a nineteen-year cycle with *luna* XIV-XXI as limits for the Easter moon, with the Resurrection celebrated on the Sunday following. Both Bede and the *Vita sancti Wilfridi* have also described how cleverly he trapped Colman into the unanswerable question of whether Peter holds the keys to the kingdom of heaven. Oswiu drew the conclusion, rather flippantly, that therefore the Roman bishop must surely know the right date for Easter, smiling as he did so, according to the author of the *Vita*.[12] But does any historian know what system was then used in Rome? About sixty years after Whitby, Bede could argue that the Dionysian system was best, with its eight columns of data for ninety-five years, lunar limits of XV-XXI for the Easter moon, and he could imply that it was this which Wilfrid had meant by his appeal to Rome. But that implication is hard to credit, when the evidence is assessed for the Roman practice at that time.

During the previous century Roman bishops were defending the use of the Victurian tables in Irish schools.[13] When Columbanus brought the Bangor *computus* to Gaul for use in his new foundations of Annegray, Luxeuil, and Bobbio, he found that the Frankish bishops expected him to follow the Victurian *computus*. He could object to Gregory the Great forcefully in 599/600 that his northern Irish school had tested the Victurian cycles and rejected them, but he was not going to receive any support from Rome.[14] A century later and over thirty-seven years after Whitby, Bede's friend Huaetbercte was probably one of those monks of Wearmouth and Jarrow who traveled to Rome and observed at Christmas 701 in St. Peter's Basilica that the great candle bore an inscription proclaiming the day not in terms of the Dionysian *aera Incarnationis* but in terms of an *aera Passionis*.[15] From the second to fifth centuries there were quartodeciman and other early forms of reckoning from the year of the Passion being used in Christian communities, but at the beginning of the eighth century such a practice in Rome probably required the system of Victurius, which observed *luna* XVI-XXII for the Easter moon during a ninety-five-year cycle.

Thus Acgilbert's withdrawal from the Whitby debate on grounds of inability to express himself in local language and Wilfrid's appeal to Rome may not be as informative as historians have hoped. These two must have agreed to oppose the pseudo-Anatolian system of the Irish Colman and to promote Alexandrian paschal usages, but that is not sufficient to inform us whether each one preferred (1) the Victurian tables prevalent in Gaul, (2) the Victurian form still considered viable in some schools of Ireland though rejected in Bangor, or (3) the Dionysian form then being studied in some schools of Gaul and southern Ireland and preferred in England by students of Bede, though possibly not yet either in Canterbury or Whitby.

Major differences between these four systems of computing—the pseudo-Anatolian, the Alexandrian nineteen-year cycle, and the Victurian and Dionysian systems based upon the Alexandrian cycle—were well known in Anglo-Saxon England, and they have been clarified by modern scholarship. Each was difficult and required long instruction and practice to understand. The choice between them cannot have been made on literary grounds. It is necessary to recognize many schools at work behind the personalities named at Whitby, each school or group with its own network of communications and influence. As Ceolfrith said to Nechtan, there was a crowd of calculators who "were able to continue the Easter cycles and keep the sequences of sun, moon, month, and week in the same order as before."[16]

That "crowd of calculators" for each paschal system had to be able to keep the bissextile or extra solar day every fourth year, a task that is actually not so easy to do as it sounds. They must know how and when to omit the one day for *saltus lunae* at the correct time during any nineteen-year cycle (and the *saltus* varies for each system) in order to keep a calendar in close accord with the actual course of sun and moon. Therefore they must know well how the sun moves relative to the stars and how the circle of the sun itself moves to extremes, the solstices, as that circle tilts about 23 1/2 degrees to the north and 23 1/2 degrees to the south of the celestial equator. They ought to be able to explain how the solar cycle twice annually passes a midpoint, the equinoxes, on each of which it may be observed anywhere on the face of the earth that the hours of light and the hours of darkness are the same. An understanding of Hellenistic astronomy as taught in Anglo-Saxon schools would allow anyone to travel safely for thousands of kilometers across continents of land or desert spaces of sea and to return home safely by other routes and without confusion.[17] At Jarrow a great monastic scholar could carefully observe, count, and measure the lunar cycle on the zodiacal scale and draw the relations between it and the mysterious motions of the sea to create a scientific theory of tides[18] that remains to this day the basis for British Admiralty Tide Tables, used by all harbor pilots in the world without acknowledging their debt to the work of the Venerable Bede.[19] These several paschal systems were each set within a broad range of Hellenistic science, and some of them brought forth new scientific knowledge of considerable significance.

The Need for Sidereal Reckoning

Yet another bit of ancient scientific research in astronomy from the schools of Anglo-Saxon England is the measurement of time, both synodical time and sidereal time. In the Hellenistic model of the heavens, lunar and solar cycles were usually correlated in terms of the number of solar days between recurring appearances of the moon above the earth's horizon. As the first sliver of the new moon may be observed sometimes after 29, sometimes after 30 days, and usually in the regular alternation of 29- and 30-day periods, the mean lunar month was taken as 29 1/2 solar days in synodical time. Twelve such lunar months, however, results in only 354 days and does not complete a solar year. For calendar purposes, therefore, the position of the moon in synodical time was accounted for annually as 365 less 354 or 11 days, called *epactae*; after the second year, 11 more days would accumulate, making up 22 epacts, and so forth. Further adjustments are also made in keeping track of epacts in the Alexandrian nineteen-year cycle. This synodical time was assumed in all four of the calendar systems discussed above.

Synodical time, however, did not allow computists to reckon lunar positions with the accuracy many of them desired. Therefore, sidereal time was introduced in order to coordinate the lunar cycle not with the terrestrial horizon but with the position of the stars. This position was expressed in terms of the zodiacal scale, whether or not the moon was visible at the time. On this scale, the lunar month in sidereal time was discovered to be 27 solar days and 8 hours. Computistical tracts will often discuss the Hellenistic model of the heavens and its applications in greater detail and complexity than this, and they give many sets of *argumenta* that explain the problems of synodical and sidereal time, along with procedures for solving them. Therefore, *computus* manuscripts often gather further tracts devoted exclusively to basic astronomy for study in Anglo-Saxon schools.

In three of his works, Aldhelm (640?–709/10) listed the major categories of knowledge, the *disciplinae philosophorum*, to be *physica, ethica,* and *logica*. The first of those categories included seven *fisicae artes,* which he gave as *arithmetica, geometrica, musica, astronomia, astrologia, mechanica,* and *medicina*. All seven terms are found and defined in the several works of Isidore of Seville that were known to Aldhelm. *Geometria* concerns measure of lengths and the terms of measurement with reference to the earth's surface — it sounds something like civil engineering; *astrologia* pertains to the rising, falling, and visibility of the stars and their courses through the heavens as they circle the earth, while *astronomia* accounts for the movements of planets and their periods of orbit. Although these terms had been common to Roman *mathematici* and *magi* (that is, astrologers and magicians), they do not suggest any number mysticism or astral influences when mentioned by either Isidore or Aldhelm, who stay with descriptive accounts of stellar phenomena.[20]

When he went to study at the Canterbury abbey of Saints Peter and Paul for the first time about 670-72, the mature Aldhelm must have received additional instruction "in the art of meter, astronomy and *computus*."[21] Although he may already have been elected abbot of Malmesbury in 670, the arithmetic that he had learned and practiced there may not have given immediate satisfaction to his master Hadrian, newly arrived at Canterbury. One of Aldhelm's complaints was about those *partes numeri* to be carried over in addition, subtraction, multiplication, or division, which could be kept in mind only with difficulty and when "sustained by heavenly grace." But he must have learned well, for the *computus* was a subject he pursued further. As a student writing to his West Saxon bishop, he emphasized the "intense disputation of computation" at the Canterbury school, the profound subject of the "Zodiac, the circle of twelve signs that rotates at the peak of heaven," and "the complex reckoning of the horoscope," which he said "requires of the expert laborious investigation."[22] *Horoscopus* in this context means an instrument for reckoning *astronomica phenomena*, perhaps a sundial or a table of data recording stellar motions.

Did Aldhelm pursue this sort of study of arithmetic and of astronomical phenomena later in his life? He seems to have known the letter sent by Bishop Vitalianus of Rome (657-72) to King Oswiu of Northumbria before the Council of Whitby.[23] He heard the appeal of Theodore of Canterbury "that we all keep Easter Day at the same time, namely on the Sunday after the fourteenth day of the moon of the first month," and he appears to have carried out the directions of the Synod of Hertford about this question by writing to Geraint, king of Devon and Cornwall, and to his bishops, who were using an eighty-four-year cycle with different lunar limits for setting the times in order (probably *luna* XIV-XX) and who were willing to observe Easter Sunday on the fourteenth day of the moon.[24] From this evidence one should not expect from Aldhelm a profound knowledge of Hellenistic astronomy.[25] But after studying with Hadrian he must have exercised his school astronomy to some extent before becoming bishop of Sherborne in 705, for there is extant in several ninth-century manuscripts a *Cyclus Aldhelmi de cursu lunae per signa XII secundum grecos*.[26] The earliest transcription of the *Cyclus Aldhelmi* that survives was written between 836 and 848 in MS Karlsruhe Landesbibliothek Aug. 167, perhaps at Peronna Scottorum.[27] The purpose of this table of data is to determine the relation of the moon to the stars throughout the nineteen-year Easter cycle by use of the zodiac, and this relation is based upon a synodical lunar period of 29 1/2 days. There are nineteen vertical columns and thirty horizontal rows. The rows are designated by fifteen letters of the alphabet alternated with blanks; year 2 begins with a blank space on the top row and continues with letter L; epacts are given at the foot of each column for use at commencement of each successive year. This cycle thus generated the lunar A-P series, which survives in many calendars without the table.[28] Several other efforts were made in Continental schools to achieve the same goal, and none were successful if they were based upon the synodical period of 29 days and 12 hours, rather than upon the sidereal period of 27 days and 8 hours.[29] Thus the *Cyclus Aldhelmi* and its synodical time adjustments dropped out of use very early in most Anglo-Saxon schools. Bede, however, recognized the problem of synodical time and proposed to use sidereal time.

Astronomia in the Age of Bede

The works of Bede could supply much evidence for the practice of *astronomia*. In *De natura rerum* liber (hereafter cited as *DNR*) written about A.D. 701, he explained the axis of the cosmos and its poles as theoretical constructs; that is, the true North Pole is near to the pole star but must be located geometrically.[30] He described the five-zone model of the heavens and its projection upon the earth with equator, two tropics, and two arctic circles.[31] All constellations and planets of course were seen to pass daily from east to west.[32] Thus he could describe motions of sun and moon in detail and gave a classic description of both lunar and solar eclipses.[33]

For anyone seeking the date of Easter, the west to east motions of planets other than sun and moon against the stellar background would be of no importance at all. Nevertheless, Bede informed his students and his readers of the long periods required by each planet to complete its west to east circuit, along with its much shorter periods of visibility.[34] He used the scale of the zodiacal band of *ccclx partes* (360 degrees) to track these longitudinal motions, but he also used its breadth of *xii partes* for an account of latitudinal *apsidae* (apogees and perigees) for the planetary orbits on that oblique band of stellar space.[35] Writing in 701, he seems to have assumed with Pliny the Elder that the stars are brighter or dimmer because of their various distances from the earth[36] and that planets move about the earth on eccentric circles.[37] But from Isidore he added a description of retrograde motion and stations for some planets,[38] implying an epicyclic theory of planetary motions that may not be consistent with eccentric circles without some mechanism for reconciliation, but he offered no explanation. Bede also noted the maximum elongations of the orbits of Venus and Mercury relative to the sun,[39] but he did not mention the model of planetary cycles by which those two planets could be thought to circle the sun, while the three of them circled the earth together as a subsystem — a model that became very popular in ninth-century Frankish schools and that came to Wales from Limoges, perhaps in the tenth century.[40]

With some of Bede's astronomy thus in mind, we may turn again to the coordination of lunar cycles with solar cycles by use of the zodiacal band. In *DNR* XXI, "Argumentum de cursu lunae per signa," Bede had accepted from Pliny a formula for the moon's circuit through the zodiac thirteen times during twelve lunar months. By the use of Roman fractions, he found that the moon would travel through one sign of the zodiac in two days, six and two-thirds hours. He considered that he could simplify the operation of finding the number of signs of the zodiac through which the moon had progressed by using a ratio of 4:9. Thus he would multiply the number of lunar days that had passed from the starting point by four and then divide by nine, in order to find the number of signs and *partes* through which the moon had progressed from the stellar starting point on the zodiacal scale.[41] But even at the time of writing in 701, he recognized that this solution was not adequate for the purpose.

Coordination of lunar and solar cycles was becoming known in the schools through excerpts of Pliny and also through attention to the writings of Ambrose and Isidore. There were young men at Malmesbury and at Sherborne during Aldhelm's lifetime who were trained in the disciplines of *arithmetica*, *astronomia*, and *astrologia*, such as Pechthelm and possibly Pleguina, both of whom later came north,[42] and they could well have brought Aldhelm's new table with them to Hexham and Jarrow. How would Bede respond to it?

Early in the period 721-25 when his *De temporum ratione* was being composed, Bede had become more careful about his reckonings and insistent about the necessity of avoiding miscalculations concerning the course of the sun and the moon through the zodiac and its twelve signs (chapter XVI, lines 23-25). The turning of the spherical ball of the heavens can be followed by taking the circuit of twelve distinct and large signs, as divided each into 30 separate and small parts (lines 25-27), since the sun gives light for 30 days in each sign. When this is observed for a full 24 hours, however, the sun's course will have actually run 10 1/2 hours more per sign than you might have expected, but you do not want to include those several 10 1/2s until the sun has passed through all twelve signs and a total of 126 hours or 5 1/4 days have accumulated. Then you add the 30 parts per sign and the extra 10 half-hours per sign twelve times, and you get 365 1/4 days for the sun's course (lines 27-33). This is an approximation that will be used to coordinate 365 1/4 days with 360 parts of the zodiac in one year.

Bede then proceeded to describe something about each of the twelve signs (lines 33-64). But he also returned to discuss their movement in quantifying terms and introduced the significance of sidereal months (lines 65-79). He noted that the sun's course through the total zodiac requires 365 days and a quarter (or 6 hours), while the moon takes only 27 days and one-third (or 8 hours). More precisely, the sun passes through one sign in 30 days and 10 1/2 hours, while the moon needs only 2 days and 6 2/3 hours per sign (lines 68-69).

There are those who assert that the moon takes 30 days to complete the same course that the sun completes in 365 days, but they err if they do that, according to Bede (lines 74-75). This general notion could have been found in Ambrose or Isidore, for example,[43] but he could have also been referring to the *Cyclus Aldhelmi*, which attempted to apply that relationship. He also warns in this case against using the data for synodical lunar months of 29 or 30 days, which only coordinate the appearance of sun and moon without reference to the stars, for it is the more exact sidereal data that are gained by reference to the stars and applied on the zodiacal scale (lines 76-79). He reaffirmed the lunar sidereal cycle of 27 1/3 days, which is obviously nearer to the fraction 1/13 than to 1/12 of a solar cycle, and actually the solar cycle would correspond with about 13 1/3 lunar sidereal cycles (lines 71-74). If this scientific effort to account for the sun's movement relative to the stars still seems unclear, that is because it is indeed confusing. It was an explanatory effort that failed. Happily Bede did not give up his efforts as a teacher and scholar of applied astronomy at this point.

After some further approximate guidelines for tracking the sun and moon across the face of the heavens, Bede finally offered in chapter XIX the *pagina regularum* and its explanation[44] as an improvement upon the *Cyclus Aldhelmi*. It guides the user by the letter series A-O, alternating fourteen letter spaces with thirteen blank spaces, coordinated with twelve zodiacal signs on the left and twelve solar months on the right. This table or cycle was offered with Bede's rather plain words that it had been created *ad capacitatem ingenioli*, and indeed it was surely an improvement for those like myself and many of my readers who may feel unsure of their ability to follow those previous calculations. Bede's *pagina regularum* became a very popular table and seems to have been taken into many other *computi* written during the next four centuries. But as Bede himself pointed out, this too is inadequate; and he invited others to try their hands at it and bring forth a better rule.[45]

Manuscript Evidence for Anglo-Saxon Computistical Activity

Unfortunately, there is in England no longer a single copy of any of Bede's scientific works written before the end of the eleventh century or the beginning of the twelfth.[46] Norse invasions and the wars of Alfred and many others were not good for schools and libraries. But probably more destructive than enemy attack were the many fires that resulted from ordinary human work, accident, or carelessness. Yet many coals are still glowing

amongst the ashes, and much science survives in Anglo-Saxon manuscripts. In 1981 Helmut Gneuss included, in his "Preliminary List of
Manuscripts," not only manuscripts containing Anglo-Saxon texts and
glosses but also Latin manuscripts, fragments, and charters, written or
imported, with practically no exclusions.[47] Because of the cooperation of
a great number of scholars, this work was able to rely less upon older cat-
alogs and more upon the direct studies of individual scholars concerning
scripts, contents, and codicological detail that reveal dating and provenance than had Neil R. Ker's 1941 *Medieval Libraries* (revised 1964, 1987)
and his 1957 *Catalogue of Manuscripts*.[48] As a result, the number of
books that are known to have been available for study in Anglo-Saxon England has grown spectacularly. Supposing (wrongly) that Ker's 1957 list of
manuscripts were representative, one could have counted only 37 books
containing Anglo-Saxon texts or glosses that may have been written or
used in Canterbury. From Gneuss's list in 1981, however, one may locate
190 texts known during that period at Canterbury: about 90 from the library of Christchurch and about 100 from the monastic library of Saints
Peter and Paul (later called Saint Augustine's). With only slightly better
indication of contents, it may easily be seen that the theological tracts
expected in that library have been joined by 23 books in the scientific categories of seven *fisicae artes* named by Aldhelm. While some of these surviving manuscripts are fragmentary, the texts contained in many of them
are multiple in number, diverse in content, and often very rich in scientific interest.

In the schools of other parts of England many and diverse works of
computus and astronomy could reveal further studies that developed better understanding of natural phenomena in our period. Only a few examples are necessary to illustrate the breadth and depth of scientific studies
in Anglo-Saxon England. The first 39 folios of MS Oxford BL Digby 63
contain computistical materials apparently written during 844-55 but
transcribed about 867 (*annus praesens*, fol. 20v) by the Frankish scribe
Raegenbold, who brought them with him to England. There he transcribed other computistical tracts from both south and north of the
Humber estuary during successive periods of his life until his final entry
at the end of the ninth century.

The first eight folios of this booklet supply Dionysian Easter tables
with eight columns of data from the third year of a nineteen-year cycle in
229 through thirty-three more cycles to the year 872. This was followed
by a *Computatio Grecorum*, a series of computistical *argumenta* known
as *Lectiones*, a set of *Versus computistica* perhaps from Verona and Saint
Gallen, and a *Tractatus de solesticia*. None of these contents were known
in Britain in another manuscript before the middle of the tenth century,
so far as I know, and it should be assumed that Raegenbold brought folios
1-39v with him from the continent.[49] But the last folio or two of his book
may have been blank when he finished. A table is found on folios 38v-39v

that is headed *Transitus lune per signa* and is based upon the sidereal lunar month of 27 days and 8 hours. Until I am able to inspect this manuscript again, I could not attempt to say whether Raegenbold also brought the sidereal table with him from the continent or found and added it in England.

Folios 40-48, however, contain a calendar whose origins have attracted considerable interest; historians may wonder whether it derives from Northumbria and came into the southern area of Wessex during the reign of King Alfred.[50] I do not wish to intervene in that discussion but should note at least that the calendar page for January concludes with "Nox horam XVI die hora VIII" (*sic*), which must indicate a southern latitude, but the page for December concludes with "Nox hora XVIII die hora VI," which could correspond with a northern latitude such as Aberdeen. One might suppose that the writer began in the south and migrated north, but he also might have adapted some of the latitudes of a calendar to the lunar table on folios 46-48 without traveling at all. Thus it cannot prima facie be taken to indicate origin of the codex or even of this part.

The third booklet in MS Digby 63 comprises folios 49-71 and contains some of the African and Spanish computistical materials that seem to have passed through Ireland (Ráth Maélsigi?) to the library of Jarrow and that were used by Bede.[51] They include *Acta synodi*, version III; letters of Pascasinus, Proterius, and Cyril; two letters of Dionysius Exiguus; *Argumentum de nativitate: Querenda est nobis nativitas lune XIIII . . .* ; the African letter of Felix and the related *Prologus Sancti Felicis Chyllitani*, also known as "Successor Dionisi"; along with other items of interest. But there is also a part of the letter from Vitalianus of Rome to Oswiu of Northumbria, omitted by Bede and apparently unknown to him. These tracts are not in the same order as they appear with other *computi* in the so-called Sirmond manuscript, Oxford BL Bodley 309 (s. XI 2 Vendôme), folios 82v-90 and 94v-95v, which has been called the computistical library of Bede, nor were they copied in the same order as they appear in the related MS London British Library Cotton Caligula A.XV. Charles W. Jones therefore could speculate that MS Digby 63 represented a separate line of transmission from Ireland to Canterbury. Unfortunately the evidence cannot settle the question of whether the writer had gone north or the calendar and *computi* had come to him in the south of England from Ireland.

In 892 Raegenbold was still working on these materials and decided to quit. Thus he wrote on folio 71:

Finit praestante. Finit liber de conputacio.
Raegenbold[us].Sacerdos. [. . . . .]
Scripsit.Istum.Libellum. et q[u]icumque legit.
Semper pro illum orat. // // // : —

Nevertheless, the same writer added yet a fourth booklet on folios 72-83. He copied the nine authentic Dionysian *argumenta*, as well as three more from other writers; a *Calculatio quomodo . . .*; the *Disputatio Morini*; an entry associated with Cummian; the beginning of a *Tractatus de celebratione paschae* (completed, however, by a second writer on folios 83-87); and other items that were also scattered through either MS Bodley 309 or MS Caligula A.XV. By 1000 this set of four booklets in 83 plus 4 folios was being used at Winchester, where several words were erased after Raegenbold's name and *de Pentonia* was added, as was the name of Baernini, who asked the reader to pray for him and wrote a few more words on folio 71 that are now illegible.[52] It was quite a respectable collection of computistical literature and was much studied.

Another important manuscript for the *fisicae artes* in Anglo-Saxon England was the Exeter Cathedral MS 3507, written about 960-86 in a beautiful English square minuscule.[53] This codex contains two significant works, Isidore's *De natura rerum* and Hraban's *De computo*, along with a collection of computistical verses[54] and geographical texts of interest for scientific instruction in the schools. A complete transcription of these materials was made toward the end of the eleventh century in MS London BL Cotton Vitellius A.XII, folios 10v-64, not taken directly from the MS Exeter 3507 but from a common exemplar no longer extant. Analysis of the text of Isidore's schoolbook *De natura rerum* in the Exeter and Vitellius manuscripts has shown that this is not the "recension longue" expected from the theories of three versions and their diffusion offered by Jacques Fontaine in his excellent critical edition of Isidore's work.[55] Rather it is a more elaborate version than has been found anywhere else. Especially notable for Anglo-Saxon studies is the earliest copy of this English version of Isidore's schoolbook in an Insular Carolingian script from mid–tenth century, MS London British Library Cotton Domitian I; its writer shared the same exemplar soon to be used for MS Exeter and then later for MS Vitellius. Further comparison with the manuscripts used by Fontaine also had interesting results, which may only be summarized here. It can be demonstrated that Bede used the earliest and shortest version prepared by Isidore in Seville in 612, whereas Aldhelm used a version in the next stage of development that had been augmented in 613 by Isidore with information from Pliny's *Historia naturalis* and that also contained astronomical verses from which Aldhelm selected a few lines. The verses have been identified in a letter from Isidore's student to whom the work had been addressed, the young Visigothic king Sisebuto.[56] The versified epistle explained both lunar and solar eclipses and included an excellent diagram of these phenomena of a type still used by astronomical societies and their publications.[57] Although Fontaine speculated that this "recension longue" could have been composed in Ireland and passed through southern England or moved directly to Northumbria, there is no evidence to connect it with either Ireland or Northumbria at all. No manuscripts survive for Fontaine's putative "recension moyen," which Aldhelm could have quoted. What he used, however, would have been present in the "recension longue" manuscripts that were written in Anglo-Saxon minuscule or in Fulda Insular minuscule during the eighth century.[58] None of these show any relationship with Northumbria or Bede. Thus we have identified four different versions of an important schoolbook for basic instruction in the understanding of natural phenomena, versions that were being used by Angles and Saxons in several parts of England during the eighth, ninth, tenth, and eleventh centuries.

The *computus* of Hraban, written at Fulda during 819 and 820, was fairly well known in Carolingian schools. Although only two copies survive in England, in the Exeter 3507 and Vitellius A.XII manuscripts, two more copies are of English origin: the MS Avranches Bibliothèque Municipale 114 (post-1128), folios 98-132, perhaps from Mont-Saint-Michel, and MS Firenze Biblioteca Medicea Riccardiana 885 (s. XIV in), folios 312-46, with the Prologus and partial capitula repeated on folio 349; both are glossed like the earlier Exeter and Vitellius copies.[59] There are also excerpts from Hraban's *computus* in marginal glosses to a calendar in MS Oxford Saint John's College Library XVII (1102-10), folios 16-22, copied at Ramsey Abbey for Thorney Abbey, and in the Cerne Abbey MS Cambridge Trinity College O.2.45 (post-1248), pages 19-20, 182-86.

However, Hraban had not explained the difference between synodical and sidereal lunar months. He did select many of the problems and the calculations set out by Bede's *De temporibus ratione* XVII and XVIII, but he passed over all references to sidereal time and omitted the *pagina regularum* and its practical applications. This aspect of Bedan science was not furthered by the books in MS Exeter 3507 and apparently not by the school and library of Leofric at Exeter, though it was taught in other schools of tenth- and eleventh-century England.

Tenth to Eleventh Centuries

Communications between the several parts of Great Britain and the several parts of Francia were lively during the tenth and eleventh centuries, and several travelers from the Continent came north by invitation of Oswald of York. One of them was Abbo (ca. 945–1004), who had known both Oswald and Germanus before 985 when they were unwilling *peregrini* in the abbey of Saint Benoît-sur-Loire at Fleury near Orléans. There Abbo taught with particular attention to mathematical and scientific subjects. At Ramsey Abbey in Lincolnshire near East Anglia and elsewhere in England from 986 to 988, he wrote *Quaestiones grammaticales* and four *Sententiae*. Both works are found in English manuscripts from our period.[60] For example, the exemplar from which MS Exeter 3507 had been copied was later wrapped by several more bifolia before being copied again in southern England over a century later into MS Vitellius A.XII (s. XI ex), folios 10v-64; the wrapper was transcribed into MS Vitellius, folios 8-10v and 64-64v. Those bifolia contained the *Sententiae* of Abbo: "De differentia circuli et sperae," 'De cursu septem planetarum per zodiacum circulum" (with figure), "Signa in quibus singuli planetarum morentur scies," and "De duplici signorum ortu vel occasu."[61]

It may also have been Abbo who introduced to English masters and students another schoolbook, the *De computo lunae* or *Ars calculatoria*. Probably written or at least completed about 883 by Heiric or Helperic (ca. 841-903) in the Abbey of Saint Germain at Auxerre and presented about 900 to Asper, *dominus* of Grandval, this *Ars calculatoria* was much used in Anglo-Saxon schools from the tenth century onward. Two English manuscripts used *annus praesens* 975, and the year 978 was given in ten more; the latter date probably stems from Abbo's own copy from Fleury.[62] In his chapter XVI: "Cur nunc XXX, nunc XXIX pronuncietur, vel quantum in unoquoque signo, vel in toto zodiaco moretur," that author included his own discussion of the sidereal lunar month of twenty-seven days and eight hours as the moon moved through the zodiac. His intention was to explain how there could be thirteen lunar months during approximately the course of twelve solar months, rather than to provide Bede's quantifying explanation of the moon's observed annual progress relative to the starry background.[63] He did not provide or discuss the *pagina regularum* or its A-O series. Thus a student was introduced to the concepts of sidereal time by Helperic's *computus* but was not carried forward to understand their usefulness.

Having been introduced to Anglo-Saxon England in 986, the *Ars calculatoria* was actively studied in its several regions and continued to be used during two subsequent centuries. *Anni praesentes* of 900, 903, 975, 977, 978, 980, 990, 994, and so on to 1155 are variants that indicate that scribes were not merely copying a text but were putting its contents to current applications. There are several versions of the text, and the manuscripts provide quite diverse series of final chapters and explicits. No careful analysis of contents has yet distinguished these versions properly.[64]

Abbo taught arithmetic from the *Calculus* of Victurius of Aquitaine and wrote a commentary on its prologue,[65] and he used the writings of Dionysius Exiguus and Bede heavily in works that were copied into MS Berlin Staatsbibliothek Phillipps 1833 [Cat. 138] (s. X ex, Fleury), folios 1-58. He was one of the earliest scholars who proposed to revise the *aera Incarnationis*, and he identified several reasons for doing so. When he projected the ninety-five-year Dionysian Easter tables from year 531 back to their beginning, Abbo did not pass over from $+1$ to -1 in the Roman style, as had Dionysius, but used the nul point to enumerate the year of the Incarnation. Adjustments to the Bedan calendar that this required for three nineteen-year cycles, together with two of Abbo's letters explaining them, survive in MS Vat. Regin. lat. 1281 (s. XII), folios 1-3, from the school at Hereford.

He did not accept the Dionysian A.D. XXXIII as the putative year of Christ's death. He had noticed that the death in the year DXXVIIII of Dionysius's contemporary, Benedict of Nursia, was reported to be XII Kal. Aprilis, feria VII (= 21 March, Saturday); unfortunately that weekday and that day of the month would not correspond with DXXVIIII but required year DVIIII in the Dionysian cycle, a difference of twenty years. If this difference were applied to the Passion, its year should have been given as A.D. XIII rather than XXXIII in that cycle. Therefore Abbo implied that Bede must have erred by accepting Dionysian chronology without correction.

On the other hand, Abbo took Bede's approach to sidereal time quite seriously. In his *Computus vulgaris qui dicitur ephemerida*, Abbo devoted ten paragraphs to the sidereal lunar month of twenty-seven days and eight hours, the *pagina regularum* with its letter series A-O for twenty-seven lunar days, and especially problems of continuing from O to A for only eight hours, or one-third of the twenty-eighth day, in order to track the moon's course relative to the stars.[66] Sidereal time provided astronomical justification for Abbo's corrections of epacts, concurrents, and lunar regulars in the Bedan calendar.

One of Abbo's English students at Ramsey Abbey, Byrhtferth, undertook to prepare an *Enchiridion* or *Handboc*, which survives in MS Oxford Bodleian Library Ashmole 328 (s. XI med), pages 1-247, in four books.[67] This may have been a useful schoolbook because it was written in the form of commentaries upon works of Bede, Hraban, and Heiric/Helperic — often quoting or epitomizing a passage in Latin and then translating or summarizing in English. There are also passages similar to parts of the *computi* by Abbo and Ælfric. This work contains not only computistical materials but also various bits of natural history, grammar, rhetoric, and exhortations against worldly evils, but the surviving portions of the text have omitted any reference to the sidereal lunar months and year, even the leading query by Helperic. Thus, despite its positive values for school teaching, it is a disappointing work for modern research, as there are really no advances in the level of scientific learning, and the sources were more sophisticated than the teacher who was making use of them. The *Enchiridion* together with its sources, however, represents the development of a substantial library of mathematical, astronomical, and specifically computistical texts in the school at Ramsey Abbey after Abbo left in 988 and through the entire eleventh century. Those many tracts and tables gathered for study at Ramsey were then copied into MS Oxford St. John's College XVII about 1102 to 1110 and must have been intended to stimulate further such studies in the school of Thorney Abbey.[68]

Another *computus* that alternates Latin with English materials is Ælfric's *De anni temporibus*. Ælfric (ca. 955–1020/25) apparently came from the North, entered the monastic school at Winchester under Æthelwold (abbot ca. 971-1005), and then lived at Cerne Abbey, where this short treatise was written between 992 and 995. He discussed divisions of the year along with a bit of astronomy and other natural phenomena by quoting passages from the two *computi* of Bede, augmenting this sometimes from the two school-books *De natura rerum* of Bede and Isidore. He also discussed corrections to be made in other Anglo-Saxon *computi*, supplied his own computistical *argumenta* concerning the beginning of the year and the bissextile (a day added in leap year), and firmly distinguished between effects of the moon on persons and nature and some superstitions about these effects. But he was not concerned with adjustments of the calendar to a new year for the Incarnation. Nor did he teach about the sidereal lunar month or its significance for lunar and other planetary positions on the zodiac that reveal sidereal time. Eight manuscripts and surviving fragments show that Ælfric's work was used in several different schools during the tenth and eleventh centuries.[69]

Abbo was not the only scholar who directly challenged the Bedan *computus* concerning the date of the Incarnation. Gerlandus compotista (ca. 1015-1102) wrote his *Computus Bedam imitantis* in England before the mid–eleventh century and taught there for twenty years, from 1038 to 1057; then he moved to Besançon, where he was teaching before 1066. After acknowledging the authority of Dionysius, Bede, and Helperic, he set forth causes and techniques for revising the Bedan *aera Incarnationis* by seven years. Gerland's work went through several versions within the author's lifetime, including revisions on the Continent that used the *annus praesens* 1081 or reference to an eclipse, possibly of 1086. Gerland's first version listed twenty-seven chapters, but he added others, including "Item de cursu solis et lunae," which elaborates his teaching in astronomy. From many detailed calculations of the sun and the moon moving through the zodiacal band and with data refined in terms not only of *horae* and *puncti* but even of *momenta*, *ostenta*, and *athomi*, this chapter demonstrated that the moon passed through the zodiac in twenty-seven days and eight hours, explaining its periodic displacement.[70]

Gerland was cited as an authority by 1102, and parts of this *magister's* *computus* and his tables of data were being used and commented upon by scholars pursuing their studies in the *corpus astronomicum* at Oxford and Paris during the twelfth and thirteenth centuries. The *computus* has not yet been published in any version, but it certainly stirred controversy in the schools.[71] His proposals to revise the calendar were incorporated into many other *computi*, some of which undertook to apply, while others wanted to refute, his system.

Abbo and Gerland raised their question about the *aera Incarnationis* on the basis of chronology but supported their proposals to correct the Bedan calendar with arguments from the data of sidereal time, tracking the movement of sun and moon against the stars and using for that purpose the ecliptic scale of the zodiac. This had a further consequence. Whether or not Dionysius had set the year of the Incarnation rightly, their astronomy demonstrated that the Bedan calendar had eventually departed from its stellar point of reference.

Another migrating scholar computist was Robert de Losinga, who came to England in the wake of or possibly as chaplain for William the Conqueror and who became bishop of Hereford (1079-95). In the school of Hereford he could have used the works of Heiric/Helperic and Gerland, but he also brought from Thuringia and Lotharingia an interest in Marianus Scottus. Marian was a sometime hermit and *peregrinus* who wished to revise the reckonings of Dionysius and Bede in order to relocate the birth of Jesus properly, this time by a change of twenty-two years. About 1086 Robert quoted a large part of Marian's computistical arguments in twenty-two of the twenty-four chapters in his *De annis domini*.[72] Marian and Robert, however, did not make use of the difference between synodical and sidereal lunar months and did not support their argument for calendar revision by sidereal time references. Nearby, however, a new instrument and new tables of data would open a different era of astronomical science for these Anglo-Saxon schools.

By use of an astrolabe, Walcher, prior of Malvern Abbey (fl. 1092-1112), could determine the dates of eclipses and could be certain that an eclipse that he had seen as a traveler in Italy on 30 October 1091 had been noted later on that same day at home in his English abbey. Lunar tables *De naturali cursu cuiusque lunationis*, which he calculated in A.D. 1092 for a seventy-six-year period (A.D. 1037-1112), provided a new form of cycle that would change computistical studies significantly. For some time he worked with Peter Anphus or Alphonsus, a Jewish astronomer and physician who had become a Christian and migrated from Spain to England. One of Peter's works, *De dracone*, gave the motions of sun and moon through the zodiac and discussed lunar nodes, not in Roman fractions as Walcher had used, but in degrees, minutes, and seconds.[73] This type of analysis would be found also in the work of Roger of Hereford (fl. A.D. 1176-1195), who used astronomical tables of Marseilles,[74] and seen again in the scientific works of Robert Grosseteste with his development from the basic terms of *Compotus* I (A.D. 1195-1200) to the Ptolemaic assumptions of his more sophisticated *Computus correctorius* (about 1220).[75]

Conclusion

From Ceolfrith and Aldhelm in the seventh century to Gerland and Robert in the eleventh, computistical and astronomical studies were actively pursued in many schools of Anglo-Saxon England. The masters and students were not only concerned with predicting the dates of future Easter Sundays but were also interested in identifying stellar and planetary regularities and in applying them to the study of natural phenomena in the context of *computus*. Manuscript records of their studies survive in every period from many parts of Britain.

Normally the masters in these schools taught their students to account for the mean lunar cycle from the first appearance of the new moon until its reappearance and often to account for the periods of appearance for the other planets, and their positions were often remarked on the Zodiacal scale. This system is called synodical time, especially with reference to the longitudinal course of the moon. With a mean lunar cycle of twenty-nine solar days and twelve hours, the system of synodical time was assumed by all those computists who met at Whitby in A.D. 664. In order to track the course of any planet by synodical time, the solar months and the zodiacal signs were coordinated in the tabular form of the A-P series by Aldhelm during the last quarter of the seventh century.

Bede was not satisfied with synodical time, however, when it was applied to the continuous motions of the planets, and he offered an alternative way to account for them, which we call sidereal time. In this system lunar and other planetary positions were also read on the zodiacal band, but with reference to the stars the moon was observed to have a complete cycle of twenty-seven solar days and eight hours. Bede presented his system also in the tabular form of a *pagina regularum*, coordinating months and signs with the A-O series for improved observations of the planets.

Considerable knowledge of the moon's cycle and its correlation with the solar cycle is necessary for the *computus*, but not knowledge about the cycles of other planets. In fact, most questions about lunar motions are adequately handled in terms of synodical time. The *Cyclus Aldhelmi* was tried by various computists in Anglo-Saxon and Carolingian schools during the eighth and ninth centuries, and many other schemes of synodical time were known, including Bede's. In the long run, however, they were displaced by sidereal time, and Bede's table and relatively difficult explanations were often transcribed and used.

Because basic procedures of the Bedan *computus* can be followed in terms of synodical time, it is not surprising that many of the masters offered brief explanations of sidereal time without including the *pagina regularum*, or that some may have copied the table without explaining it, and that others may even have omitted all reference to sidereal time from their teaching.

Abbo's two years in English schools toward the end of the tenth century, however, were different. Not only did he teach the system of sidereal time in the *computus*, but he also offered new examples of how useful it could be in astronomy and justified his questions about the Dionysian and Bedan *aera Incarnationis*. Likewise Gerland used it as the basis for radical revision of the Bedan calendar in the eleventh century.

Bede had not been satisfied with his own explanations and applications of sidereal time, and he had invited other scholars to improve upon them. Not even Abbo or Gerland had been able to do that. More exact observations with the astrolabe, however, did allow both Englishmen and Continental immigrants to England to make more refined observations. They also began to develop longer data series, along the lines of those used by Syrian, Greek, Hebrew, and Arab astronomers in Toledo and Marseilles.

One important result of this more accurate astronomy was the use of a seventy-six-year period for the lunar cycle and a new *computus* being taught in the arts curriculum of new universities during the twelfth and thirteenth centuries, a *computus* to which Robert Grosseteste made a primary contribution.

As with all research enterprises, some of the labors of Anglo-Saxon schools succeeded, some did not, and the best scholars could have both successes and failures. The manuscripts offer evidence that scientific research abounded in the schools of England, as the chronological uncertainties of historical events interacted conceptually with computistical and astronomical studies. One aspect of their research, concerning which the manuscripts will have more to reveal, was the discovery and application of sidereal time.

Notes

1. Some indication of scientific labors by Scots, Britons, Saxons, and Angles has been offered by the author in "Scientific Instruction in Early Insular Schools," in *Insular Latin Studies*, ed. Michael Herren (Toronto, 1981), pp. 83-111. Also in preparation is "A Catalogue of Computistical Tracts, A. D. 200–1200," which will include at least forty-five manuscripts written in Anglo-Saxon England containing sixty-two independent *computi*, in addition to many different *versus computistica* and diverse series of *argumenta paschalia*.

2. Biscop Baducing (ca. 630-89) became a monk and took the name Benedictus about 652. He founded the North Sea monasteries of Wearmouth (674) and Jarrow upon Tyne (681), which Bede later entered as a child. Concerning Biscop's trips to Lyons, Arles, Lerins, and Rome, see W. Levison, *England and the Continent in the Eighth Century* (Oxford, 1946), pp. 38-42, and chapter 6, "Learning and Scholarship," especially pp. 132-34 and 143; P. Hunter Blair, *The World of Bede* (New York, 1970), pp. 155-87, especially pp. 156-60, 168-69, 176-77, and 186-87; J. Campbell, "The First Century of Christianity in England," *Ampleforth Journal* 76 (1971): 12-29; H. Mayr-Harting, *The Coming of Christianity to Anglo-Saxon England* (London, 1972); P. Wormald, "Bede and Benedict Biscop," in *Famulus Christi*, ed. G. Bonner (London, 1976), pp. 141-69, especially pp. 149-52; and J. M. Wallace-Hadrill, "Rome and the Early English Church: Some Problems of Transmission," *Settimane di studio del Centro italiano di studi sull'alto medioevo* 7 (Spoleto, 1960): 519-48, reprinted in his *Early English History* (Oxford, 1975), pp. 115-37.

3. See the collection of materials sent by Aldhelm to Aldfrith, king of Northumbria (685–705), and addressed *ad Acircium*, as well as the letters to Wihtfrith and Heahfrith, ed. R. Ehwald, in *Monumenta Germaniae Historica, Auctores Antiquissimi* 15 (1919) (hereafter cited as *MGH, AA*), and the English translations and annotations of Michael Herren in *Aldhelm, the Prose Works*, trans. M. Lapidge and M. Herren (Ipswich, 1979); and Bede, *Historia ecclesiastica* III.27, IV. 4, 26, and V.15, ed. Charles Plummer (Oxford, 1896) (hereafter cited as *HE*).

4. Many of the sources for Bede's computistical studies were copied into the MS Oxford, Bodleian Library, Bodley 309, probably of Vendôme provenance in the second half of the eleventh century. They were identified by Charles W. Jones, "The 'Lost' Sirmond Manuscript of Bede's Computus," *English Historical Review* 52 (1937): 204-19, and described more fully in section 6 of the introduction to his *Bedae Opera de temporibus* (Cambridge, Mass., 1943), pp. 105-13.

5. Ceolfrith was a teacher of Bede and then abbot of Wearmouth and Jarrow, 688-715. His letter to Nechtan provided a clear explanation for the significance of *luna* XIV and of the *termini paschales luna* XV-XXI in order to celebrate Easter during the third week of the first

month of the Jewish year, and it rejects other limits as unbiblical. It was transcribed by Bede, *HE* V.21, and is found separately in MS Montpellier B. Fac. Méd. 157 (s. IX), fols. 55v-60.

6. Christine E. Fell, "Hild, Abbess of Streonæshalch," in *Hagiography and Medieval Literature*, ed. H. Bakker-Nielsen et al. (Odense, 1981), pp. 76-99; and P. Hunter Blair, "Whitby as a Centre of Learning in the Seventh Century," in *Learning and Literature in Anglo-Saxon England: Studies Presented to Peter Clemoes*, ed. M. Lapidge and H. Gneuss (Cambridge, Eng., 1985), pp. 3-32, especially pp. 3-14.

7. Bede, *HE* III.25-26 on Colman's teaching. There was indeed a bishop Anatolius who set forth a *computus*, some of which survives in Eusebius, *Historia ecclesiastica*, ed. E. Schwartz in *Eusebius Werke* (Leipzig, 1903-4), VII.32, 14-19; this was discussed by C. H. Turner, "The Paschal Canon of Anatolius of Laodicea," *English Historical Review* 10 (1895): 699-710. But the *Canon paschalis* used by Colman had been attributed falsely to Anatolius, either by the Brittoni in Wales or the Scotti in Ireland, perhaps in order to fend off the teaching introduced earlier by Patrick; see C. H. Turner, "The Date and Origin of Ps-Anatolius De Ratione Paschali," *Journal of Philology* 28 (1901): 137-51; and Jones, *Bedae Opera de temporibus*, pp. 82-87. Three manuscript fragments of the *Canon paschalis ps-Anatolii* have been identified from eighth-century Echternach and early ninth-century Flavigny, and the full text is found in MS Köln Dombibliothek LXXXIII/2 (Cologne, ca. 805), fols. 188-91v, Geneva University Lat. 50 (second quarter s. IX Massai), fols. 127-28, and four later manuscripts. There is no adequate edition, but see B. Krusch, *Studien zur christlich-mittelalterlichen Chronologie: Der 84jährige Ostercyclus und seine Quellen* (Leipzig, 1880), pp. 316-27; and August Strobel, *Texte zur Geschichte des fruhchristlichen Osterkalendars* (Münster in Westfalen, 1984), pp. 1-42.

8. MS Köln Dombibliothek LXXXIII/2 (Cologne, ca. 805) is a collection of texts from Irish and Anglo-Saxon schools; a table of comparisons of the Victurian and Dionysian data for Alexandrian cycles was added to a *Computus Grecorum* in the same manuscript on fol. 59v, and fol. 211v has a table of lunar epacts for the first day of each month in Alexandrian terms but adjusted to the Victurian cycle. The Victurian cycle was worked out by Victurius of Aquitaine in 457. See further C. W. Jones, "The Victorian and Dionysiac Paschal Tables in the West," *Speculum* 9 (1934): 408-21; and more recently M. Walsh and D. Ó Cróinín, introduction to *Cummian's Letter De controversia paschali and the De ratione conputandi* (Toronto, 1988), pp. 42-45 and 87 n. 216.

9. Acgilbert's family abbey of Jouarre may have been within the range of Irish influence through Luxeuil, according to J. Guerout, "Les origines et le premier siècle," in *L'abbaye royale Notre Dame de Jouarre* (Paris, 1961), pp. 41-45, cited by Wormald, "Bede and Benedict Biscop," pp. 145-46. However, Acgilbert had studied for some time in southern Ireland, possibly at Ráth Maélsigi, according to D. Ó Cróinín, "The Irish Provenance of Bede's Computus," *Peritia* 2 (1983): 229-47, especially pp. 224 and 245. See also Hunter Blair, "Whitby as a Centre of Learning," pp. 30-32.

10. Bishops of Gaul, meeting at Orléans in 541, preferred the *Laterculus Victurii*; according to the earliest surviving letter of Columbanus, some bishops in that region were using Victurian tables about 599-600 and complained mightily that he would not do so. According to his second letter they wished to question him about his practice in a synod at Chalons-sur-Saône in the summer of 603 or possibly winter of 603-4. A late copy of each letter is found in MS St. Gallen Stiftsbibliothek 1346 (s. XVII in), pp. 109-19; and the second also survives in MS Biblioteca Apostolica Vaticana Vat. Lat. 9864 (s. XVIII), fol. 28; they were edited and translated by G. S. M. Walker, *Sancti Columbani Opera* (Dublin, 1957), pp. 2-15.

11. Victurian and Alexandrian Easter tables were set in parallel columns in the MS Milano Biblioteca Ambrosiana H. 150 inf. (s. IX in), fol. 125; most texts in this manuscript appear to derive from Irish and Anglo-Saxon schools, but these tables may be Frankish, and there are later Frankish manuscripts with similar comparisons. See also note 8 above. Historians have usually designated paschal tables as Dionysian when the columns of data were organized in Alexandrian style, but there are significant variations of tables within that

style, and those that were specifically designed by Dionysius Exiguus have not yet been distinguished.

12. Bede, *HE* III.25; *Vita sancti Wilfridi* 10, ed. W. Levison, *M. G. H. Scriptores rerum Merovingicarum* 6 (1913): 202-4; see also D. P. Kirby, "Northumbria in the Time of Wilfrid," and D. H. Farmer, "Saint Wilfrid," in *Saint Wilfrid at Hexham*, ed. D. P. Kirby (Newcastle upon Tyne, 1974), pp. 8-12, 18-20, and 43.

13. Ó Cróinín, "The Irish Provenance of Bede's Computus," pp. 229-47.

14. Note the response conveyed to Columbanus by Candidus, Gregory's diocesan officer in Gallia: " . . . temporis antiquitate roborata mutari non posse," *Columbani Epistola ad Gregorium*, ed. Walker, p. 12; this letter was written within the years 597-600.

15. Bede, *De temporum ratione* XLVII.61-71, ed. C. W. Jones, *Bedae Opera de temporibus* (Cambridge, Mass., 1943) (hereafter cited as *DTR*). Bede dedicated his work to Huaetbercte, who had become abbot of Jarrow in 716.

16. Bede, *HE* V.21. About the Dionysian cycle Ceolfrith said, "Quibus termino adpropinquantibus, tanta hodie calculatorum exuberat copia, ut etiam in nostris per Brittaniam ecclesiis plures sint, qui mandatis memoriae veteribus illis Aegyptiorum argumentis facillime possint in quolibet spatia temporum paschales protendere circulos, etiam si ad quingentos usque et xxx duos voluerint annos; quibus expletis, omnia quae ad solis et lunae, mensis et septimanae consequentiam spectant, eodem quo prius ordine recurrunt," according to Bede, *HE* V.21, p. 341.

17. Two practical systems for calculating latitudes were provided by Bede, *De natura rerum* XLVII (hereafter cited as *DNR*), and enlarged upon in his *De Temporibus* VII, *DTR* XXX-XXXIII, and *HE* I.1. The two systems have been explained in modern terms by Wesley M. Stevens, *Bede's Scientific Achievement*, the Jarrow Lecture for 1985 (Jarrow upon Tyne, 1986), pp. 7-10 and 43-44.

18. Stevens, *Bede's Scientific Achievement*, pp. 10-18.

19. See the *Admiralty Tide Tables*, vol. 1 (1985), *European Waters Including Mediterranean Sea*, published by the Hydrographer of the Navy (London, 1984), pp. vi-xi, "Introduction," and pp. xii-xxx, "Instructions for the Use of Tables." This volume was presented to me in Dublin on 10 February 1986 by Willie Donahoe, harbor pilot, Dublin Bay.

20. Isidore, *Differentiæ* 149-52, *De natura rerum* XVIII. 24-26, and *Etymologiae* III.10.3. These could have been the sources for Aldhelm, *Epistola* 1, written in 675, possibly to Leuthere (bishop of Winchester, 670-76?), ed. Ehwald in *MGH, AA*, p. 475-78, trans. Herren in *Aldhelm, the Prose Works*, pp. 152-53. Concerning the absence of astral influences in Isidore, see J. Fontaine, "Isidore de Séville et l'astrologie," *Revue des Etudes Latines* 31 (1954): 271-300. Both Isidore and Aldhelm have been discussed by Stevens, "Scientific Instruction in Early Insular Schools," pp. 96-98.

21. Bede, *HE* IV.2: "Ita ut etiam metricae artis, astronomiae et arithmeticae ecclesiasticae disciplinam inter sacrorum apicum volumina suis auditoribus contraderent." In general see V. R. Stallbaumer, "The Canterbury School of Theodore and Hadrian," *American Benedictine Review* 22 (1981): 46-63; the use of glossaries in the Canterbury schools has been explained from the manuscripts by Michael Lapidge, "The School of Theodore and Hadrian," *Anglo-Saxon England* 15 (1986): 45-72.

22. Aldhelm, *Epistola* 1, ed. Ehwald, in *MGH, AA*, pp. 475-78, especially pp. 476-77, trans. Herren in *Aldhelm*, pp. 152-53.

23. Aldhelm, *Epistola ad Geruntium* (690?), ed. Ehwald in *MGH, AA*, pp. 483-86, especially pp. 483-84, trans. Herren in *Aldhelm*, pp. 158-59. Other parts of that letter survive in Bede, *HE* III.29, and MS Oxford Bodleian Library Digby 63 (s. IX/2), fol. 59v, ed. B. Krusch in *Studien zur christlich-mittelalterlichen Chronologie: Die Entstehung unserer heutigen Zeitrechnung* (Berlin, 1938), p. 86. See also Jones, *Bedae Opera de temporibus*, pp. 18 and 102-4; and Herren, *Aldhelm*, pp. 140-43.

24. Aldhelm, *Epistola ad Geruntium*, ed. Ehwald in *MGH, AA*, pp. 483-84, trans. Herren in *Aldhelm*, pp. 158-59.

25. It should not be supposed that his knowledge was limited to poetic imagery such as he used in the *Carmen rhythmicum*, ed. Ehwald in *MGH, AA*, pp. 524-28, trans. M. Lapidge in *Aldhelm: The Poetic Works* (Cambridge, Eng., 1985), pp. 177-79; Lapidge has pointed out (p. 262) that similar imagery could have been found by Aldhelm in Isidore, *Origines* III.71, 6-9 and 13-15, and also XIII.11.

26. *Cyclus Aldhelmi* is found in six manuscripts of the ninth, tenth, eleventh, and twelfth centuries and was edited by C. W. Jones, *Bedae Pseudepigrapha* (Ithaca, N.Y., 1939), p. 70; see also his comments in *Bedae Opera de temporibus*, pp. 353-54.

27. Michael Lapidge, "The Present State of Anglo-Latin Studies," in *Insular Latin Studies*, ed. Herren, pp. 45-82, notes that the *Cyclus Aldhelmi* is found "in a number of manuscripts either of English origin or from continental centres with English connections" and states that "although this table was not known to Ehwald, I see no reason not to regard it as Aldhelm's" (p. 49).

28. An early user of the *Cyclus Aldhelmi* also created a lunar series of data organized by the fifteen letters A through P. The Series A-P helps one coordinate the synodical month of 29 1/2 lunar days with 30 degrees per sign and 360 degrees of the zodiacal band. It has been noticed in MS Paris, Bibliothèque National Lat. 5543 (847 Fleury), fols. 95-100v; Vat. Regin. lat. 309 (s. IX/2 St. Denis), fols. 128-40; Chartres, Bibliothèque de la Ville 19 (26) (s. X), fols. 3v-8v (destroyed in 1944); Biblioteca Apostolica Vaticana, Vat. Lat. 644 (s. X St. Gallen?), fols. 24v-28v; Milano, Biblioteca Ambrosiana D. 48 inf. (s. X/2), fols. 101-8; Leiden, Bibliotheek der Rijksuniversiteit Scaliger 38 (s. XI), fols. 7v-13; and ed. *Patrologia Latina* (*PL*) 90 (1850), 759-84, col. 2, but with a line of data omitted. See Jones, *Bedae Pseudepigrapha*, pp. 108-10.

29. Lunar letter series are often found with twelve-month calendars. See H. Leclercq, s.v. "calendars," in *Dictionnaire d'archéologie chrétienne et de liturgie*, ed. F. Cabrol and H. Leclercq (Paris, 1907 seq.), 8:624-67, and Jones, *Bedae Pseudepigrapha*, pp. 108-10.

30. Bede, *DNR* VI, from Pliny, *Historia Naturalis* (*HN*) II.71, 177, and 76, 183-85.

31. Bede, *DNR* IX and XLVII.

32. Bede, *DNR* III, and V-VI.

33. Bede, *DNR* XXII and *DTR* XXVII.2-22. Both explanations were drawn from Pliny, *HN* II.47-50 and 56-57, rather than from Isidore, *De natura rerum* XX-XXI or *Origines* III.58-59. Added by Bede, *DNR* XXIII, from Pliny, *HN* II.72-73, 180-81, was the example of observation of the longitudinal passage of an eclipse that had been recorded at two distant places on the eleventh night before Alexander's victory over Darius at Arbela (Gaugamela), 20/21 September 331 B.C.

34. Bede, *DNR* XII.2-8, from Pliny, *HN* II.4, 12 and 6, 32-33 (planetary circuits); *DNR* XIII.1-11 on the time required for each circuit, from Pliny, *HN* II.6, 32-41; and *DNR* XIII.11-14 on the periods of visibility, from Pliny, *HN* II.15, 78 and 12, 59-61. These excerpts from Pliny were available in several manuscripts and were edited by Karl Rück, *Auszüge aus der Naturgeschichte des C. Plinius Secundus* (Munich, 1888), pp. 34-35.

35. Bede, *DNR* XVI.5-7, used Pliny, *HN* II.13, 66-67 to explain the range of wandering for the seven planets within the zodiacal band, or beyond it in the case of Venus. Bede, *DTR* VII.31-32 and XXVI.15-19, states that the band has a breadth of *xii partes* (twelve degrees), which were alluded to in *DNR* XVI only as *superior et inferior*. The two Bedan texts written in 701 and then 721-25 repeat from Pliny the faulty notion that the sun varies its course from the median by two degrees: "Sol deinde medio fertur inter duas partes flexuoso draconum meatu inaequalis" — perhaps a misunderstanding of the Pliny excerpt. However, it is uncertain whether observation could correct this mistake with instruments available prior to the seventeenth century.

36. Bede, *DNR* III, from Pliny, *HN* II.4, 10-11; Bede, *DNR* V.7-9, from Augustine, *De Genesi ad litteram libri* II.10, 23, and Pliny, *HN* II.13, 63; and Bede, *DNR* VI.2-8, from Pliny, *HN* II.71, 177 and II.76, 183-85.

37. Bede, *DNR* VI and XIV.2-20, the latter from Pliny, *HN* II.13, 63-64 and 68; as he often did elsewhere, Bede then referred the reader to his source: "De quibus si plenius scire velis, lege Plinium Secundum ex quo et ista nos excerpsimus." Similar excerpts were published by Rück, *Naturgeschichte des C. Plinius Secundus*, pp. 39-40. The colors of the planets helped in understanding these phenomena of various and variable distances, according to Bede, *DNR* XV, from Pliny, *HN* II.16, 79.

38. Bede, *DNR* XIV.20-21, from Isidore, *De natura rerum* XXII.3, about retrograde motion and stations of planets.

39. Bede, *DNR* XIII.13-14, from Pliny, *HN* II.15, 78.

40. Concerning the origins and early medieval interest in the planetary configuration of Venus and Mercury with the sun, as a group that travels together around the earth, see Bruce S. Eastwood, "Plinian Astronomical Diagrams in the Early Middle Ages," in *Mathematics and Its Applications to Science and Natural Philosophy in the Middle Ages*, ed. E. Grant and J. Murdoch (Cambridge, Eng., 1987), pp. 141-72; Eastwood, "Plinian Astronomy in the Middle Ages and Renaissance," in *Science in the Early Roman Empire: Pliny the Elder, His Sources and Influence*, ed. R. French and F. Greenaway (London, 1986), pp. 197-251; Eastwood, "The Chaster Path of Venus (orbis veneris castior) in the Astronomy of Martianus Capella," *Archives Internationales d'Histoire des Sciences* 32 (1982): 145-58; idem, "Mss Madrid 9605, Munich 6364, and the Evolution of Two Plinian Astronomical Diagrams in the Tenth Century," *Dynamis, Acta Hispanica ad Medicinae Scientiarumque Historiam Illustrandam* 3 (1983): 265-80; Patrick McGurk, "Germanici Caesaris Aratea cum scholiis, A New Illustrated Witness from Wales," *National Library of Wales Journal* 18 (1973): 197-216; and Eastwood, "Notes on the Planetary Configuration in Aberystwyth N. L. W. ms. 735 C, f. 4ᵛ," *National Library of Wales Journal* 22 (1981): 129-40.

41. Bede, *DNR* XXI.2-7: "Luna zodiacum tredecies in duodecim suis conficit mensibus, duobus scilicet diebus et sex horis et besse, id est octo uncii unius horae, per singula signa decurrens. Si ergo vis scire in quo signo luna versetur, sume lunam quam volueris computare, utpote duodecim, multiplica per quattuor, fiunt XLVIII. Partire per novem (novies quini quadragies quinquis)."

42. *HE* V.13. 18, 23: Pechthelm had been with Aldhelm as deacon and monk; he was well known to Bede and was probably his primary informant for West Saxon affairs; he may have been active in Galloway and Dumfriesshire before he became bishop of Whithorn (ca. 730-34). Bede, *Epistola ad Pleguinam*: Pleguina came north of the Humber about 707.

43. Ambrose, *Hexaemeron* IV.5, 24; Isidore, *De natura rerum* XIX.1 or *Origines* V.36, 3.

44. Bede, *DTR* XIX and accompanying table, pp. 218-20, and brief notes on p. 354.

45. The *pagina regularum* will be further considered on another occasion.

46. Stevens, *Bede's Scientific Achievement*, pp. 33-38, Appendix 1: "Bede's Scientific Works," is organized by title, incipit and explicit, extant manuscripts, and editions of his scientific tracts and letters, with a brief guide to some of the questions of text and authorship of each. Several fragments of Bede, *DTR*, in Northumbrian uncial and minuscule scripts survive at Bückeburg, Münster in Westfalen, Darmstadt, and Vienna, but none in Great Britain; see ibid., pp. 39-42, Appendix 2: "Bedae De temporum ratione liber, Manuscripts Dating from the Eighth and Ninth Centuries." Several historians have cited the complete text of *DTR* in MS Salisbury Cathedral 158 (s. IX 2), fols. 20-83; the earlier part of that manuscript may have been written in England, but those folios containing *DTR* display Carolingian script from the Continent (pp. 35 and 41).

47. Helmut Gneuss, "A Preliminary List of Manuscripts Written or Owned in England up to 1100," *Anglo-Saxon England* 9 (1981): 1-60. At least seventy-nine of those manuscripts are reported to contain scientific works, and many of them are said to contain several such works.

48. Neil R. Ker, *A Catalogue of Manuscripts Containing Anglo-Saxon* (Oxford, 1957); idem, *Medieval Libraries of Great Britain: A List of Surviving Books*, Royal Historical So-

ciety Guides and Handbooks 3 (London, 1941; 2nd ed., 1964; supp. ed., Andrew G. Watson, 1987).

49. E. W. B. Nicholson made several entries in the "official copy" of the Digby Catalogue kept in the Bodleian Library, but I should be loath to follow them: what he saw as underlining of a date on fol. 8, for example, is actually the reverse of a trough from dry point lining done on the verso, and the tiny black points of ink under the numerals for year 844 on fol. 36v cannot provide "evidence that the MS was copied from an earlier one written in 844, the first year of Adelhard abbot of St. Bertin's," as he thought. There are similar black points beneath numerals in most nineteen-year cycles, especially from 855 to 876, and they do not necessarily suggest an *annus praesens* for either scribe or user. On fol. 36v and fol. 37 is a list of indictions from 844 to 892, corresponding with the end of the nineteen-year cycles, and I assume that Raegenbold thought his work done by 892 or 893. Nevertheless he added another indiction for each year until 899. In the meantime he or someone else had begun to recopy the Dionysian Argumentum I from fol. 72v onto fol. 8, applied it to the year 867 but with incorrect data, erased, and then abandoned the item. These several observations leave us with the period from 844 to 892/93 within which Raegenbold worked, and they suggest that he may have lived until 899.

50. There is a special feast of John of Beverly and another for Cuthbert in the calendar, which suggest Northumbrian origins. Thus Kenneth Sisam, *Studies in the History of Old English Literature* (Oxford, 1953), p. 71, thought that this collection was Northumbrian and contained "a calendar that reached Southern England about Alfred's time." But this is uncertain.

51. Jones, "The 'Lost' Sirmond Manuscript of Bede's Computus," pp. 204-19; Jones, introduction to *Bedae Opera de temporibus*, pp. 105-13; Stevens, introduction to *Rabani mogontiacensis episcopi de computo*, in *Corpus Christianorum continuatio mediaevalis*, vol. XLIV (Turnhout, Belgium, 1979) pp. 170-71, and 177-84; and Ó Cróinín, "The Irish Provenance of Bede's Computus," pp. 229-47.

52. Raegenbold's odd practice of writing *qi* for *qui*, *qando* for *quando*, and so on, is just one of his peculiarities of orthography and grammar, which have not found parallels in other ninth-century manuscripts. Despite the possibilities outlined by David Dumville, "Motes and Beams," *Peritia* 2 (1983): 249-50, the script does not allow one to expect an English background for this writer.

53. David Dumville has shed much light on the development of this script and may soon clarify the origin of this manuscript. His "English Square Minuscule Script: The Background and Earliest Phases," *Anglo-Saxon England* 16 (1987): 147-79, is a brilliant discussion of "the complex evidence attesting scribal efforts at reform and progress in the period c. 890-c. 920 . . . " and "a beginning made in charting the early history of the new Square minuscule" (p. 179). He finds that "the creation of a new canonical English script form had been achieved by c. 930" (p. 178). MS Exeter 3507 should be included soon in his studies.

54. Some of the same verses were also found in MS Oxford BL Bodley 579, fols. 53v-54v: "Linea Christe . . . ," "Prima dies Phoebi . . . ," "Bes sena mensium . . . ," and "Primus Romanas . . . " — the last from Ausonius but with an extra line; the verses "Ianus et october binis . . . " and "September semper quinis . . . ," however, are not found in the Exeter manuscript, although they were copied into the later MS London BL Sloane 263 (s. XI), fols. 21v-22, and other English manuscripts. MS Bodley 579 is commonly called the Leofric Missal because fols. 1-37 contain a service book and it was listed with Bishop Leofric's gifts to Exeter Cathedral . That part of the codex was written about s. IX/X in northeastern France (perhaps in the region of Arras/Cambrai) and may have been brought from that region to England by Leofric himself. But fols. 38-58 compose a separate codex that was also written in a different Continental minuscule probably of late tenth century. Fol. 49 displays a large *dextera domini* with dates written on each finger of the hand, and this opens a section that applies some computistical knowledge to liturgical practices. The very common nineteen *Termini Paschales* ("Nonae Aprelis . . . ") are found on fol. 52. There are a calendar and Eas-

ter tables for 969 to 1006 on fol. 53, but fols. 54v-58 have additional prose passages with *argumenta* that serve specifically liturgical rather than computistical interests. This part of MS Bodley 579 therefore cannot properly be called an "Anglo-Saxon *computus*," and its presence or use at Exeter has not yet been demonstrated. MS Bodley 579 was published as *The Leofric Missal* (Oxford, 1883) by F. E. Warren, who hoped that the calendar and Easter tables had been prepared for "Glastonbury before 978." His wish has often been repeated as if it were fact by other scholars without citing evidence to support the proposal.

55. J. Fontaine, *Isidore de Séville, Traité de la nature*, (Bordeaux, 1960) pp. 164-327, Latin text and French translation. See also the sections of his introduction, pp. 38-45: "Les 'accidents massifs' et les trois recensions"; pp. 69-83: "La diffusion du De Natura rerum en Europe de Sisebut à Charlemagne"; and pp. 75-78: "Le problème de la 'méditation irlandaise.'"

56. Fontaine, *Isidore de Séville*, pp. 328-35.

57. The earliest manuscript of Isidore, *De natura rerum* (612, first version), and of the verse *Epistola Sisebuti* (613, response) is MS El Escorial, Real Biblioteca de San Lorenzo, R.II.18, fols. 9-24, in a single Visigothic script within the period 636-90. The drawing on fol. 24 represents the positions of sun, moon, and earth in positions of either solar or lunar eclipses; later users of this manuscript also noted on fol. 66 the eclipses of 778 and 779. Unfortunately, Fontaine did not reproduce the manuscript diagram but created his own explanatory schema on p. 337.

58. The manuscripts are Basel Universitätsbibliothek F.III.15f (Anglo-Saxon minuscule s. VIII), fols. 1-13; København Universitetsbibliotek Lat. 19 (Anglo-Saxon minuscule s. VIII 2), fragment VII; Basel F.III.15a (Fulda Insular minuscule s. VIII ex), fols. 1v-16v; and Weimar Landesbibliothek Fragment 414a (Fulda Insular minuscule s. VIII ex). Insular exemplars appear to have been used for two other manuscripts with this version: St. Gallen Stiftsbibliothek 238 (750-70), pp. 312-84, written by Winithar; and Besançon Bibliothèque Municipale 184 (Eastern France s. IX in), fols. 1v-55v. MS Paris Bibliothèque National Lat. 10616 (Verona 796-99) fols. 1-93v, deriving from an exemplar of the "Recension courte" that had received the long version additions before being transcribed at Verona during the episcopacy of Egino, reveals no Insular traces.

59. *Rabani mogontiacensis episcopi de computo*, ed. Stevens, pp. 163-331; see pp. 190-94 for manuscripts and pp. 322-23 for glosses.

60. Abbon de Fleury, *Quaestiones Grammaticales*, ed. Anita Guerreau-Jalabert, Collection auteurs latins du moyen âge (Paris, 1982); Henry Bradley, "On the Text of Abbo of Fleury's Quaestiones Grammaticalae," *Proceedings of the British Academy* 10 (1921-23): 126-69; M. Manitius, *Geschichte der lateinischen Literatur des Mittelalters* 2 (Munich, 1923), pp. 664-72; A. Van de Vijver, "Les oeuvres inédites d'Abbon de Fleury," *Revue Bénédictine* 47 (1935): 126-69; and Ron B. Thomson, "Two Astronomical Tractates of Abbo of Fleury," in *The Light of Nature*, ed. J. D. North and J. J. Roche (Dordrecht, Netherlands, 1985), pp. 113-33. Thomson (pp. 116-18) listed eighteen manuscripts for his edition of two *Sententiae*, of which at least twelve were written in England.

61. Edited by Thomson, "Two Astronomical Tractates of Abbo of Fleury," pp. 113-33, and "Further Astronomical Material of Abbo of Fleury," *Mediaeval Studies* 50 (1988): 671-73.

62. Ludwig Traube,"Computus Helperici," *Neues Archiv* 18 (1893): 73-105, reprinted in *Vorlesungen und Abhandlungen* 3, ed. Paul Lehmann (Munich, 1920), pp. 128-56; Patrick McGurk, "Computus Helperic: Its Transmission in England in the Eleventh and Twelfth Centuries," *Medium Aevum* 43 (1974): 1-5; Arno Borst,"Computus: Zeit und Zahl im Mittelalter," *Deutsches Archiv* 44/1 (Munich, 1988): 1-81, esp. 25. W. M. Stevens, "Catalogue of Computistical Tracts, A.D. 200-1200," currently lists seventy-eight manuscripts, but more will be located.

63. MS Oxford St. John's College Library XVII (1102-10), fols. 123-37, especially fols. 127-28: "... fiunt XXVII. Superest in singulis signis, bisse unius horae. ... "

64. Heiric/Helperic Autissiodurensis, *Liber de arte calculatoria*, explicits (1) " . . . de his omnibus quicquid quesierit procul dubio repperturus erit"; (2) " . . . ut his primum quasi quibusdam alphabeti characteribus inducti, illa deinceps facilius assequantur"; (3) " . . . adventum domini celebrare valebit"; (4) " . . . sequentes post se terminos in aliam feriam mutaverit"; and others. One version was prepared by Abbo of Fleury from an exemplar that used *annus praesens* 946, and the text reveals adjustments of dates from 898 to 912; see MS Biblioteca Apostolica Vaticana Vat. Lat. 3101 (1077 from Ilmunster?), fols. 42-62, cited by Traube, "Computus Helperici," p. 136. Abbo added the preface, "Me legat annotes qui vult cognoscere ciclos. . . . "

65. MS Berlin Deutsche Staatsbibliothek Phillipps 1833 [Cat. 138] (s. X ex Fleury), fols. 7v-20v; his dialectical and rhetorical justifications for arithmetic have been studied by G. R. Evans and A. M. Peden, "Natural Science and the Liberal Arts in Abbo of Fleury's Commentary on the *Calculus* of Victorius of Aquitaine," *Viator* 16 (1985): 109-27; see also Borst, "Computus," pp. 27-28.

66. MS Berlin, fols. 33v-43, ed. *PL* 90 (1850), cols. 727-60, especially cols. 757-60. This manuscript was transcribed either near the end of Abbo's life or shortly thereafter. As his computistical works have not yet found a modern editor, it is not altogether clear whether these paragraphs are directly from Abbo or from his students at Fleury. I am aware of twenty-nine manuscripts of the *Computus vulgaris* in several versions, five manuscripts of his preface to Dionysian Easter tables, seven manuscripts of his *Tabula lunaris*, seven manuscripts of his first letter to Gerald and Vitalus (1003) about altering the date of the Incarnation, and five manuscripts of another letter (ca. 1004?) to the same recipients, with further discussion of that question. No reliable editions of these works are available, and the final letter seems not to have been published.

67. S. J. Crawford, ed., *Byrhtferth's Manual*, Early English Text Society (EETS) 177 (London, 1929; repr. in EETS Original Series [Oxford, 1966], with notes and errata by N. R. Ker). The exemplar from which the Ashmole manuscript was transcribed was in disarray and so is the edition, which should be read in the following sequence: p. 2, line 1, to p. 30, line 9; 44.28 to 56.29; 30.9 to 44.27; 56.30 seq.; and passages of a folio or more are missing in several places. The manual was illustrated, but most figures have been torn out of the Ashmole manuscript in modern times. On the basis of Ashmole 328, pp. 173-74, Crawford dated the whole work to 1011, and this was repeated by Ker, *Catalogue*, no. 288, but it is difficult to see how the data would support this assertion. Various entries must have been made by the author in different years. Peter Baker has announced the preparation of a new edition.

68. Peter S. Baker, "Byrhtferth's Enchiridion and the Computus in Oxford, St. John's College 17," *Anglo-Saxon England* 10 (1982): 123-42. The earlier proposal to date that manuscript to 1081-92 by Cyril Hart, "The Ramsey Computus," *English Historical Review* 85 (1970): 29-44, depended upon an assumption that the four leaves of MS London British Library Cotton Nero C. VII (Ramsey, 1086-92), fols. 80-84, were missing folios from the Saint John's College codex, as had been proposed by N. R. Ker, "Membra disiecta," *British Museum Quarterly* 12 (1938): 130-35. Baker has demonstrated, however, that this could not have been the case and accepted the dating clause on MS fol. 3v "ad praesens tempus I. CX" or 1110. Nevertheless, the annals and the texts transcribed reveal numerous details of dating between 1102 and 1110, with a few entries extending to 1113. This has been demonstrated very well in the recent study of the manuscript by Faith E. Wallis, "Ms Oxford St John's College 17: A Mediaeval Manuscript in Its Context" (Ph.D. diss., University of Toronto, 1984), especially pp. 122-29. Therefore the transcription of computistical texts into MS St. John's College XVII occurred during the period of 1102-10.

69. *Aelfric de temporibus anni*, ed. H. Henel, Early English Text Society 213 (London, 1942), from MS Cambridge University Library Gg. III.28 (s. X ex), fols. 255-61v; this manuscript has a collection of Ælfric's early writings, made perhaps at Cerne Abbey by one of his students. See also M. R. Godden, "De temporibus anni," in *An Eleventh-Century Anglo-*

Saxon Illustrated Miscellany: British Library Cotton Tiberius B. V, part I, ed. Patrick Mc-Gurk, Early English Manuscripts in Facsimile 21 (Copenhagen, 1983), pp. 59-64.

70. MS Cambridge St. John's College Library I.15 (s. XII ex), pp. 353-402, esp. p. 396: "Unde patet lunam peragere zodiacum annum XXVII dies et octo horas." See Borst, "Computus," p. 35; on dating of Gerland's work, see idem, "Ein Forschungsbericht Hermanns des Lahmen," *Deutsches Archiv* 40 (1984): 379-477, esp. 465-66. Thus far, I have recorded only twenty-six manuscripts of the *Computus Gerlandi Bedam imitantis* in the "Catalogue of Computistical Tracts, A. D. 200-1200," mostly from the twelfth and thirteenth centuries, but there may well be at least a hundred more for this popular work, which has not been published. Cataloguers have sometimes mentioned *Tabulae Gerlandi* without determining whether the accompanying text or various texts are by the same author.

71. For example, the *Computus Cunestabuli* (Constable, s. XII Canterbury) and the work by Salomon of Canterbury (fl. 1185-98) in MS London BL Egerton 3314 (s. XII 2), fols. 1v-8v, argue strongly against Gerland. These texts have not been published. See C. H. Haskins, *Studies in the History of Medieval Science*, 2nd ed. (Cambridge, Mass., 1927), p. 87; and P. J. Willets, "A Reconstructed Astronomical Manuscript from Christ Church Library Canterbury," *British Museum Quarterly* 30 (1965-66): 22-30.

72. Robert de Losinga, *De annis domini* (1086), MS Oxford Bodleian Library Auct. F.1.9 (1120-30), fols. 2v-12v, and seven other manuscripts. The MSS Oxford BL Digby 56 (s. XII), fols. 162-219, and Vat. Regin. lat. 1281 (s. XII), fols. 1-4v, show that the *computi* of Heiric/Helperic and of Gerland and the letters of Abbo about the *aera Incarnationis* were available at Hereford while Robert was bishop; the latter manuscript contains Robert's work on fols. 4v-5. See W. H. Stevenson, "A Contemporary Description of the Domesday Survey," *English Historical Review* 22 (1907): 72-84; and A. Cordoliani, "L'activité compotistique de Robert, évêque de Hereford," in *Mélanges René Crozet* (Poitiers, 1966), pp. 333-40. The manuscripts of Robert's *computus* also give dates for movable feasts in three great (532-year) Dionysian cycles with corresponding Marian years rubricated in the right column: Dionysian year 1086 would be Marian year 1108 of the Incarnation. See Anna-Dorothea van den Brincken, "Marianus Scottus," *Deutsches Archiv* 17 (1961): 191-238; and Borst, "Computus," pp. 37-38.

73. *De naturali cursu cuiusque lunationis* is known in four manuscripts, of which the earliest is MS Cambridge Trinity College O.7.41 (s. XI 2), fols. 54v-58; it is unpublished. *Sententia Petri Ebrei cognomento Anphus de dracone quam dominus Walcerus prior malvernensis ecclesie in latinam transtulit linguam* is known in MS Oxford Bodleian Library Auct. F.1.9 (s. XII med), fols. 96-99, and MS Erfurt Wiss.-Bibl. Amploniana Q. 351 (s. XIV), fols. 15-32; ed. J. M. Millás-Vallicrosa, in "La Aportación Astronómica de Pedro Alfonso," *Sefarad* 3 (1943): 87-97; I owe this citation to Charles S. F. Burnett and J. B. Trapp of the Warburg Institute. Another work of Walcher is *De bipertita discretione horarum* (1108-12?), known in two English manuscripts but unpublished. See L. Thorndike, *A History of Magic and Experimental Science*, vol. 1 (New York, 1923), pp. 68-73, concerning Peter; and Haskins, *Studies in the History of Medieval Science*, pp. 113-17, who discussed both Walcher and Peter and quoted from the *Sententia*.

74. *Praefatio magistri Rogeri infantis in compotum* (1124, 1176?), MS Oxford BL Digby 40 (s. XII/XIII), fols. 21-50v, and Cambridge University Library Kk. I. 1 (s. XIII), fols. 222v-239, partly published by T. Wright, *Biographia Britannica Literaria* (London, 1846), 2:89-91. Roger used and corrected the works of Heiric/Helperic and Gerland. See also Roger's *Tabula astronomica* in MS London BL Arundel 377 (s. XIII), fols. 86v-87 (1120-1400), but adjusted for the meridian of Hereford in 1178 (fol. 86v apud Toletum et Herefordiam), unpublished. See C. H. Haskins, "Introduction of Arabic Science into England," *English Historical Review* 30 (1915): 65-68, and his *Studies in the History of Medieval Science*, pp. 124-26.

75. Concerning Robert's early life at Hereford where he may have written the *computi*, see R. W. Southern, *Robert Grosseteste: The Growth of an English Mind in Medieval Europe* (Oxford, 1986), pp. 63-82 and 127-31. Richard C. Dales, "The Computistical Works Ascribed to Robert Grosseteste," *ISIS* 80 (1989): 74-79, dates the so-called *Computus I* shortly after 1200; because of its use of Arabic sources he places the *Computus correctorius* after 1217 and probably about 1220. The *Kalendarium* is left undated by Dales, but he thinks that it "is nearly identical with that of Roger of Hereford" (citing a paper by Jennifer Moreton, to be published). The so-called *Computus minor* was found to be a post-1220 abridgment of Robert Grosseteste's *Computus I*; it refers to yet another *computus* for common rules of calendar reckoning (Heiric/Helperic, Abbo, Gerland?), but not to any of Robert's works. The *Computus correctorius* of Robert Grosseteste displaced other works, such as *De anni ratione liber* of Johannes de Sacrobosco, and brought new English computistical scholarship into the core of the *corpus astronomicum* of Oxford, Paris, and other medieval universities. See Olaf Pedersen, "The Corpus Astronomicum and the Traditions of Mediaeval Latin Astronomy," in *Colloquia Copernicana* 3: *Astronomy of Copernicus and Its Background* (Wroclaw, 1975), pp. 57-96, especially pp. 73-82.

PART IV

✣

Sutton Hoo and Archaeology

CHAPTER 9

✛

Princely Burial in Scandinavia at the Time of the Conversion

Else Roesdahl

Research into Conversion-era Scandinavian princely burials and into Sutton Hoo involves many of the same problems: considering the results of old excavations, interpreting the absence of human bones, identifying the dead person, and taking into account the political and religious background of new burial customs and of particularly splendid burials, as well as possible Christian elements in a generally pagan-type burial. Unanswered questions and uncertain answers are many, but our understanding might be made clearer if late pagan princely burials were studied in a broader context, for despite the differences in time between the conversion of the individual Anglo-Saxon kingdoms and each of the three Scandinavian kingdoms, some of the same social mechanisms were probably at work—there as well as in Continental western Europe and elsewhere—at the time of the conversion of the various realms. One such mechanism might have been a pagan reaction and revival against Christianity, which threatened to destroy the old order—a revival also reflected in new and extravagantly pagan princely burial customs and monuments, often based on ancient types in order to focus on tradition and recall the old order. In addition, such princely burials and monuments might have had an important function as dynastic or family symbols in the power politics of their time.[1]

Researchers of Conversion-era Scandinavian and English princely burials also face the common problem of interpreting and identifying such graves in the light of histories and of heroic or court poetry, some of which is of uncertain date. This poetry (for example, *Beowulf* and the Old Norse skaldic poems *Ynglingatál*, *Hákonarmál*, and *Eiríksmál*) is intensely concerned with the death, burial, and reputation of named kings. It clearly demonstrates a deep fascination with such matters, which is fully shared by today's and yesterday's archaeologists. For instance, could the Queen Åsa mentioned in *Ynglingatál* be the woman buried in that splendid ship in the ninth-century Oseberg mound in south Norway? Was the rich woman of the mound that tough queen, who (among many other things) arranged the assassination of her husband King Gudrød?[2]

In an introduction to princely burial in Scandinavia a few points should be clarified. First, although Scandinavia (Figure 9.1) is a very vast area,

Figure 9.1. Scandinavia.

constituting about half of Europe's length, and although the main foreign contacts of Denmark, Norway, and Sweden were widely different (as determined by geography), there were easy connections by boat among the various parts of Scandinavia, and it did share much of a common culture distinct from the rest of Europe. Second, it was during the Viking Age that the three Scandinavian countries started to take form, and Christianity was introduced in all three countries by a native king, but never by one of an ancient and established local royal lineage. Christianity came — as far as we can see — hand in hand with a new power politics: it meant a break with traditional power structures, as well. Third, the chronology of the conversion of the three Scandinavian countries is not quite the same. Denmark was first, in about 965. Norway was converted about fifty years later, at the beginning of the eleventh century. Last came Sweden, which had a Christian king from about the year 1000, but where important parts of the country remained partly pagan until around 1100. And while there are hardly any contemporary written sources about the conversion of Sweden, or about Sweden in the Viking Age generally (apart from rune-stones), we do have — by Scandinavian standards — quite a few about Norway and Denmark.

Monument types and burial customs used in late pagan and early Christian Scandinavia's princely burials appear nonetheless to be largely uniform: fashions spread from one region or country to others through close contacts between their ruling classes. Pagan princes received monumental mounds and rich grave goods (often including ships), while Christian kings were buried in churches from the very beginning. It is also a common Scandinavian phenomenon that the first suitable king to die by violent means became a saint: St. Olav of Norway was martyred in 1030 and St. Canute of Denmark in 1086, although Sweden had no royal saint until St. Erik, killed in 1160.[3]

The monuments of Adelsö in Uppland, Sweden, are characteristic of late pagan princely burial places in Scandinavia: a group of large mounds (possibly built over a rather long span of years) located on an important royal manor not far from a large trading center or trade route. It is also characteristic that a church was built close to the mounds at a later date. The largest of the Adelsö mounds, known collectively as the Kings' Mounds, is about fifty meters in diameter and of unknown date. Only the smallest of them has been excavated: Skopintull, about twenty meters in diameter, excavated in 1917. Skopintull held a cremation burial from the tenth century, with human bones and the remains of unusually rich grave furnishings, such as fragments of gold, fine textiles, belt mounts, gilt bronze mounts for a splendid horse harness, many animal bones, and possibly a boat.[4] There can be no doubt about the princely character of the burial.

It is not known who was buried here, but we know the names of some of the ninth-century kings connected with Birka on the nearby island of Björkö in lake Mälaren, one of Scandinavia's most important trading centers in the Viking Age. It is very likely that Adelsö was the seat of the kings connected with Birka: the estate was not too close, but close enough to benefit from all the commodities and luxuries arriving at the trading center and close enough to exercise oversight over local affairs and to guarantee market peace.

Figure 9.2. Burial mounds at Borre, Norway. (Photograph: Ove Holst, the University Museum of National Antiquities, Oslo, Norway, 1970.)

Because of the very few written sources on early Sweden, the Adelsö mounds and other large Swedish burial mounds of probable Viking Age date (such as the very large Nordian's mound in Åshusby, Uppland) will remain anonymous. The first historically known Swedish king whose burial place is noted in written sources (albeit later ones) is Olof Skötkonung, the first Christian king, who died in about 1022. He is said to have been buried in the church of the royal estate of Husaby in Västergötland, where a fine Romanesque church now stands. While Adelsö was in the original territory of the Svear, not far from the pagan cult center of Old Uppsala, Husaby lay in the original territory of the Götar; it was here that Christianity was first generally accepted, and here that King Olof Skötkonung's power was based.[5]

The most famous Norwegian Viking Age princely burials are the ship graves in Oseberg, Gokstad, and Borre. They are all inhumation graves in large mounds, situated in the southern part of the country not far from present-day Oslo and close to Kaupang, which functioned as a trading center in the eighth and ninth centuries.[6] Borre (Figure 9.2) has a fine group of mounds and cairns near a medieval church, as at Adelsö. We know of nine large mounds and two cairns here (of which some have been destroyed) and of more than twenty-five smaller mounds and cairns. The large mounds are up to forty meters in diameter and four to five meters high.

From a large mound destroyed in 1852, iron ship nails and some very fine grave goods have been preserved, including gilt bronze mounts from a horse harness whose ornaments gave the name to the Borre art style. It is clearly a princely grave from the late ninth or early tenth century – about one hundred years before the conversion of Norway, but certainly a time when Christianity was well known in the country through its many contacts with the British Isles and the Continent.

Borre must have been a royal estate in the Viking Age. The skaldic poem *Ynglingatál* of the late ninth century mentions Borre as the burial place of two former kings, Halvdan and Øystein. Of course, every effort has been made to figure out in which of the large mounds they were placed, and a number of very ingenious but not very convincing theories have been launched. This is also true of the other two ship burials mentioned above, Oseberg and Gokstad, for Ynglingatál celebrates not only the death and burial place of Kings Halvdan and Øystein, but also those of a long line of petty royalty in the area, whose splendid ancestry is traced to the old Swedish royal dynasty of Uppsala and further back to the gods themselves.[7]

It may well be that the prestigious Borre mounds are the manifestations of a new dynasty that introduced splendid new burial customs and monuments in the area, in order to mark the new times and to support their family prestige. The Borre mounds, some of which are probably of Migration-period date, may have been inspired by the large royal mounds in Uppsala, which date from the fifth or sixth centuries and reach up to sixty meters in diameter. This would chime with the Swedish ancestry of the dynasty, as claimed in *Ynglingatál*. It must, however, be borne in mind that Norway also had large old mounds that could have been the inspiration, such as Raknehaugen north of Oslo. This is about ninety-five meters in diameter and fifteen meters high and is probably of the sixth century. It is Scandinavia's largest man-made mound, but it held no grave.[8]

The whole Borre complex, with its links to religion, royalty, and skaldic poetry, is central to our understanding of princely burial in Scandinavia, yet far too little is known about it. New results, however, are on their way: a large research program on Borre with new excavations and reevaluations of the old evidence has begun, directed by Björn Myhre of Oslo University.[9] It is also to be hoped that dendrochronology (the technique of dating by tree rings) will provide exact dates in years to come for the Oseberg and Gokstad burials, traditionally dated from the early ninth and tenth centuries, respectively.[10] They might be studied on a safer basis then, and thus their relation to skaldic poetry and sagas, as well.

The dead person in each of the graves (a woman in one, a man in the other) had been placed in a specially built chamber in the ship. Both chambers had been broken into long before the excavations; the bodies had been disturbed, and a number of valuables undoubtedly removed. We are left with the question of who was responsible for the mound-breaking. Were they grave-robbers, or could they have been the members of the family that had since become Christian, trying to remove the remains of their pagan ancestors and give them a Christian burial, perhaps in a nearby church? The question is still open, especially for Oseberg,[11] but it will be discussed further below, in connection with Jelling.

The Oseberg and Gokstad burials also provided a wealth of grave furnishings: a large ship and all the other equipment necessary for the journey to the next world and for a suitable life upon arrival. The Oseberg burial held a whole wagon and several exquisitely carved sledges, all sorts of household goods for both kitchen and table, beds, a chair, fine textiles embroidered with elaborate procession scenes, and much else besides. It seems reasonable to conclude from these and from other late pagan burials in Scandinavia that the pagan concept of death included the idea of a journey to the next world (by ship, by horse, by wagon, or by a combination of these means) and of an afterlife there along the lines of real life.[12]

It is generally accepted that the late pagan realm of dead warriors, chieftains, and kings was Valhalla, the Hall of the Slain, where the chief god Odin presided and where the dead heroes spent their time fighting and feasting till the end of the world. The closely related skaldic poems *Eiríksmál* and *Hákonarmál*, composed for two Norwegian kings and brothers in about 960, the eve of the adoption of Christianity, provide very important information on Valhalla. Eirík was Erik Bloodaxe, who was expelled from Norway, became king in York, and was killed at Stainmore in 954. He was a pagan, and the location of his grave is unknown. Hákon, his half brother, was brought up as a Christian in England at the court of King Athelstan. When he returned to Norway, it was as Christian king of a pagan country. *Hákonarmál* and later sagas relate how well he managed this difficult situation, and how after being killed in battle in about 960, he was buried the pagan way and received by Odin in Valhalla. Odin had decided that the brave Christian king Hákon should lose his life in order to go to him.[13]

It would be extremely interesting to have direct knowledge of this princely burial from the time of the conversion; sagas from around 1200 locate it at Seim, not far from the town of Bergen in western Norway. Yet the only known mound of any size (known in 1824 as Kongehøjen) in the area of Seim is only twenty meters in diameter, and it was already badly damaged in 1879 when it was first excavated. Nothing important was found then, and a reexcavation in 1958 by the late Egil Bakka had no important results either. So whether or not this was in fact the grave of the Christian king Hákon the Good remains in question.[14]

Norway has many other large burial mounds of probable Viking Age date, such as the enormous Herlaugshaugen in Trøndelag, northern Norway, with a diameter of about seventy meters. But little synthetic work has been done on them in recent times, and excavations are usually old, if the mounds have been excavated at all.[15] The first Christian king of Norway to receive Christian burial was Olav Haraldsson, later Saint Olav, who was killed at Stiklestad in 1030. His relics were taken soon after that to Trondheim, the later archbishop's seat, where he was worshipped as a saint.[16]

Our understanding of Conversion period princely graves in Norway and Sweden can be broadened by studying the evidence of Danish graves from the tenth century. Much work has been done on these during recent years, including new excavations, republications of old excavation results, and the establishment of exact dates through dendrochronology. We can begin to glimpse how the advent of Christianity affected burial customs, and I think that we can also start to understand some of the ideas behind monuments, grave furnishings, and rituals.

It is known from written sources that Denmark was converted at the command of King Harald Bluetooth around the year 965. But through many foreign contacts to the south and west, Denmark (like Norway) had long known about the new religion, and many Danes abroad had been baptized or received the *prima signatio* (the sign of the cross, a fairly noncommittal precursor to baptism). There had also been missionaries in Denmark, and a few churches had already been built there. An earlier king, Gnupa, had been forced to receive baptism in 934 after his defeat at the hands of the German king Henry the Fowler.

Christianity was thus well known as an approaching religion, and against this background it is interesting to note that a new burial custom for the upper classes appeared in Denmark around 900 or slightly later. It was a rather extravagant and stereotyped form of burial custom, lasting until Christian burial customs took over in the second half of that century. This new burial custom may have been partly inspired by the great Norwegian ship burials. For the men it was certainly a burial fit for warriors, and it clearly involved transport facilities for both men and women. This burial custom can be studied on at least two levels, the upper-class and the princely.

The upper-class male grave furnishing can be described thus: a horse, riding equipment, and food for the journey; weapons and entertainments (like a game board or a hunting dog) for the next life. This is in accordance with what we believe to be the concept of Valhalla, an afterlife of strife and good social entertainment among equals. The graves never contain a helmet or a mail shirt, perhaps because such would not be necessary in Odin's realm, where the slain would wake up again.

Upper-class women were usually buried in a wagon body, a substitute for a whole wagon, as their means of transportation to the other world. Ladies did not ride; they traveled by wagon, just as in their lifetimes. They brought fine textiles and textile implements, often a box with small necessities, some nice tableware, perhaps a roasting spit, and perhaps a lapdog (instead of a man's hunting dog). Thus women were also prepared for a comfortable life after death, though it is hardly known where they went.[17]

These men's and women's graves were often in mounds, and many are known from this short period. They were probably cheaper versions of the true princely graves that appeared in Denmark for the first time during this same period. Of these, the finest are from Hedeby, Ladby, and Jelling — all male burials, though the woman's grave at Søllested,[18] dug up in the nineteenth century, probably equaled them. The oldest of these graves, dating from about 900, is the so-called boat-chamber grave found under a mound just outside the semicircular rampart of Viking Age Scandinavia's largest trading center, Hedeby. The mound contained a burial chamber (Figure 9.3), above which was placed a whole ship, of which only the clench nails have survived. There were three horses, and there had been three men: two men, each with a sword, in one part of the burial chamber, and the main person with his own unusually fine sword in a separate compartment. Their bones did not survive, but the grave goods were undisturbed and seem to be suited to travel in style and ceremonies for fine receptions, as known from Frankish sources. According to the theory published by Detlev Ellmers, the two extra men may have been the marshal and the cupbearer.[19] If this is really a Valhalla burial (and I believe it is), the dead prince or king intended to travel in style to Odin's Hall, followed by two high-ranking men killed for the occasion.

The slightly later ship burial from a mound in Ladby had once been even more splendid. Here were found no less than eleven horses and several dogs, but there had clearly been intruders, and the human bones and many grave goods were missing. What is left, however, demonstrates extreme richness and quality. The dead prince has tentatively been identified with King Gnupa, the Danish king mentioned above, who was forced to baptism in 934 by Henry the Fowler.[20] His dynasty was soon to be overthrown by that of King Gorm the Old and his son Harald Bluetooth.[21]

The grandest and also the most thoroughly investigated royal burials from the time of the conversion of Scandinavia are in Jelling; they form part of a large, partly pagan and partly Christian complex of monuments (Figure 9.4). These comprise two large mounds, the remains of a stone-setting, two royal burials, two rune-stones, and a church (there may, of course, have been more monuments, which have since disappeared). All those mentioned were erected during the decades around and after the middle of the tenth century, at the very time of the conversion of Denmark, and most of them were built by King Harald Bluetooth. These clearly celebrate his parents and also himself, his rule over a very large territory and his great achievements, including military conquests and the conversion itself. They are the monuments of the new prosperous dynasty at its height, displaying its power, wealth, and prestige on a scale never before seen in Scandinavia. And here a pagan monument complex was changed into a Christian one.

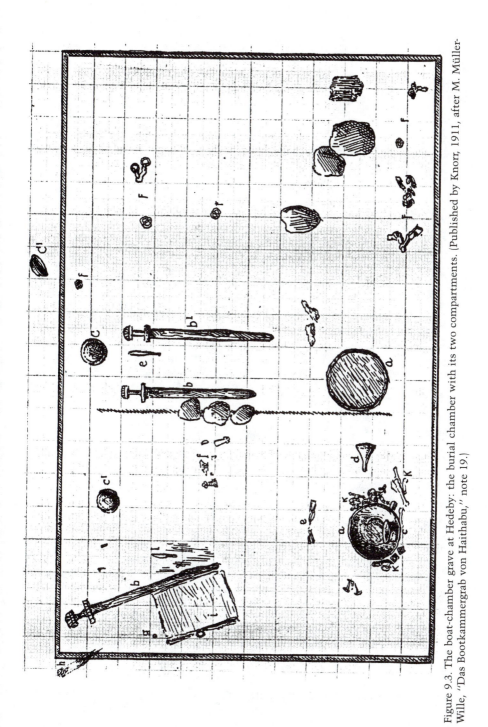

Figure 9.3. The boat-chamber grave at Hedeby: the burial chamber with its two compartments. (Published by Knorr, 1911, after M. Müller-Wille, "Das Bootkammergrab von Haithabu," note 19.)

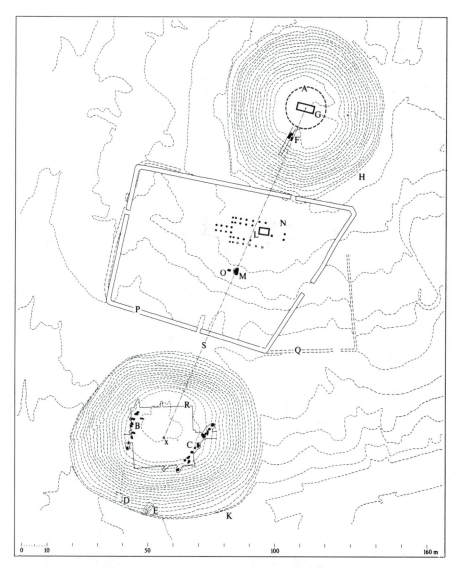

Figure 9.4. Plan of Jelling, Denmark. *A*, Bronze Age mound. *B, C, D, E*, rows of standing stone, probably remains of ship-setting. *F*, six large stones. *G*, burial chamber. *H*, North Mound. *K*, South Mound, with *x* indicating the post in the center of the mound. *L*, burial in the church. *M*, King Harald's rune-stone. *N*, outline of the present church and roof bearing posts from the earliest building below it. *O*, King Gorm's rune-stone. *P*, extent of the churchyard in 1861. *Q*, extent of the churchyard today. *R*, area excavated inside the South Mound in 1942. King Harald's rune-stone stands at the midpoint of a line *S* connecting the center of the burial chamber in the North Mound and the post in the center of the South Mound. (After E.Roesdahl, *Vikingernes verden*.)

Jelling has been investigated many times. The latest excavations were carried out in the late 1970s and in 1981 by Knud Krogh of the Danish

National Museum, and recently dendrochronology has provided some exact dates. A modern publication, by Knud Krogh and others, is in progress.[22]

The monuments belong to at least three phases, and the clue to the whole complex is the two rune-stones. The inscription on the smaller stone says, "King Gorm made this monument in memory of Thorvi (Thyre) his wife, Denmark's adornment." The large stone says, "King Harald commanded these monuments to be made in memory of Gorm his father and in memory of Thorvi (Thyre) his mother — that Harald who won the whole of Denmark for himself and Norway, and made the Danes Christian."

The smaller rune-stone raised by King Gorm must be among the oldest elements from pagan times, but it is not known for certain where Thyre was buried, nor is the original place or context of the stone known. The once enormous stone-setting must also be early and pagan. Only part of it is preserved, however — the part covered by the South Mound. It was presumably a ship-setting, and if so the largest known in Denmark.[23]

The stone-setting seems to relate to the North Mound, which is the largest burial mound in Denmark, about sixty-five meters in diameter and eight and one-half meters high. It held a chamber grave for a very high-ranking man. Dendrochronology provides a terminus post quem for the closing of the chamber of either late 958 or early 959, a date fully corroborated by those few objects that were found in the chamber in the nineteenth century (it had clearly been broken into at an earlier stage). The date 958/59 accords with what little is known from written sources about the date of the death of the pagan king Gorm, Harald's father. All available evidence suggests that it really is King Gorm, who was buried with splendid pagan ceremonies in the North Mound of Jelling by his son. It is the only royal grave from pagan Scandinavia in which the dead person has been convincingly identified. The North Mound is the grandest late pagan princely grave known in Scandinavia, and it is contemporary, within five years or less, with the two greatest skaldic poems on the afterlife of kings in Valhalla, *Eiríksmál* and *Hákonarmál*, both mentioned earlier. The years around 960 must have seen a vigorous outburst of pagan revival and display on the highest social levels.

But within six or seven years of the great pagan burial in Jelling, King Harald and the Danes converted. Written sources imply that it happened after the year 958 and before 965, which is in full accordance with the dendrodate given for the North Mound. Against this background, the dendrodates from the South Mound are very interesting: according to them, the erection of this enormous mound (about seventy-seven meters in diameter and eleven meters high) probably started and certainly finished after the conversion, although the concept of a mound is basically pagan. No grave was found here during extensive excavations in 1942. This mound was probably built as a memorial, and possibly also for ceremonies on its large flat top. It was certainly a power symbol meant for display, and it was a work of architecture, like other mounds, carefully constructed of enormous numbers of grass turfs and shaped by using template structures.

King Harald's rune-stone mentioned above clearly dates from after the conversion. It was placed exactly between the centers of the two mounds, and it is the finest of all rune-stones—a large pyramidical boulder with script on one side, a lion and snake on the other, and Christ on the third side (Figure 9.5). Like so many other rune-stones it was presumably painted in vivid colors, but no trace of paint has been found.

Between this stone and the North Mound a large wooden church was built, at least thirty meters long and with a wooden burial chamber. It was found when the floor of the present stone church from about 1100 (the fourth church on the site) was excavated. In the grave were remains of the bones of a middle-aged man—who had first been buried elsewhere—as well as remains of rich textiles and two fine strap ends, which correspond closely in style to some of the objects from the chamber grave in the North Mound (Figure 9.6).

All available evidence suggests that this was also King Gorm's grave—that King Harald had his pagan father removed from the North Mound (hence the early intrusion) in order to give him a Christian burial and thus secure an afterlife for him. The grave was prominently placed in the east end of the nave of the new church, between the two mounds, and there was room for yet another grave by its side. Perhaps this space was reserved for Harald himself and the Jelling church was planned as a dynastic burial church, as in other Christian countries. But when Harald died about twenty years later, circa 987, after a successful rebellion led by his son, he was buried in Roskilde (the first precursor of the present Roskilde cathedral, where kings and queens are buried today). The great days of Jelling were over.

The Jelling complex seen as a whole, with its pagan and Christian monuments side by side, expresses the power of the mightiest Scandinavian king of its time.[24] Jelling also expresses the religious policy of the king who converted Denmark, the first Scandinavian country to become Christian. This must have been a policy of tolerance and peaceful transition—a pragmatic ruler's view, rather different from the ideologies expressed in some of the poetry and by the Christian church.

Being the most prestigious royal burial place in Scandinavia, Jelling presumably set some fashions, including perhaps the notion of translating pagan ancestors from mounds to churches. This may be the reason for some of the many intrusions in burial mounds where human bones are missing: they may instead be resting in a nearby church.

As elsewhere, Scandinavian kings and princes built churches and were buried in churches after their conversion. But whichever beliefs they or

Figure 9.5. King Harald's rune-stone in Jelling, Denmark. Under the picture of Christ are the last words of the runic inscription: ". . . and made the Danes Christian." (Photograph: Erik Moltke, National Museum of Denmark.)

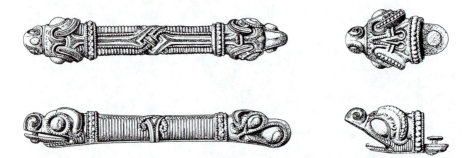

Figure 9.6. Silver cup from the burial chamber in the North Mound in Jelling and two strap mounts of gilt silver from the grave in the church; all are examples of the Jellinge art style and come from the graves attributed to King Gorm. (After M. Müller-Wille, "Königsgrab und Königskirche.") Scale 1:1.

others had, a basic function of burial was still the performance of religious and social ceremonies and the veneration of the dead man on a scale suitable to his reputation and to the reputation of those responsible for the burial, usually the family. Extravagant princely burial also provided a memorial to the dead man or woman and his or her descendants, as did princely poetry and literature – a memorial that helped to build up and sustain family prestige and reputation and to avoid oblivion, a basic human problem at the time, as expressed so clearly in its poems.[25]

Notes

1. Some important surveys or discussions of Scandinavian as well as other European material of the Viking Age and other periods include: M. Müller-Wille, "Bestattung im Boot:

Studien zu einer nordeuropäischen Grabsitte," *Offa* 25-26 (1970): 7-203; idem, "Pferdegrab und Pferdeopfer im frühen Mittelalter," *Berichten van de Rijksdienst voor het Oudheidkundig Bodemonderzoek* 20-21 (1970-71): 119-248; idem, "Königsgrab und Königskirche: Funde und Befunde im frühgeschichtlichen und mittelalterlichen Nordeuropa," *Bericht der Römisch-Germanischen Kommission* 63 (1982): 349-412; *Vendel Period Studies: Transactions of the Boat-Grave Symposium in Stockholm, February 2-3, 1981*, ed. J. P. Lamm and H.-Å. Nordström (Stockholm, 1983); J. Werner, "Adelsgräber von Niederstotzingen bei Ulm und von Bokchondong in Südkorea. Jenseitvorstellungen vor Rezeption von Christentum und Buddhismus im Lichte vergleichender Archäologie," *Bayerische Akademie der Wissenschaften, Philosophisch-Historische Klasse Abhandlungen, Neue Folge*, Heft 100 (Munich, 1988), pp. 1-20.

2. For example, A. W. Brøgger, *Borrefundet og Vestfoldkongernes graver*, Skrifter utgit av Videnskapsselskapet i Kristiania 1916, II. Historisk-Filosofisk Klasse 1 (Kristiana, 1917).

3. E. Roesdahl, "Prestige, Display and Monuments in Viking Age Scandinavia," in *Les Mondes Normands*, ed. H. Galinié (Caen, 1989), pp. 17-25; idem, *The Vikings* (London, 1991), published in Danish as *Vikingernes verden* (Copenhagen, 1987); and P. Sawyer, "The Process of Scandinavian Christianization," in *The Christianization of Scandinavia*, ed. B. Sawyer et al. (Alingsås, 1987), pp. 68-87. Müller-Wille, "Königsgrab und Königskirche," has many maps and full bibliographies and provides a valuable introduction to the topic of Scandinavian princely burials.

4. H. Rydh, *Förhistoriska undersökningar på Adelsö* (Stockholm, 1936), pp. 104ff.

5. B. Ambrosiani, "Aristocratic Graves and Manors in Early Medieval Sweden," *Archaeology and Environment* 4, in Honorem Evert Baudou (Umeå, 1985), pp. 109-18; Ambrosiani, *Birka*, Svenska Kulturminnen 2 (Stockholm, 1988); and P. Sawyer, *The Making of Sweden*, Occasional Papers on Medieval Topics 2 (Alingsås, 1988).

6. C. Blindheim, "Introduction," in *Proceedings of the Tenth Viking Congress*, ed. J. Knirk (Oslo, 1987), pp. 27-42.

7. Snorri Sturluson, *Heimskringla. Sagas of the Norse Kings*, trans. S. Laing, rev. P. Foote (London and New York, 1961, and later eds.); A. W. Brøgger, *Borrefundet: Reallexikon der Germanischen Altertumskunde*, ed. H. Beck et al. (Berlin and New York, 1973), s.v. Borre, article by C. Blindheim; and B. Myhre, "The Royal Cemetery at Borre: A Norwegian Center in a European Periphery," forthcoming in the proceedings of the Sutton Hoo symposium in York, October 1989, ed. M. Carver.

8. Myhre, "The Royal Cemetery at Borre"; and B. Magnus and B. Myhre, *Norges Historie* 1: *Forhistorien*, ed. K. Mykland, 2nd ed. (Oslo, 1986), pp. 389-93.

9. Myhre, "The Royal Cemetery at Borre."

10. N. Nicolaysen, *Langskibet fra Gokstad ved Sandefjord* (Kristiania, 1882), full text in both Norwegian and English; and A. W. Brøgger, H. Falk, and H. Schetelig, eds., *Osebergfundet* 1-5 (Oslo, 1917-28).

11. A. W. Brøgger, "Oseberggraven—Haugbrottet," *Viking* 9 (1945): 1-44.

12. O. Almgren, "Vikingatidens grafskick i verkligheten och i den fornnordiska litteraturen," *Nordiska Studier*, tillegnade Adolf Noreen (Uppsala, 1904), pp. 309-46; M. Müller-Wille, "Frühmittelalterliche Prunkgräber im südlichen Skandinavien," *Bonner Jahrbücher* 178 (1978): 633-52; D. Ellmers, "Fränkisches Königszeremoniell auch in Walhall," *Beiträge zur Schleswiger Stadtgeschichte* 25 (1980): 115-26; E. Roesdahl, *Viking Age Denmark* (London, 1982), pp. 159-71; and idem, *The Vikings*, pp. 147-58.

13. P. G. Foote and D. M. Wilson, *The Viking Achievement* (London and New York, 1970; rev. ed., 1980), pp. 361-62 and 391; E. Marold, "Das Walhallbild in den Eiríksmál und den Hákonarmál," *Medieval Scandinavia* 5 (1972): 19-33; Ellmers, "Fränkisches Königszeremoniell"; E. Roesdahl, "Fra vikingegrav til Valhal," in *Beretning fra Andet tværfaglige Vikingesymposium*, ed. T. Kisby et al. (Århus, 1983), pp. 39-49.

14. E. Bakka, "Kongshaugen på Seim i Alversund, Nordhordland," in *Frå Fjon til Fjusa* (1958), Årbok for Nord-og Midhordland Sogelag, 11. årgang, pp. 19-35.

15. Magnus and Myhre, *Norges Historie*, pp. 377-87 and 411-27.

16. E. Hoffmann, "König Olav Haraldsson als Heiliger des norwegischen Königshauses," *Acta Visbyensia* 6, ed. G. Svahnström (Visby, 1981): 35-44.

17. M. Müller-Wille, "Prunkgräber"; idem, *Das wikingerzeitliche Gräberfeld von Thumby-Bienebek* 1-2 (Neumünster 1976, 1987); E. Roesdahl, review of Müller-Wille, *Thumby-Bienebek* 1, in *Zeitschrift für Archäologie des Mittelalters* 11, 1983 (1986): 175-79; Roesdahl, *Viking Age Denmark*, pp. 159-83; idem, "Fra vikingegrav"; idem, *The Vikings*, pp. 154-58; and H. H. Andersen, "Vorchristliche Königsgräber in Dänemark und ihre Hintergrund – Versuch einer Synthese," *Germania* 65 (1987): 159-73.

18. *Antiquarisk Tidsskrift* 1861-63, pp. 16-22; H. H. Andersen, "Kongsgårdshøjen," *Skalk* 4 (1987): 9-13; and idem, "Vorchristliche Königsgräber."

19. M. Müller-Wille, "Das Bootkammergrab von Haithabu," in *Berichte über die Ausgrabungen in Haithabu* 8, ed. K. Schietzel (Neumünster, 1976); Ellmers, "Fränkisches Königszeremoniell"; and Andersen, "Vorchristliche Königsgräber."

20. K. Thorvildsen, *Ladbyskibet* (Copenhagen, 1957); and Andersen, "Vorchristliche Königsgräber."

21. Andersen, "Vorchristliche Königsgräber."

22. There is a vast literature on Jelling. The following titles give an introduction and further references: J. Kornerup, *Kongehøiene i Jellinge* (Copenhagen, 1875); Karl Martin Nielsen et al., "Jelling Problems. A Discussion," *Mediaeval Scandinavia* 7 (1974): 156-234; Roesdahl, *Viking Age Denmark*, pp. 171-76; idem, *The Vikings*, pp. 67 and 162-65; K. J. Krogh, "The Royal Viking-Age Monuments at Jelling in Light of Recent Archaeological Excavations," *Acta Archaeologica* 53 (1982): 183-216; E. Moltke, *Runes and Their Origin. Denmark and Elsewhere* (Copenhagen, 1985), pp. 202-23; K. Christensen and K. J. Krogh, "Jelling-højene dateret," *Nationalmuseets Arbejdsmark* (1987): 223-31.

23. See also T. Capelle, "Schiffsetzungen," *Præhistorische Zeitschrift* 61 (1986): 1-63.

24. E. Roesdahl, "The Danish Geometrical Viking Fortresses and Their Context," *Anglo-Norman Studies* 9, ed. R. A. Brown (Woodbridge, 1987): 208-26; and P. Sawyer, "Da Danmark blev Danmark," in *Gyldendal og Politikens Danmarks Historie* 3 (Copenhagen, 1988), pp. 221-45 and passim.

25. E. Roesdahl, "Prestige, Display and Monuments."

✤

The Archaeology of Danish Commercial Centers

Henrik M. Jansen

New Discoveries at Lundeborg on Funen

New archaeological evidence in Denmark helps to provide a context in which to view the Scandinavian connections so apparent in the Sutton Hoo burial. In 1986 one of the most important Danish finds in recent years was made close to Lundeborg on Funen. After a few weeks of excavations, we knew that we were excavating the oldest commercial center in Denmark, situated in the richest area of Migration-period Denmark, the Gudme region in southeast Funen.[1] So far, both chance finds and archaeological investigations in this area have led us to believe that this part of Funen can shed light on important occurrences in Danish history and on the exceptional social position of the region between 300 and 600. No other place in Denmark has yielded such rich archaeological material for an understanding of the period.

The area had already attained significance by the first century B.C., as is attested by the rich cremation burials at Langå, containing imported metal vessels from the Roman Empire and the remnants of a magnificent wagon of the Dejbjerg type. Investigations of Møllegårdsmarken, the largest burial place in Denmark, indicate a gradual increase in population to A.D. 400.[2] In graves at this cemetery we have found the greatest concentration of imported Roman luxury items in Scandinavia. Judging by gold finds and Roman coins, during the Migration period the Gudme area enjoyed a degree of wealth found nowhere else in northern Europe. Many treasure hoards from the Migration period contain items that come from areas outside the Roman Empire (such as eastern Europe), serving to underscore the international connections of the Gudme region. The discovery of this commercial center at Lundeborg has given us a chance to explore these long-distance connections, thus changing our understanding of the contemporary community and the way it was organized.

The entire Lundeborg complex stretches over 800 meters along the coastline of Store Bælt. Lundeborg was a seasonal settlement, characterized by a collection of small temporary stalls and huts. The oldest and best-preserved part of the site, dated from the third to the fifth centuries, is situated south of the brook, extending about 300 meters in a north-south direction and just over 60 meters to the west. North of the brook—

about 500 meters along the coast and about 100 meters inland – the structure of the community is somewhat different, and finds made here date from the fourth to the ninth centuries. At the mouth of the brook there was probably a good natural harbor. Results of excavations during the summer of 1992 should give a final verdict on this assumption.

In this coastal settlement there are traces of many kinds of crafts. The majority of the finds consist of craft materials such as ingots, preliminary products and partly made goods, fragments of crucibles and molds, drops from casting, and bronze and iron slag, as well as other refuse from metalworking. A remarkable number of small objects have been recovered, such as finger rings of gold, silver, and bronze; fibulae of iron and bronze; bronze pincers and small fittings; ornamental nails for shields; sword sheaths; and chests (Figure 10.1). Many of the metal items had been imported. Bronze and lead weights, gold objects from which pieces had been cut, and Roman denarii (Figure 10.2) bear witness to an exchange of goods among the merchants. Also among the imported items were numerous colored glass beads and fragments of glass beakers.

The presence of pieces of amber, as well as finished beads, leads us to believe that amber cutters were among the local craftsworkers. Pieces of bone and antler that had been worked give evidence of the activities of comb makers, who also produced gaming pieces. Some finds indicate that ships were repaired here, and perhaps new ships built (Figure 10.3). The leading role of shipbuilders is proved by the presence of many thousands of iron nails, the oldest in Scandinavia. We have also found many traces of repair work – chisels for splitting riveting plates and mandrels for hammering rivets through planks.

Our knowledge of ships and shipping during the period from 200 to 400 is extremely limited, derived mainly from the large fourth-century ship found in the Nydam bog. It was clinker-built like Viking ships, with planks held together by rivets, and it was propelled by sails rather than oars. Studies of the rivets will contribute to an understanding of Migration period shipping; for instance, by helping to determine the varying sizes of the ships.

Further inland, close to Gudme, we have recently found traces of houses, farms, and villages.[3] The Gudme-Lundeborg region offers many opportunities to broaden our understanding of economy, trade, and community during one of the most dynamic periods of early Danish history. The name "Gudme" can be glossed as "Home of the Gods," which indicates a possible role for the area as the location of heathen cults. Such a combination of sanctuary and central marketplace supports the proposition that the area was home to an early political and religious center of power – perhaps even a royal residence.

Figure 10.1. Lundeborg. One of about one hundred "guldgubbe" recovered in 1989. Seventh century. Size 1 × 1.5 cm. (Drawing by Benno Blæsild.)

Archaeology of the Eighth Century in Jutland

There seems to be no doubt of the existence of a monarchy when we examine southern Jutland, with its well-known and important defense of the Danevirke (Figure 10.4). Danevirke is one of the biggest defenses in northern Europe, effectively blocking access to Denmark for southern enemies.[4] According to dendrochronological determinations, the oldest

173

Figure 10.2. Lundeborg. Roman denarii. Most were struck in the second century A.D. and were in circulation until entering the archaeological deposit during the third and fourth centuries. The scale is in centimeters. (Photograph: Svendborg County Museum.)

large rampart was built in circa 737, of earth and oak timber. This rampart is about seven kilometers long, ten meters wide, and two meters high. On the front it was securely boarded with wood. Where the rampart crossed marshy areas there are special foundations – the rampart was replaced by an embankment in swampy areas, permitting passage along the line of defense. On the mainland there was a wall in front of the rampart. The oldest Danevirke rampart may have been built as a defense against at least three possible enemies: the Slavs, the Saxons, or the Frankish Empire, all of whom tried with varying success to force this important rampart complex over the course of the next five hundred years. One possible builder is a Danish king mentioned in Frankish sources, Ongendus (Angantyr?), who expelled the Frisian missionary Willibrord in 715.

Frankish chronicles also reveal that shortly before 800, the Danish king

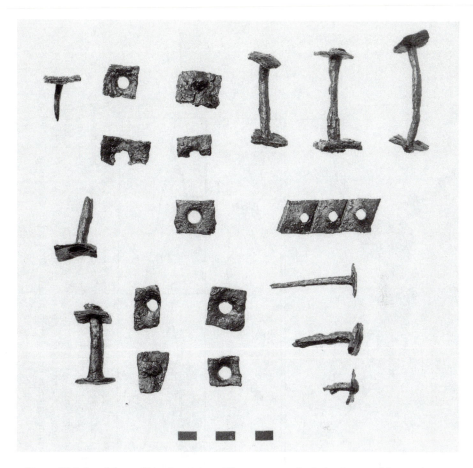

Figure 10.3. Lundeborg. Ship rivets, iron. The presence of whole rivets and intact rivet plates indicates that ship repairs were made here on the site. The scale is in centimeters. (Photograph: Svendborg County Museum.)

Godfred built a frontier rampart from the Baltic to the North Sea, which was to have only one gate. Perhaps this was an addition to the 737 rampart or a reconstruction of the Kovirke rampart. Ruler straight and about seven kilometers long, Kovirke has only one building phase, although its age has never been clearly established.

Dendrochronological datings attribute another impressive structure to the eighth century: the Kanhave Canal on the Samsø River, dated at 726. Its extensive engineering was meant to ensure that the Danish fleet could move rapidly from the western to the eastern shores of the island in order to defend the inner waters against intruding enemies. An enterprise of this scale can be attributed to the presence of a strong royal power.

There seems to have been some sort of central rule in Jutland, possibly

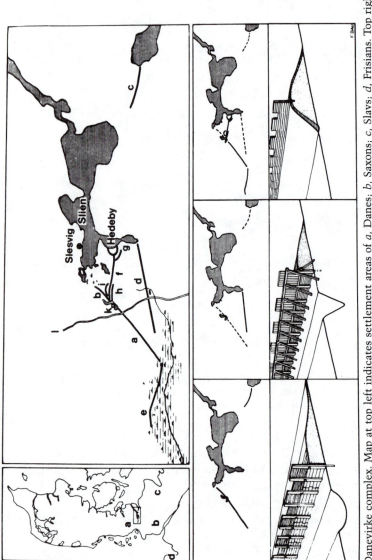

Figure 10.4. The Danevirke complex. Map at top left indicates settlement areas of *a*, Danes; *b*, Saxons; *c*, Slavs; *d*, Frisians. Top right map shows the position of the ramparts: *a*, main rampart; *b*, the northern rampart; *c*, the eastern rampart; *d*, Kovirke; *e*, Krumvolden, i.e., the curved rampart; *f*, the connecting rampart; *g*, the semicircular rampart around Hedeby; *h*, the twin rampart; *i*, the curved rampart; *k*, Thyraborg; *l*, the Army- or Ox-road, i.e., indicates a road probably for movement of either military units or livestock. The total length of the ramparts is about 30 km. The maps in the middle and the bottom illustrations show to the left the rampart from 737, in the center Kovirke, and to the right the ramparts in use about the year 1000 — building phases and reconstructions. (Drawing by Flemming Bau. From Else Roesdahl, *Vikingernes verden* [Copenhagen, 1987].)

a monarchy, during the first half of the eighth century. This hypothesis is supported by excavations at Ribe, where compact layers containing workshops situated in measured lots have been found.[5] The presence of specialized craftsworkers, such as bead makers, manufacturers of amber items, comb makers, and bronze founders, has been established. Although the site was a seasonal trading center, this does not exclude the possibility that it existed in association with a permanent settlement or a major estate. The fact that its division into areas was maintained over approximately one hundred years is best explained by the presence of some permanent authority, which must also have been able to ensure peace in the marketplace and access to the site. The numismatist D. M. Metcalf suggested in 1986 that the appearance of Wodan/monster sceattas could be explained by their having been struck in Ribe by a king in the first half of the eighth century. It might be reasonable to imagine that a center of trade and craft activities might grow into a true Viking Age town, yet the following centuries provide only few and scattered finds.

Ribe is situated where north-south land traffic crosses the Ribe River, directly connected with the tidal sea. The artifact material, which includes glass beakers, pottery, and basalt lava quernstones from the Rhineland, reflects contact with Frisia and Saxony. The same area was probably a source of jewelers' raw materials, such as glass for bead making and bronze and precious metals for casting. The craftsworkers seem to have produced their wares for the local Danish market and not for foreign merchants, but whether Ribe thus served as a transit point for Scandinavia is as yet an open question.

Later Archaeology in the Light of Historical Tradition

The site of Hedeby (Haithabu) is situated on a brook near the western end of the Schlei, a long, narrow inlet of the Baltic Sea in the south of the Jutland peninsula.[6] The Frankish Chronicles record that King Godfred moved merchants from Reric to Hedeby in 808 and had the first rampart at the site built. Archaeological finds from the extensive excavations at Hedeby corroborate the written sources to provide a picture of a well-organized and sizable settlement.

Some 340,000 artifacts have been recovered in the Hedeby excavations, providing rich documentation of daily life, craft activity, and trade. The 200,000 animal bones attest to the subsistence economy, showing a strong preponderance of pigs. Only portions of the extensive cemeteries at the site have been investigated; on the basis of the cemetery research, it has been estimated that over ten thousand individuals were buried at Hedeby over a period of nearly three hundred years. Among the excavated burials, marked social differences are apparent in the grave equipment, especially during the tenth century.

The commercial importance of Hedeby is shown by its establishment at this harbor location, by large quantities of trade goods recovered on the site, and by coins minted locally. The intensive commerce and craft activities make apparent the well-developed division of labor in this period. The residents of Hedeby probably imported their food from surrounding agricultural communities rather than producing their own.

Other major monuments dating to the tenth century further attest to the political, military, and religious changes that were taking place in Denmark. King Harald Bluetooth felt the need for increased security to protect his kingdom from enemies both within his lands and beyond them. Around 980 he oversaw the construction of four great circular fortifications, at Trelleborg on Zealand, Fyrkat in northeastern Jutland, Nonnebakken on Fyn, and Aggersborg at Limfjorden (Figure 10.5). Size and arrangement of individual fortresses vary, but all were built on the same geometrical plan. The precise source of their design is disputed, but it no doubt has its origin in contemporaneous European monumental architecture or in the Slavic circular camp.

At about the same time, King Harald had additions made to the Danevirke, the greatest fortification that protected the Danish border in southern Jutland.

Around 979, according to dendrochronological dating, Harald had a long bridge built across the Ravning River near Jelling. Enormous expenditures of labor and oak timber were required for this bridge, about a kilometer long and over five and one-half meters wide. The bridge builders used an estimated seventeen hundred posts for about four hundred spans and eight hundred props, as well as timber for the superstructure. The posts are preserved to a depth of two to four meters; in cross section they are square and measure about one foot on a side. The carrying capacity of the bridge is estimated at five tons, suggesting that it was used to support heavy traffic.

At Jelling are significant monuments that represent stages in the introduction of Christianity into Denmark. During the ninth and tenth centuries we have a number of written records of early missionary efforts, and by the middle of the tenth century we know of the existence of bishops in Aarhus, Ribe, and Schleswig. In Jelling, where King Harald had his residence, are the two largest burial mounds in Denmark; between them stand the rune-stones of King Gorm and King Harald beside the early church. While much research has been devoted to study of the mounds, the stones, and the church, only recently has the settlement at Jelling come under study. Early results suggest that the community was sizable. It was strategically situated at the center of Danish territory, on the military road where it lies closest to the Kattegat on the stretch between Viborg and Hedeby.

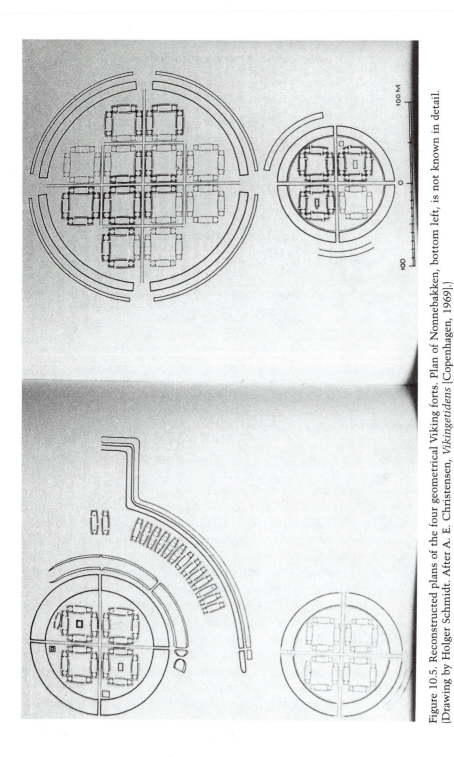

Figure 10.5. Reconstructed plans of the four geometrical Viking forts. Plan of Nonnebakken, bottom left, is not known in detail. (Drawing by Holger Schmidt. After A. E. Christensen, *Vikingetidens* [Copenhagen, 1969].)

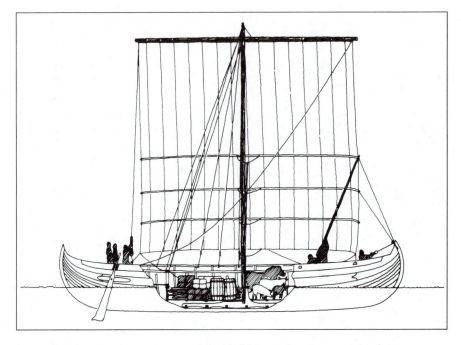

Figure 10.6. Reconstruction drawing of the Skuldelev 1 ship. It was made of pine, probably in western Norway.

The reign of King Harald thus left a substantial number of major archaeological monuments in the Danish landscape. In addition to Christianizing Denmark, Harald employed thousands of men, probably as forced labor, in the great building projects at Danevirke and Hedeby, the bridge at Ravning, the five circular camps, the burial mounds at Jelling, and great wooden churches at Jelling and other sites.

After Harald's death in 987, his son Svend took power. In the new period of stability and prosperity, new towns were established and grew in commercial and political activity, including Lund and Viborg, and slightly later Slagelse, Aalborg, and Ringsted. Increasing national wealth is also reflected in the ships built, including big freighters like that found at the site of Skuldelev 1 (Figure 10.6), capable of carrying twenty-five tons with a crew of four to five, or the Hedeby freighter, twenty-two to twenty-five meters long, which could carry forty to fifty tons. These large ships could carry anything from live cattle and horses to soapstone from Vestfold in Norway, millstones of basalt lava from the Rhineland, and iron and other metals. Large-scale transportation had grown in order to satisfy increasing demand for cheaper consumer goods.

The processes of change that led to the birth of the Danish kingdom remain a subject of debate. Many different disciplines need to be brought into the discussion, including history, philology, archaeology, and place-name studies. This contribution is intended to provide an overview of some of the relevant archaeological material.

Notes

1. Preliminary reports in *Årbog for Svendborg og Omegns Museum, 1986-90*, with English summaries, by Per O. Thomsen et al.; Per O. Thomsen, "Ein neuer Stierkopf aus Fünen," *Frühmittelalterliche Studien* 23 (1989); and idem, "Lundeborg: A Trading Centre from the 3rd–7th century A.D.," *Shipping and Society in Scandinavia* (1989-90).

2. Excavations are still in progress here, directed by Henrik Thrane of the Fyens Stiftsmuseum.

3. Anne Kromann and Peter Vang Petersen, "Romerske mønter, skatefund og jernalder-huse," in *Nationalmuseets Arbejdsmark* (1985): 194-206; Anne Kromann, "A Fourth Century Hoard from Denmark," *Rivista Italiana di Numismatica E. Scienze Affini* 90 (1988): 239-61; Ole Crumlin-Petersen, "Havne og Søfart i Romersk og Gremansk jernalder," *Skrifter fra Historisk Institut*, Odense Universitet, no. 33 (1985): 68-91; and Peter Vang Petersen, "Gudme II, en guldskat i hus!" *Årbog for Svendborg og Omegns Museum* (1988): 42-51.

4. Else Roesdahl, "The End of Viking-age Fortifications in Denmark, and What Followed," *Chateau Gaillard* 12 (1985): 39-47.

5. Lene B. Frandsen and Stig Jensen, "Pre-Viking and Early Viking Age Ribe: Excavations at Nikolajgade 8, 1985-86," *Journal of Danish Archaeology* 6 (1987): 175-89; and Mogens Bencard, ed. *Ribe Excavations, 1970-76*, vols. 1-2 (1981-84). In the summer of 1989 a series of precise dendrochronological datings of structures were made. Timber from a well was dated to 705-10. The above-mentioned parceling-out seems to to have taken place around 710, which makes Willibrord's presumed journey to Ribe even more interesting, because now written sources and dendrochronological datings concur. Later in the summer of 1989, remnants of a rampart and wall around the oldest buildings in Ribe were investigated.

6. The archaeological investigations in Hedeby from the 1960s and later are currently being published in *Berichte über die Ausgrabungen in Haithabu*, ed. Kurt Schietzel, which have appeared in more than 20 volumes since 1969.

Conclusion

❖

The Future of Sutton Hoo

Martin Carver

One of the central problems of archaeology is how to use our monuments for a greater understanding of early society, and the problem is particularly acute when the investigation of the monument means its destruction and the society in question is that of the Anglo-Saxons. If a monument is excavated in pursuit of a prognosis, it does not normally survive the operation, and we have effectively killed it, even if we killed it out of love. There is no recourse in the future to this monument, only to such records as were made, which in turn depended on such research concepts as prevailed at the time. And of all past cultures that we can confront by archaeological methods, the early Anglo-Saxon remains one of the most opaque. It lacks stone buildings, prominent earthworks, and large assemblages of widely distributed finds. It was a culture whose physical imprint is elusive but whose historical significance is permanent. When doing archaeology, we therefore have to match the research urgency provoked by historical and literary questions about the Anglo-Saxons with the techniques required to make them visible and the ethics of destruction. Nowhere is this dilemma revealed in such an acute form as at the site of Sutton Hoo.[1]

Of course, we would hardly be aware of the existence of such an unusual source of evidence without the cavalier curiosity of an earlier age. When Edith Pretty, landowner and magistrate, decided to investigate the unpretentious cluster of earth mounds on her estate in 1938, there was little thought of deliberate inquiry into the character of Anglo-Saxon kingship or social structure. The tumuli (Figure 11.1) might well have been Bronze Age, like those across the river Deben on Martlesham Heath, and Anglo-Saxon archaeology itself had then a far less ambitious agenda than we have now. Her excavator, Basil Brown, employed through Ipswich Museum, used a most traditional excavation technique, cutting or driving trenches through Mounds 2, 3, and 4 to locate and empty the central burial pits that lay beneath. All had been robbed, but his work showed clearly that the mounds were of Anglo-Saxon date and of high status, sufficient stimulus to return in the spring of 1939 to open the mound that was to make the site famous, Mound 1.[2]

Figure 11.1. The Sutton Hoo burial mounds looking southwest in 1983. (Photograph: C. Hoppitt.)

Mound 1 was also broached by trench, but Basil Brown and his team very quickly recognized the presence of ship rivets and, leaving them in situ, were able to trace the outline of a ninety-foot-long vessel buried in the sand, even though no timber survived (Figure 11.2). At the center of this enormous ship, still the largest known from the European Dark Ages, lay a rectangle of dark humic sand "exactly above the place," as Basil Brown noted in his diary on 3 July, "where I expect the chief lies."[3] This, the burial chamber, was excavated by a hastily convened team of prehistorians under the direction of Charles Philips between 21 and 31 July, an astonishing ten days in which 263 finds were recovered.[4]

The discovery, thrilling no less for the richness and rarity of its objects than for the circumstances of their retrieval in the long, hot summer preceding the outbreak of World War II, was the point of departure for fifty years of research and speculation: historical, anthropological, literary, and aesthetic. A preliminary publication in *Antiquity* for 1940, equally remarkable for its speed and its prescience, has been followed by Bruce-Mitford's monumental study of the finds and their context.[5] Here Mound 1 is carefully argued to be the resting place of Rædwald, king of East Anglia and a "Bretwalda," possibly aspiring to leadership of the British Island, who, after a brief flirtation with Christianity, died in 624 or 625. He was neither the first recorded king of East Anglia nor the last, so that it is reasonable to suppose that East Anglia was perceived as a kingdom by

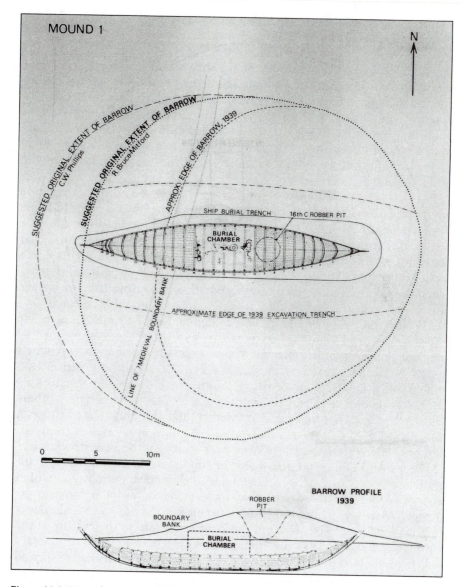

Figure 11.2. Mound 1: the ship burial. (*Bulletin* 4, figure 28.)

the early seventh century and that Sutton Hoo, which has no obvious equivalent in the territory, was the burial ground of its kings. For many this will be, of itself, sufficient explanation of the monument, and indeed it has been vehemently argued that no further work was or is necessary at the site. To dig up the graves of more kings would be at worst serendipitous and at best a shameless attempt to acquire more treasures. Much better to search for a palace or investigate Anglo-Saxon agriculture, the source, presumably, of the wealth that made these extravagant funeral rites possible.

Bruce-Mitford and colleagues from the British Museum returned to the site from 1966 to 1971 to reexcavate the ship-burial site (abandoned since the war) and to investigate Mound 5 and the prehistoric settlement encountered by Basil Brown.[6] Flat graves, cremations, ditches, and postholes appeared beside and beneath the burial mounds, and it at once became plain that the archaeological terrain was difficult and that unusual techniques would be required to master it. No simple string of barrow excavations would suffice either to understand the whole purpose of the burial ground or to give it a context.

In 1983, with the benefits of forty years of copious and scholarly study and publication behind them, the members of the Sutton Hoo Research Trust began a new project, appointing me as its director. What could be achieved that had not been achieved already? What could be known, that could not easily be known or guessed from a scrutiny of documents, place names, or poetry? How far was such a project an act of political therapy, launching an archaeological flagship, guaranteed to return from its voyage laden with treasure, and how far was it serious, innovative research?

My reaction to the challenge was to demand time to make a plan. We knew a great deal about a very small part of the Deben Valley, just as, thanks to the ship burial, we knew a great deal more about a very small part of Anglo-Saxon society. We knew very little about how Sutton Hoo related to the East Anglian territory, or how the East Anglian territory related to kingdoms to the north, south, and west of it in Britain or to others across the North Sea in Norway, Sweden, and the northwest European continent. Did the East Angles always have kings, or were they an invention of the late sixth century? What was a king in the seventh century? Did he govern? Did he tax? How did the Anglo-Saxons exploit the agricultural wealth of East Anglia? Using what settlement hierarchy and which social and economic system? Did trade exist, or only diplomatic exchange? What was the relationship between East Anglia and Sweden; was it special or fortuitous? How did the kingdom relate to the culture of the Britons and the politics of the Franks? Above all, how did such things vary and change between the fifth and the eighth century, the formative period of the nation of England?

It was clear enough that Sutton Hoo had a role to play in confronting some of these big questions. It was very much less clear how archaeology, a lengthy and expensive public performance, could be deployed to provide independent answers to them. The material correlates of kingship, kingdoms, taxation, and diplomacy were hotly debated, and it was by no means certain that Sutton Hoo could offer them. We knew very little about the extent or archaeological character of the site itself.

Accordingly, the first three years of the project were dedicated to *evaluation*, the nondestructive mapping of the extent and quality of archaeological deposits in the general area of the burial mounds. From this it could be predicted that there were two principal phases of use: a prehistoric settlement, extending to 14 hectares and dating to around 2000 B.C., and an early medieval cemetery, containing burial mounds, flat graves, and possibly cremations, and extending to 4.5 hectares (Figure 11.3). The soil was an acid sand in which organic material and human bone rarely survived. The prehistoric episode was expressed as an array of postholes, pits, and ditches, belonging to round houses and field boundaries, associated with pottery and flint implements, while the early medieval site consisted mainly of "sand bodies" without grave goods on flat ground (Figure 11.4) and burial mounds covering both cremations and ship burials, for the most part thoroughly robbed.

These were our raw materials. How could they be interrogated to throw new light on Anglo-Saxon society? The principle applied was simple. The research target would be social formation and social change in East Anglia between the fifth and eighth century and how East Anglian society interacted during this period with neighboring polities. The project would be of finite length and apply itself to field operations in the East Anglian region and at the site of Sutton Hoo itself. These operations would be carefully targeted and nondestructive wherever possible. Excavation would use a scale and technique appropriate to confront the research questions. Nothing would be done without purpose.

Such an approach was dubbed "cautious" or even "timid," although it was in reality simply scientific. Sutton Hoo is itself an epitome of the development of archaeology, the theoretical basis of which has changed a great deal since 1939. The assumptions made about the relationship between people and their material culture are quite different now, and they will no doubt have changed again by 2039. To eliminate an entire site to satisfy a research agenda of the 1990s, with techniques belonging only to that time, would be reprehensible arrogance.

The results of these deliberations were published in 1986 as a research design,[7] the arguments of which can be briefly summarized. Early Anglo-Saxon society, like any other, depended on natural resources on which it constructed an economy. The exploitation of these resources would be archaeologically visible in pollen reservoirs and on settlement sites, and the articulation of the economy would be visible as assemblages of animal bone, plants, pottery, metalwork, and so on. The changing economy would also be reflected in a changing social structure, visible in the way space was used by and within settlements: their distribution in the landscape and the disposition of different sizes of buildings within them. If a society altered its ranking, this would also be reflected in changing settlement plans and in cemeteries, too, since an equation could be made with the richness of graves and the wealth available to a buried party. The relationship of the early Anglo-Saxon community to others, its communal politics, could also be read in the archaeological record. Not only were

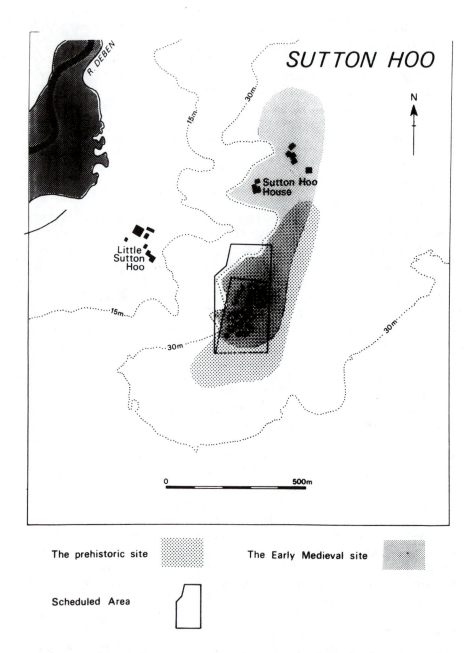

Figure 11.3. Evaluation of Sutton Hoo: the prehistoric and early medieval sites mapped by remote sensing. (*Bulletin* 5, figure 2.)

exotic objects to be found in cemeteries and settlements, but also exotic burial rites, indicating contact, whether by embassy, emigration, trade, or

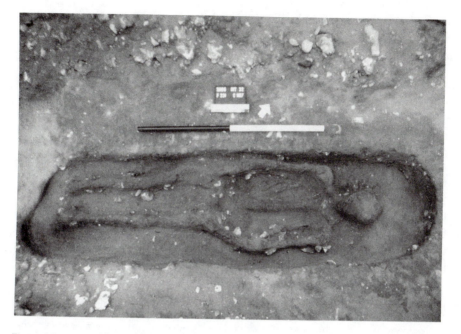

Figure 11.4. A sand body. (Photograph: N. Macbeth.)

simply cultural emulation. Lastly, a community, particularly a nonliterate community, could manifest, in its material culture, the expression of a shared ideology. We know this to have been true of Christian peoples, and the interpretation of churches, monasteries, baptismal fonts, the crucifix, relics, and even fish ponds has an ideological basis that is not in doubt. Why should the early Anglo-Saxons have been less superstitious, less prone to investment in extravagant ideological signals than succeeding generations? Modern archaeological interpretation would therefore place a new construction on an Anglo-Saxon cemetery. Its burial rites and grave goods may certainly be an index of cultural or ethnic affiliation or social difference or belief, but we are inclined now also to credit a burial party with a less passive role. Burial, particularly high-status burial, may be a deliberate statement with an ideological message. And a cemetery like Sutton Hoo is a theater in which each episode, each burial mound, is potentially a fossilized political attitude belonging uniquely to a moment in history. The Sutton Hoo ship burial in this interpretation is no routine cultural procedure, providing an anchor in reality for the *Beowulf* epic. It is in itself a poem, constructed from artifacts, mortuary structure, and, for all we know, dramatized ritual on the day of the funeral and after.

Such observations show that, no less than for historical or literary studies, archaeological fieldwork requires source criticism—an evaluation of the potential yield of the strata and a theoretical assessment of the context of their meaning. The research design also implies that a portfolio of field operations would be required at different scales: comparative studies in the Scandinavian countries, settlement mapping in East Anglia, samples of settlement types, their plans and assemblages, samples of cemeteries, a coarse mapping of the Sutton Hoo area, a refined mapping of the Sutton Hoo cemetery, and a meticulous record of major burials. Much of this work was already in train in the East Anglian region, thanks to the activities of a number of diligent archaeologists, not least in the Archaeological Units of Norfolk and Suffolk County Councils. Coincident with the new Sutton Hoo project, an "East Anglian Kingdom" project began, which set out to map the settlement pattern in six representative zones.[8] Excavations have been completed and published of a whole cemetery at Spong Hill, and of numerous other cemeteries with which partial contact had been achieved. Settlement sites had been excavated and published at West Stow and North Elmham. Work was meanwhile in progress at the adjacent Anglo-Saxon cemetery at Snape, at the settlement and cemetery at Burrow Hill and Brandon, and at the early Anglo-Saxon port and town of Ipswich.[9] All this work will be vital to the future interpretation of Sutton Hoo, and it is to this wider picture that studies at the site itself intend to make their contribution.

As proposed by the research design, that contribution was an excavation lasting six years. Our objective was to examine the changing social structure and ideological signals of the Sutton Hoo community, and it was contended that this could be done by revealing a sample of the mortuary behavior practiced from the beginning to the end of the cemetery's use. This was realized by a transect thirty-two meters wide crossing the site from east to west, that is from one edge to the other (Figure 11.5). The assumption made was that the cemetery would grow inland, from west to east, but since no such ordered development could be guaranteed, a comparable transect was added that ran from north to south. The cruciform area so formed was one hectare in extent, about one quarter of the whole cemetery as so far known; it included six known burial mounds of which one (Mound 2) had been previously excavated by Basil Brown, three had been leveled (Mounds 5, 14, and 18) and two were upstanding, although most probably robbed (Mounds 6 and 7). In addition to the excavations, the twelve-hectare area around the burial mounds would be extensively mapped by nondestructive means, in order to establish the plan of the prehistoric settlement and to recreate the landscape that the Anglo-Saxons saw when they came to found their cemetery there.

Although the excavation has two more seasons to run as of this writing, it might be useful here to attempt a brief account of the story so far, since 75 percent of the proposed sample has now been brought to light of day (Figure 11.6 and Table 11.1). The eastern transect (sector 1 on Figure 11.6) is scheduled to open in the summer of 1990. [Now open. — EDS.]

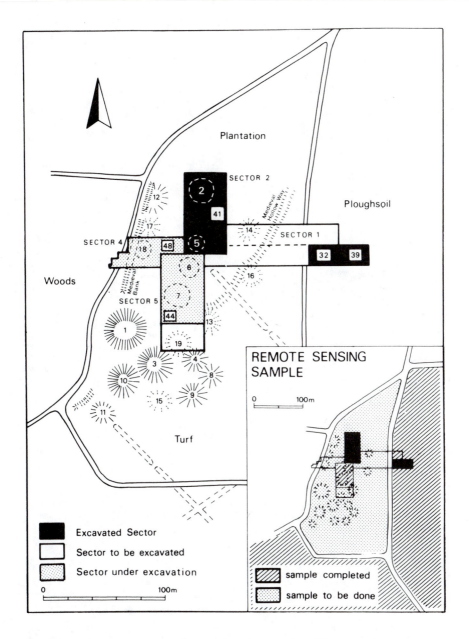

Figure 11.5. Excavation strategy: the sample to be investigated by excavation and remote mapping, 1989. (*Bulletin 7*, figure 1.)

The excavations began with the expectation that Sutton Hoo would be a mixed folk cemetery of long duration (fifth to seventh centuries) com-

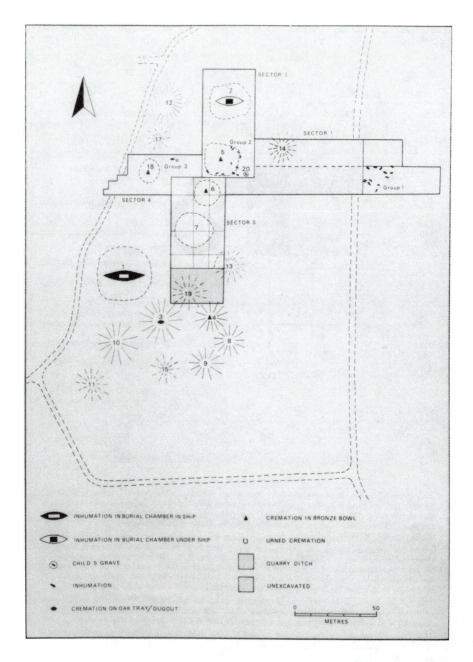

Figure 11.6. Early medieval burials at Sutton Hoo: the story so far. (*Bulletin* 7, figure 6.)

parable with Spong Hill or Snape. This is not the case. No certain urned cremations or accompanied inhumations belonging to the East Anglian cultural norm in the fifth and sixth centuries have been contacted. The burials are varied, thinly spread, peculiar, and generally badly disturbed.

The burial mounds are of three types. Mounds 3, 5, 6, and 18 contained cremations, in the case of Mound 3 placed on an oak tray and in the case of the other mounds wrapped in cloth and placed in a bronze bowl. All were accompanied by grave goods of high status, but, like the burials themselves, these were thoroughly disturbed and dispersed by the activities of rabbits, medieval farmers, bracken, nineteenth-century excavators, and twentieth-century treasure hunters.

Mound 20, in a group of its own, is the grave of a child, who was buried in an oak coffin accompanied by a miniature spearhead and belt buckle. The mound itself, inferred from a shallow ring-ditch, was less than two meters in diameter. Mounds 1 and 2 are ship burials. Mound 1 was the burial of a man in a chamber in a ship, while Mound 2 has proved on dissection to be the equally rich burial of a man in an underground chamber with a ship placed on top of it (Figure 11.7). Mound 2 had been previously excavated, probably in the nineteenth century, as well as by Brown in 1938, so the burial rite had to be pieced together from some 650 ship rivets and fragments of weapons and other finds (see Table 11.1), which were found scattered around the mound, in the robber trench, and in the burial pit itself.[10]

Beside the burial mounds are a number of flat graves, for the most part without grave goods of any kind. They consist of "sand bodies," largely deprived of bone, which are notable for their diverse and eccentric postures. These include individuals buried prone with their hands behind their backs, supine with hands above the head, crouched, beheaded, or with broken necks (see Table 11.1, and Figure 11.4). They occur in three groups. The fifteen burials on the eastern periphery include ten where ritual trauma can reasonably be inferred; among them is the so-called plowman burial, an individual apparently buried in a plowing position accompanied by a primitive wooden ard.[11]

The second group of twelve burials is disposed radially or tangentially around Mound 5 and includes seven where ritual trauma can be inferred. These graves are contemporary, or only a little later than, the construction of Mound 5, since the outermost examples are cut into the partially silted pits originally quarried to build the mound (Figure 11.8). The remaining example of a flat grave (group 3) was a pit containing a single skull near Mound 18.[12]

The dates of the Sutton Hoo burials, whether obtained from grave goods or radiocarbon dating, all fall within a period of less than one hundred years during the seventh century. No clear sequence of construction for burial mounds or flat graves has been observed by means of stratigraphy. The mounds themselves appear to have been untidily quarried from adjacent shallow ditches, and the stratigraphic excavation of several of

Table 11.1. Inventory of early medieval burials, as of September 1989. (*Bulletin* 7, table 2.)

MOUNDS. UNEXCAVATED
Mound 8, 9, 10 (robbed?), 11 (robbed?), 12, 13, 14 (to be excavated), 15, 16, 17, 19.

MOUNDS. EXCAVATED

MOUND 1: INHUMATION W-E in chamber in ship; with sword, shield, helmet, regalia, horns, buckets, cauldron etc.
DATED: c 625 AD (grave goods).
INTACT Excavated 1939, 1965-71 (INT 5-10).

MOUND 2: INHUMATION W-E in chamber below ship; originally with sword, shield, belt buckle (?), silver buckle, horns, tub (?), bucket (?), cauldron (?), bronze bowl, blue glass jar, silver-mounted box, silver-mounted cup. 5 knives, textile, iron fragments.
Excavated and ROBBED 1860(?) (INT 1) Excavated 1938 (INT 3)
Excavated 1984, 86-89 (INT 26, 41). DATED: late 6th-early 7th C (grave goods).

MOUND 3: CREMATION on oak 'tray' or dugout boat; with limestone plaque, bone facings, bronze ewer-lid, francisca, comb, textile, pottery, horse (cremated).
ROBBED (19th C?) Excavated 1938 (INT 2). DATED: late 6th-early 7th C (grave goods).

MOUND 4: CREMATION in bronze bowl, with playing piece, textile, horse (cremated).
ROBBED (19th C?) Excavated 1938 (INT 4). DATED: late 6th-early 7th C (grave goods).

MOUND 5: CREMATION in bronze bowl; with composite gaming pieces, iron shears, silver-mounted cup, comb, knife in sheath, ivory fragment, glass fragments, textiles, dog? (cremated).
ROBBED, twice Excavated 1970, 1988 (INT 12, 41). DATED: late 6th-early 7th C (grave goods).

MOUND 6: CREMATION wrapped in cloth in bronze bowl; with copper alloy sword-pyramid.
Excavated and ROBBED (19th C?) Under excavation 1989 (INT 44). DATED: late 6th-early 7th C (grave goods).

MOUND 7: Reticella bead.
ROBBED (19th C?) Under excavation 1989 (INT 44). DATED: late 6th-early 7th C.

MOUND 18: CREMATION originally in bronze bowl, with textile fragments and (cremated) comb.
PLOUGHED AWAY Excavated 1966, 1989 (INT 11, 48). DATED: Anglo-Saxon (comb).

MOUND 20: (F114) INHUMATION W-E in oak coffin. 4-8 year old child, with iron spearhead, bronze belt-buckle and bronze pin.
INTACT Excavated 1987 (INT 41). DATED: Anglo-Saxon (grave goods).

BURIALS NOT UNDER MOUNDS

CREMATIONS
INT 11 (Aiii) Un-urned cremation. UNDATED: Bronze Age?
INT 11 (Aiv) Cremation in pot. Young male. DATED: 6-7th C AD (?)

INHUMATIONS
Group 1: In INT 32, eastern periphery of cemetery.

F9 (254) N-S flexed, on back
•F39 (101, 245, 246) W-E extended, on back, in coffin
•F40 (102, 247) E-W extended, prone, with hands tied behind back (?)
F106 (248, 249) NW-SE extended, on back, in coffin/tree-trunk with animal joint, under cairn DATED: 620±80 ad (C 14)
•F108 (251) W-E extended, on back: no head
F109 (252) W-E extended, on back: above F108, with head of F108
•F137/1 E-W extended, on back, with broken neck
•F137/2 crouched, beneath F137/1
•F146 (258) SE-NW extended, prone, with wrists and ankles tied (?) DATED: 750±70 ad (C 14)
•F154 (259) W-E extended, on back, over F146
•F161 (260, 261) W-E in 'ploughing' position, with 'plough' and rod
•F163 (262) W-E kneeling, top of head missing
•F166 (263) W-E extended on back, hands tied (?) and stretched above head

F173 (264) W-E — extended on back, wrist over wrist
F180 — empty
F226 — empty
F231 (237) W-E — extended
•F227/1 (238) W-E — extended, prone
•F227/2 (239) W-E — extended, prone, with F227'1
F235 (240) W-E — flexed, in square coffin (chest?)

Tally: 18 graves; 2 empty. 18 bodies, of which 10 show evidence for ritual trauma.

Group 2: In INT 41, associated with Mound 5.

F54 N-S — empty
•F81 (152) W-E — flexed on side in 'sleeping' posture, head detached and turned upwards through 180°
•F82 (507, 509, 510) S-N — flexed on side; with additional human limbs |cuts quarry pit F508|
•F86/1 (148) N-S — extended on back, head detached, lying with neck up
•F86/2 (149) N-S — extended, prone on top of 148, with additional human limbs.
DATED: late 6th-7th C (associated with Mound 5)

F123 NW-SE — empty
F124 (542) NW-SE — extended, on back
F154 (55) W-E — prone |= INT 12, Grave 3|
F399 — empty
F424 (499) NW-SE — flexed, on side |This grave cuts quarry pit F130|
•F435 — body piece (part of long bone?) only |This grave cuts quarry pit F133|
DATED: late 6th-7th C (associated with Mound 5)

•F486 (555) S-N — slightly flexed, on side, head detached and placed by foot
•F517 (524, 525) NW-SE — extended, on back, head wrenched (hung?), with organic collar (rope?) around neck |This grave cuts quarry pit F129, containing animal remains|
DATED: late 6th-7th C (associated with Mound 5)
F588 (INT 12, Grave 1) S-N — flexed, on side
F590 (INT 12, Grave 2) W-E — extended, on back

Tally: 14 graves; 3 empty. 12 bodies, of which 7 show evidence for ritual trauma.

Group 3: West.

•INT 11, Pit 1 E-W — skull only, detached, facing foot end; with glass bead and bronze fitting.   DATED: 746±80 AD (C 14)

* These graves show some evidence for ritual trauma.

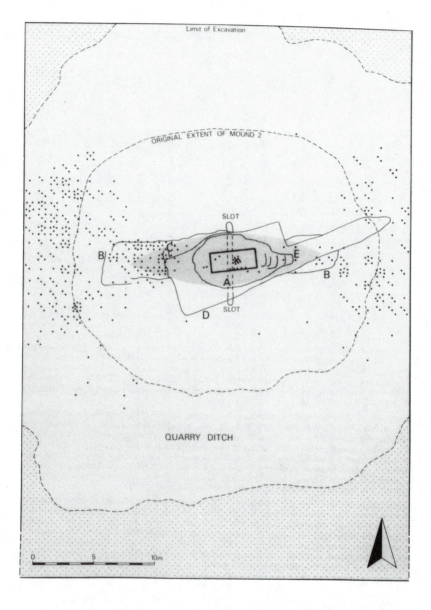

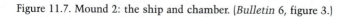

Figure 11.7. Mound 2: the ship and chamber. (*Bulletin* 6, figure 3.)

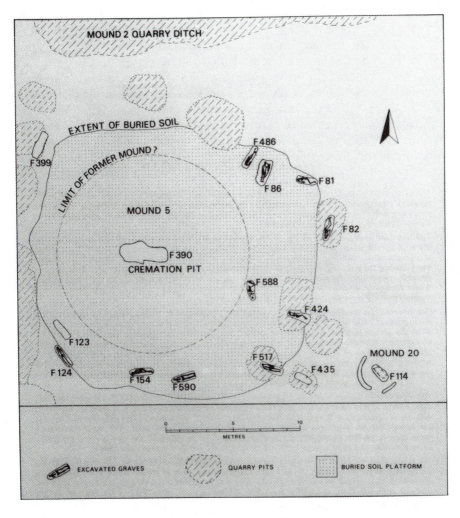

Figure 11.8. Mound 5 and its satellite burials. (*Bulletin* 7, figure 2.)

these ditches appears to indicate that Mounds 5, 6, and 7 were actually built at the same time. Preliminary analysis of the Mound 2 stratigraphic sequence suggests that the initial, if ephemeral, form of the mounds was a garish yellow cone of sand and gravel. The evidence for the chronological ordering of the cemetery is thus equivocal. It is possible to propose that an initial period of cremation under mounds was succeeded by ship burial, or that an initial ship burial (Mound 1) was followed by cremations under mounds, or that neither took precedence. It seems more prudent to

197

conclude that the burial rite employed in the mounds is neither chronologically, culturally, nor ethnically determined, but belongs to its historical context, and its principle message is ideological.

In many ways, perhaps in every way, it is unwise to pronounce on the significance of these discoveries before the excavation and its analyses are completed. The findings in sector 1 particularly, which link the burial mounds to the distinctive and presumably late graves on the periphery, will play a crucial role in its interpretation. However, interim observations can have some value if only to provide a historical rationale for what is to be done during the last phases of the present campaign.

Sutton Hoo is a seventh-century cemetery of short duration reserved for the elite. In this it provides a contrast with the three to four hundred other Anglo-Saxon cemeteries known from East Anglia, and no others are known that resemble it. It is reasonable to see it as a royal burial ground, but if so, such a signal of "royalty" is seen only in the seventh century. The evidence we have for ritual trauma, that is, persons executed or sacrificed by beheading or hanging, is not unimpeachable, but it is consistent and was practiced in direct association with one of the mounds (Mound 5). It cannot be said whether this practice was religious or punitive, or indeed how one could tell the difference, but it seems unnecessarily contrived to disregard it or to ignore it as a contribution to the ideological statements. The range of burial rites so far seen (cremation under mound, cremation under mound with satellite burials, ship burial) could be interpreted as political manifestos pertaining to high-status individuals. However, we have no direct evidence as to who these individuals were. The argument that Mound 1 contained the tomb of Rædwald can now be equally applied to Mound 2.

The ideological messages as a whole do, however, suggest particular insistence on allegiance with Scandinavia. This is encapsulated not only in the grave goods,[13] but also, and most significantly, in the rite of ship burial itself.[14] There is no evidence at all for local Christian symbolism, but a great deal that shows ritual investment of a non-Christian kind. It is only logical to read the burials as pagan and to suppose that this is how they were meant, then, to be understood, whatever the spiritual vagaries of the buried individual.

A study of early East Anglian society, from the results of the "kingdom survey" and earlier work, shows considerable changes in the material culture of both settlements and cemeteries between the fifth and seventh centuries.[15] From this it can be argued that whereas East Anglian society began as a stratified one, it initially took the form of numerous small lordships. Only in the late sixth century had any individual lord gained sufficient economic power to claim territorial control. At this point the concept of "kingship" could be promoted through genealogies and regalia; such a role would have to be supported by the reimposition of territorially based tribute, that is, tax as opposed to rent. East Anglia and its kings on this model are recent creations of the early seventh century, and Sutton Hoo is the ideological expression of their claims. It was this new fiscal and political structure that was ripe for conversion to Christianity.[16]

Such a conversion carried with it the implication of "ideological capture" by the new Roman/Frankish "empire," and was surely resisted. The extravagant character of Sutton Hoo, with its adopted superpaganism, can be seen as a token of that resistance. There is some evidence, too, that the change of allegiance from a pagan/Scandinavian to a Christian/Frankish alignment was reflected in the altered axis of exchange across the North Sea.[17] The context of Sutton Hoo is therefore political; proclaiming a pagan, maritime, and independent kingdom, and one not destined to endure.

During the next five years the present campaign of fieldwork will be completed and the results presented for publication. The conclusions then reached will vary, no doubt, from those offered here, and so they must. Thereafter the study of Anglo-Saxon England will enter a new phase, with new goals and new targets. Archaeologists no longer believe that they are on the periphery of Anglo-Saxon studies; theirs is the only evidence that is likely to increase over the years, and they now wield conceptual procedures of considerable power. But it is evidence of a peculiarly delicate and often irreplaceable kind, requiring the reconciliation of research objectives with deposit quality, techniques of investigation, and ethics. It is only right that most of Sutton Hoo should survive for the next stage of the inquiry. It is right, too, that scholars of every branch of early medieval studies should help to set the future archaeological agenda.

Notes

1. M. O. H. Carver, "Digging for Ideas," *Antiquity* 63 (1989): 666-74.
2. Rupert Bruce-Mitford, *The Sutton Hoo Ship-Burial*, with contributions by Paul Ashbee et al., 3 vols. in 4 (London, 1975-83), vol. 1.
3. R. L. S. Bruce-Mitford, *Aspects of Anglo-Saxon Archaeology* (London, 1974), p. 66.
4. Bruce-Mitford, *Sutton Hoo*, vol. 1; M. O. H. Carver, "Anglo-Saxon Objectives at Sutton Hoo, 1985," *Anglo-Saxon England* 50 (1986): 139-52.
5. Bruce-Mitford, *Sutton Hoo*.
6. Bruce-Mitford, *Sutton Hoo*, vol. 1; I. H. Longworth and I. A. Kinnes, *Sutton Hoo Excavations, 1966, 1968 to 1970* (London, 1980).
7. *Bulletin of the Sutton Hoo Research Committee*, 7 vols. (1983-90), vol. 4.
8. J. Newman, *East Anglian Kingdom Pilot Survey* (Leicester, forthcoming); *Bulletin* 4: 61.
9. For references, see M. O. H. Carver, "Kingship and Material Culture in Early Anglo-Saxon East Anglia," in *The Origins of Anglo-Saxon Kingdoms*, ed. S. Basset (Leicester, 1989), pp. 141-58.
10. *Bulletin* 6.
11. Carver, "Sutton Hoo, 1985."
12. Longworth and Kinnes, *Sutton Hoo Excavations*.
13. Bruce-Mitford, *Sutton Hoo*, vols. 1-3.
14. M. O. H. Carver, "Pre-Viking Traffic in the North Sea," in *Maritime Celts, Frisians, and Saxons*, ed. S. McGrail, CBA Res. Rep. 71 (Oxford, 1991), pp. 117-25.

15. Carver, "Kingship."
16. Carver, "Kingship."
17. Carver, *Pre-Viking Traffic.*

Contributors

❖

James Campbell is a fellow of Worcester College, Oxford University. His publications include *The Anglo-Saxons* (Ithaca, 1982).

Martin Carver is a professor of archaeology and co-director of the Centre for Medieval Studies at the University of York. His publications include *Underneath English Towns: Interpreting Urban Archaeology* (London, 1987).

Robert Payson Creed is a professor of English and Comparative Literature at the University of Massachusetts at Amherst. He is the author of *Reconstructing the Rhythm of Beowulf* (Missouri, 1990).

Roberta Frank is a professor at the Centre for Medieval Studies, University of Toronto. She is the author of *Old Norse Court Poetry* and of numerous articles on Old English and Old Norse literature and history, and is the general editor of Publications of the *Dictionary of Old English* and of the Toronto Old English Series.

Michael Geselowitz is a lecturer in the Center for Materials Research in Archaeology and Ethnology at the Massachusetts Institute of Technology, from which he holds bachelor's degrees in engineering and anthropology. His Ph.D. in anthropology was awarded by Harvard University in 1987. He has written numerous scholarly articles and, with D. Blair Gibson, edited *Tribe and Polity in Late Prehistoric Europe* (New York, 1988).

Gloria Polizzotti Greis is a Ph.D. candidate in the Department of Anthropology at Harvard University specializing in the economies and social structure of Bronze and Iron Age Europe. She is manager of archaeological collections for the Peabody Museum of Archaeology and Ethnology, Harvard University.

Henrik M. Jansen is a lecturer and assistant professor at Copenhagen and Odense Universities. He has been director of Svendborg County Museum and is currently leader of the Medieval Svendborg project. His publications include *The Early Urbanization of Denmark* (Oxford, 1985) and "Svendborg in the Middle Ages" (*Journal of Danish Archaeology* (1987).

Calvin B. Kendall is a professor of English and Germanic philology at the University of Minnesota. His publications include *The Metrical Grammar of Beowulf* (Cambridge, 1991).

Simon Keynes is a university lecturer in Anglo-Saxon history at the University of Cambridge and a fellow of Trinity College, Cambridge. His publications include *The Diplomas of King Aethelred the Unready* (1980).

Else Roesdahl is a reader in medieval archaeology at Aarhus University, Denmark, and a special professor in Viking Studies at Nottingham University, England. Publications include *Viking Age Denmark* (London, 1982) and *The Vikings* (London, 1991), published in Danish in 1980 and 1987, respectively.

Edward Schoenfeld received his B.A. in history and German from Marquette University in 1980 and his M.A. in history from the University of Wisconsin–Milwaukee in 1988. He is currently working on his Ph.D. in history at the University of Minnesota.

Jana Schulman received her B.A. in English from Barnard College in 1981 and her M.A. in English and comparative literature from Columbia University in 1983. She is currently working on her Ph.D. in Germanic philology at the University of Minnesota.

Alan Stahl is the curator of medieval coins at the American Numismatic Society, New York City. His publications on Merovingian coins include two books: *The Merovingian Coinage of the Region of Metz*, Numismatica Lovaniensia 5 (Lovain-la-Neuve, 1982), and *Monnaies Mérovingiennes*, Fonds Bourgey (Paris, in press).

Wesley Stevens is a professor of history at the University of Winnipeg and the executive secretary of the Consortium for Austro-Bavarian Studies, for which he teaches Latin paleography in Germany and Austria. He is codirector of the Benjamin Catalogue for History of Science. He has published four books, thirteen research articles, and many other reports. He has taught in Austria, Canada, Germany, and the United States and has presented twenty-eight public lectures in those countries, as well as in England, Scotland, and the Republic of Ireland.

Peter S. Wells is a professor of anthropology and the director of the Center for Ancient Studies at the University of Minnesota. His publications include *Farms, Villages and Cities: Commerce and Urban Origins in Late Prehistoric Europe* (Ithaca, 1984) and "Iron Age Temperate Europe: Some Current Research Issues," *Journal of World Prehistory* (1990).

Index

✣

Aalborg, 180

Aarhus, bishop of, 178

Abbo of Fleury, 137-40, 142; *Computus vulgaris qui dicitur ephemerida*, 139; *Quaestiones grammaticales*, 137; *Sententiae*, 137-38

Acgilbert, bishop in Paris and Wessex, 126-28; death and burial of, 126; Easter practices, 126; ordination of Wilfrid, 127

Acta Synodi, version III, 135

Adelsö, 157-58; connection to Birka, 157; kings' mounds, 157; monuments, 157; mounds, 158; Skopintull mound, 157. *See also* Skopintull

Administration, Roman, of urban centers, 7

Adomnán, 108; *Life of Columba*, 108

Adon, 126

Adriatic, 30-31

Ælfeah, will of, 19

Ælfric, *De Anni Temporibus*, 139

Aera Incarnationis, 127, 138, 140, 142

Aera Passionis, 127

Æthelberht, king of Kent, 87, 107; laws of, 87

Æthelwulf, *De Abbatibus*, 86

Afterlife, 165-66; Christian, 166; pagan concept of, 160-61

Aggersborg, fortifications, 178

Agriculture, 30; Anglo-Saxon, 185; East Anglian, 186

Aidan, 126

Akerman, John Yonge, 50; *Remains of Pagan Saxondom*, 50

Alcuin, xii, 86; *The Bishops, Saints and Kings of York*, 86

Aldhelm, abbot of Malmesbury and Sherborne, 125, 129-30, 132, 134, 136-37, 141-42; *Cyclus Aldhelmi de cursu lunae*

per signa XII secundum grecos, 130-31, 133, 142

Alexandria, 92, 126

Alfred the Great, king of Wessex, xvi, 113, 133; court of, 113; reign of, 135

Alhfrith, king of Deira, 126

Almgren, Bertil, 92

Altai, 36

Altars, xv, 86, 103; Christian, xv; pagan, xv

Amalesuntha, Ostrogothic princess, 85

Ambrose, bishop of Milan, 132

Amethysts, 81, 91

Amiens, mint at, 9

Anastasius I, emperor of Byzantium, monogram of, 17

Anatolia, 30-31

Anatolius, bishop of Laodicea, 126

Andernach, mint at, 8

Angers, mint at, 8

Angles, 92, 125, 137

Anglo-Saxon Chronicle, 80, 107, 112-13, 116; list of kings, 113; Parker manuscript, 111; translation into Latin, 111; use of *Bretwalda*, 111

Anglo-Saxons, xiv-xv, 15, 70, 73, 92, 94, 105, 112-15, 183, 186, 190; burials of, 94; cemeteries of, in East Anglia, 198; Christian culture, xiv; shipbuilding techniques of, 15; singing, 73; soldiers, 19; superstitiousness of, 189; weapons, 18

Animals, value of, 88

Annegray, 127

Annuli, 86

Annus praesens, 138, 140

Anphus or Alphonsus, Peter, 141; *De Dracone*, 141

Antioch, 91

Antiquaries Journal, x, 49

Antiquity, 49, 80, 184